CRITIQUE IS CREATIVE

critique IS CREATIVE

The CRITICAL RESPONSE PROCESS in Theory and Action

LIZ LERMAN AND JOHN BORSTEL

Edited by John Borstel

WESLEYAN UNIVERSITY PRESS Middletown, Connecticut

Wesleyan University Press
Middletown CT 06459
www.wesleyan.edu/wespress

Manufactured in the United States of America
Designed by Richard Hendel
Composed in Utopia and The Sans by Integrated Publishing Solutions

Some passages in this book have been adapted from previously published works by John Borstel: "Finding the Progress in Work-in-Progress: Liz Lerman's Critical Response Process in Arts-Based Research," in *Arts-Based Research in Education*, eds. Melisa Cahnmann-Taylor and Richard Siegesmund (Routledge, 2018); "Back to the Roots of Critical Response," in the Alternate ROOTS blog (November 9, 2017); and "The Wonderful Freedom of Not Being Finished: Four Values for Constructive Critique," in *Youth Drama Ireland*, Issue 14 (2011–12).

LIBRARY OF CONGRESS CATALOGING-IN-PUBLICATION DATA
Names: Lerman, Liz, author. | Borstel, John, author.
Title: Critique is creative : the critical response process in theory and action / Liz Lerman and John Borstel ; edited by John Borstel.
Description: Middletown, Connecticut : Wesleyan University Press, 2022. Includes bibliographical references and index. | Summary: "Comprehensive introduction to the Critical Response Process, a widely used method for giving and getting generative feedback on creative works in progress, with applications in varied disciplines and situations to foster creativity, learning, and equitable practice"—Provided by publisher.
Identifiers: LCCN 2022000613 (print) | LCCN 2022000614 (ebook) | ISBN 9780819580825 (cloth) | ISBN 9780819577184 (trade paperback) | ISBN 9780819580832 (ebook)
Subjects: LCSH: Feedback (Psychology) | Creative ability. | (Literary, artistic, etc.) | Criticism.
Classification: LCC BF319.5.F4 L47 2022 (print) | LCC BF319.5.F4 (ebook) | DDC 153.3/5—dc23/eng/20220318
LC record available at https://lccn.loc.gov/2022000613
LC ebook record available at https://lccn.loc.gov/2022000614

5 4 3 2

To everyone who has taken the risk of
putting forward work in progress
To everyone who has asked a thoughtful question
before stating an opinion
To everyone who has sought to guide a
conversation to make it better

CONTENTS

PREFACE THE CRITICAL RESPONSE PROCESS

LIZ LERMAN

The Critical Response Process came into being at a time when I was seeking the kind of critique that would make me excited to go back to work.

The Critical Response Process was born during a period when it seemed that product was everything, and process was to be kept secret. Things have changed. CRP worked then, and it works now.

The Critical Response Process is a system for feedback.

The Critical Response Process is also a collection of tools that can be applied independent of each other for a wide range of human purposes.

The Critical Response Process is a kind of ritual. Like good ritual, it holds you in relationship to values that would be otherwise hard to keep in the rush of daily living.

The Critical Response Process is a set of practices that allow you to live on the horizontal in a world dominated by the hierarchical. This means it can help you manage ambiguities, hold multiple perspectives, and function where meaning depends on context but where values and ethics still matter.

The Critical Response Process is an opportunity to rethink your aesthetics, your opinions, and your assumptions about any subject.

The Critical Response Process helps you manage your judgments, which are occurring daily in numerous different settings.

The Critical Response Process can lead to deeper conversations as well as more civil ones.

The Critical Response Process was put out into the world as a photocopied sheet of paper over thirty years ago. It is now in wide use around the world. It still holds close to its original form, but is always generating new knowledge while evolving in its purposes, adaptations, and variations. We hope you will evolve it too.

ACKNOWLEDGMENTS

The authors extend their sincere thanks to the contributing writers credited in the table of contents and contributor biographical notes. We are also grateful to those consenting to use of quotes and excerpts used in the text: James Bundy, Andrew Burke, Linda Chapman, James Darrah, Michael Despars, Brian Francoise, Ruth Fraser, Raji Ganesan, Helena Gaunt, Kristin Kjølberg, Diane Kuthy, Talia Mason, Paloma McGregor, Erika R. Moore, Roxie Perkins, Chris Postuma, Ellen Reid, Sadie Leigh Rothman, Michel A. Riquelme Sanderson, David Tinapple, Leigh-Ann Tower, and Suzannah Vaughn. For their contributions to the process and faith in the vision of this book, we thank Mary Cohen, Ellie Dubois, Christine Hamilton, Simon Hart, Falk Hübner, Jaine Lumsden, and Valeska Populoh.

Special thanks to Jane Brown and Linda Caro Reinisch for their financial support of the Critical Response Process. We are grateful for the support of the staff of Liz Lerman LLC, namely Amelia Cox, Erin Donohue, and Candice Williams. We are thankful to Dance Exchange for providing an incubator, laboratory, and an ongoing center for the practice of CRP.

We extend huge thanks to the staff and team at Wesleyan University Press, particularly to director and editor-in-chief Suzanna Tamminen whose vision and sustained support were unflagging, to production editor Jim Schley for his unique combination of precision and nurture, and to our deft and comprehensive copyeditor, Natalie Taylor Jones.

This book was supported in part by funding from the Montgomery County government and the Arts and Humanities Council of Montgomery County, Maryland.

It is not an exaggeration to say that in every encounter in which we teach or facilitate the Critical Response Process, the authors learn something new from a question, a response, an insight, an example, or a risk. With recognition of how that learning has been channeled into this book, we are deeply grateful to all the organizations that have hosted trainings and residencies focused on the Process and all the individuals who have spent time with us in CRP circles. You've helped to make this book what it is.

In Memoriam: Shula Strassfeld.

CRITIQUE IS CREATIVE

PROLOGUE OPENING CIRCLES

LIZ LERMAN

My mother believed in originality. She loved modern art and turning things into something they are not. In the first home I remember, our coffee table was an old barbeque grill that she painted. It also functioned to hold magazines. I think she just put something across it when people needed a shelf to rest their drinks. When we made the move to Washington, D.C., when I was four, and later to Milwaukee, she proudly bought doors that she turned into our kitchen table after she attached very modernistic iron legs to them. Creativity was important to her.

We often made things like paper doll clothes, cloth doll clothes, and dolls themselves out of Kleenex, rubber bands, and bits of fabric. And we always had crayons and paper at our disposal. Color, color, color. "Make a mark," she'd say. In my earliest memory of her saying anything about *how* we were doing what we were doing, I was sprawled on the floor, loose paper all around me and a pile of crayons nearby. I was busy making circles. I remember my gleeful abandon as I scribbled circles of different sizes, different colors, pushing the crayon down hard or light to get a different weight of line. After four or five pages of these, I felt my mom standing over me. She looked at what I was doing and said, "Don't just draw circles. Can't you do something different?"

Despite the fact that this event happened very long ago, when I think of it I can still feel the admonishment in my body as a distortion in the inner workings of my core. Even as a child, I knew I had somehow failed in getting my mother to see what I had created. When our creativity is made invisible by the words of another, the experience brings a grave disappointment.

I am, in the language of today, a resilient being. And even then, as a child, within seconds I had removed the overly developed circle drawings. What happened next I can't remember, but I imagine that I might have started drawing something else. It is conceivable that my mother's suggestion moved me to a new subject, which I may have attacked with joy, or newfound purpose, or with a dutiful resolve. It is possible that I was able to continue. It is, however, more likely that I put the supplies away and went outside to play.

I wish I could have told my mother to look more carefully. That if she had, she would have seen that no circle in my drawings was the same as another. She would have seen the abundant imagination at work as I formed and re-formed this amazing geometry.

It's a useful story for all kinds of reasons, one of which is that the Critical Response Process and circles often go together. Most photographs of CRP workshops feature people sitting in circles. I have now been in hundreds of them. They are never the same. Patterns emerge, of course. Much of this book is about what we have learned by doing CRP over and over and over. But the uniqueness of each event supports the creativity of that child I was so long ago. The many colors, sizes, shapes, weights, and geometries exist to aid us in pursuing what is vital, mysterious, and challenging in the act of creating something new.

INTRODUCTION

Some events elude documentation. Though the Critical Response Process came into being swiftly and decisively through pilot ventures at Alternate ROOTS and the Colorado Dance Festival, it seems no one recorded an exact birthday for it. But we're fairly confident that this system for giving and getting feedback got its start in 1990, and so has been in active use for over thirty years. It continues to thrive at its point of origin within the practice of its inventor, choreographer Liz Lerman, in her overlapping circles of influence as an artist, speaker, teacher, and out in the world. Its first decade brought a few changes in determining what was essential as opposed to auxiliary (the core Process contracting from six to four steps) and in how Liz named its components (particularly in the case of step one). But aside from those minor points of communication, CRP has required remarkably little tinkering.

It has, however, demanded some clear and detailed description. Our first CRP book, *Liz Lerman's Critical Response Process: A Method for Getting Useful Feedback on Anything You Make, from Dance to Dessert*, appeared in 2003. A quick read at sixty-four illustrated pages, the book offered a fast-track means of getting CRP into eager hands, helping to disseminate the Process into worldwide use. In its modest aspiration to serve as a user's manual, the first book offered a basic description of the Process and guidelines for facilitators, along with a few variations and sidebars featuring user insights. It has been heartening to hear from those who have been able to establish a practice of CRP based on the book alone, as it fulfilled its function as a basic primer.

But that function was limited. Even as we wrote that guide, we knew we were leaving many paths unexplored, and the passage of time has revealed an ever-broadening range of practice and theory not encompassed in the original book. As steady as its core principles have been, CRP has constantly yielded discovery about its ramifications for learning and insight, as well as its internal workings as a vehicle for personal and interpersonal intelligence. Users have increasingly come to recognize its potential as an integrated system for ethical communication, the value of its variations, and the broad applicability of its principles, both within and far beyond its original domain of the arts. Almost every CRP workshop or facilitation session raises a new question or illuminates a new angle. Some are relevant to the mechanics and inner dynamics of the Process, its three roles, and the range of options participants have in enacting them. We continue to learn about the journey of an opinion as it moves through the Process and ponder the role of clarifying questions. We regularly gain new insight into the relationship of expertise and naivete as blocks to dialogue or sources of information, and about randomness versus organization in the conversations that follow the structure of CRP. Some discoveries are relevant to applications of CRP's values beyond their original purpose for artistic critique—in particular, how regularly stating what is meaningful and resonant can enhance workplace interaction, how the attempt to remove judgment from a question can diffuse potential conflicts in a relationship, and how life changes when you ask permission to offer an opinion.

Beyond our first book, which stands as the clearest, most codified version of CRP, our distribution method has been open, informal, and highly adaptive. From the beginning the Process has been making its own progress in the world, passing from person to person and site to site with users encouraged to experiment, vary, and tailor it to their immediate needs. We have led many workshops, sometimes with a sole focus on CRP, often incorporating it with other artmaking or community-building methods, always customizing the approach and emphasis to the host organization and participants. Through the original book, articles, workshops, and user-to-user dissemination, CRP has been introduced to thousands of people and has won adherents all over the planet. It has constituted a core method for institutions like New York Theatre Workshop, has been a cornerstone of the MFA program at Yale School of Drama, and has become a fulcrum for change among the participating conservatories in Europe's Innovative Conservatoire (ICON), to mention just a few. In spite of this reception, it wasn't until 2019 that we instituted a certification program for facilitators; we are just beginning to establish an online source for literature on CRP as this book goes to press.

The upside of the loosely structured distribution system with which CRP has made its way to a wider audience is that it is constantly finding new users, both individual and institutional. In the spirit of open-source technology, CRP has thrived through adaptive usage and application to local conditions and specific challenges, compounding the volume of discovery. The downside is that the Process and its progress have been impossible to track. With equal measures of delight and consternation we watch CRP emerging in unexpected places and worry about how well or poorly its principles are being enacted.

Meanwhile, the three decades since CRP's invention have witnessed some dramatic change in the domain of the arts as much as anywhere else. In the early 1990s arts world of CRP's origins as Liz was experiencing it, *product* was everything: the primary basis for consideration in education, public perception, and professional practice. But the last twenty years have seen a growing premium placed on *process* and its value as a source of learning, a focus for documentation and analysis, a locus of public encounter, and an income-generating asset. Process, moreover, is increasingly perceived in an integrated rather than binary relationship to product—a both/and rather than an either/or. Relative to CRP, this change in our perception of process has radically repositioned the concept of a work in progress from the artist's secretive purview to a hub for public engagement, from a forum of feints, failures, and red pencil to a generative laboratory. In the neighborhoods of the art world where this new mentality has taken hold, artists can be more vulnerable, artwork more pliant and malleable, interim states of formation more exposed and appreciated, and an audience's role as a co-creator of meaning more active and overt. Work in progress has come out of its closet: rather than a focus for shame, apology, and inadequacy, work in progress can now stand as an emblem for (just imagine!) progress.

The implications for CRP have been powerful: Institutionally, it has expanded from internal functioning to public programming. It has come to anchor educational programs where artists' capacity to represent their ideas and process are valued on par with their ability to deliver a product. And, perhaps true to its roots in Liz Lerman's expansive and democratic approach to creative participation, its structure and principles have increasingly been deployed in community engagement and civic dialogue.

Other shifts have come with thirty years of generational turnover. With changing trends in parenting and education, people arriving at adulthood may not have felt the bruising criticism—both in art and life—that was typical for earlier cohorts. A gentler ethos of feedback may have prevailed in the upbringing of the generation that is taking the stage post-millennium.

But those reared in this more supportive climate face their own dilemmas. If in 1990 the emphasis in the practice of CRP was to help artists find functional meaning and to forestall defensiveness as a counter to the fractious noise of then-typical critique, the stress three decades later may well be on assuring that efforts designed to nurture can also offer challenge, substance, and discernment.

Thirty years has also brought an accumulation of variations as CRP has been channeled into the cultures of particular artistic disciplines, and ventured and interrogated in domains beyond the arts. For example, within the social sciences it has proven compatible with the values of Participatory Action Research. In the laboratory sciences it has been explored as a partner to peer review. And in educational circles, as you will see later in this book, numerous variations have informed core pedagogies, curriculum development, and formative assessment. Meanwhile, life in a globalized world increasingly calls on us to communicate across difference in a rapidly evolving conversation about history, coexistence, exploitation, redress, and the legacies of systemic racism and White supremacy. These realities heighten the challenge and potential of CRP, giving new urgency to some long-standing questions: Artmaking contexts aside, is this method of feedback relevant to cross-cultural dialogue in and of itself? Does CRP contain its own cultural biases? If so, how might they be managed or mitigated? What are the power dynamics of the Process, and can we deploy them equitably? And getting back to art, in any community from Baltimore to Phoenix to Brisbane, where cultural practitioners are grappling with cross-cultural issues in the work they make, the question arises: How can CRP support such work and the conversations it inspires, and what do artists, responders, and facilitators need to know to use it effectively?

As authors, our own points of reference have expanded over the history of CRP, also affecting the contents of this book. Through reading, conversation, artistic practice, and teaching, both of us have explored the nature of creative acts, creative tools, and creative capacities. In the process, we've discovered much that illuminates the generative nature of the principles of CRP and the creative energy of the dialogue it supports. One important idea in this regard has been that of divergent/convergent thinking. Broadly speaking, divergent thinking sounds and feels like what people often suppose creativity to be: multiple ideas, fecund production of options, flaps open, eureka, the *aha* moment, abundant fruit produced by free-flowing process. But as long as those ideas remain merely ideas, divergence is only half the story. For a creative project to evolve and progress, divergence must meet convergence, the complementary force that narrows, weighs merits, edits, moves into viable production, engineers vision into reality, and, yes, judges. Without moving through cycles of divergence and convergence, no vision becomes a reality.

CRP, we've discovered, mirrors and incorporates these forces of divergence and convergence, as well as helping the user manage their interactions in the creative process. It's easy to assume that critique and feedback reside in the realm of the convergent, but our experience in hundreds of CRP circles insists that divergent functions are consistently stimulated as well: new perceptions emerge, contrasting interpretations coexist, and we find that a problem may have multiple solutions. By observing interacting forces of divergence that are inevitably active in a Critical Response session, we have come to think of critique not as a pause button on the creative process but as a way of heightening and intensifying it into a concentrated session of time. With the Critical Response Process, critique is creative.

We have witnessed a constantly emerging and expanding body of knowledge about CRP that this volume seeks to capture, however partially, while still offering enough of the essentials to offer a point of entry for a reader new to the Process. While reflecting some of the transdisciplinary reach CRP has achieved, this text holds its center in artistic practice, generally using "artist" to designate the person presenting work in progress. With contributions from practitioners in education, science, and religious practice, we trust that this work provides examples from other fields for readers intent on broader applications to make the translation. Encouraging that kind of active engagement by the reader, and reaching beyond the functions of a primer, we suggest multiple ways to approach this book: As a travel guide, offering an armchair tour of CRP applications; as a symposium, inviting varied perspectives on a central topic and interpretations of a core text; and as a practical handbook that will get you thinking about the uses of the Critical Response Process and its values in your life and practice. Rather than representing a summation, we hope this work sparks more reflection, inquiry, and experimentation, and begins a process of gathering the literature that will support CRP and its uses over the next thirty years.

THE PRACTICE

1 FRAMING FEEDBACK

Origin stories are powerful, whether the subject is a cosmos, a culture, or a custom. It's always an interesting question as to when and how anything begins, particularly anything, like the Critical Response Process (CRP), which seeks to be generative or to harness human creative capacity. Find a starting point and you can always ask, "What happened before that . . . and what happened before *that*?" And much as we like to think of a single point of genesis—one common ancestor for all the human DNA, a single source for all the languages spoken on earth—it's worth remembering that many complex phenomena trace back to multiple causes, that as many roots twist beneath the trunk of a tree as branches spread above it.

So it is with CRP. Its roots touch into individual and collective experiences of feedback, the formalized or haphazard customs of critique, and the circumstances that gave rise to Liz's impulse to formulate this system thirty years ago. With this first chapter serving to put CRP into some perspective before exploring its particulars, we will look at some of those varied roots. In her opening words, Liz poses the constancy and centrality of feedback in any human life, as its components of judgment and reflection shape our sense of who we are and what is (or isn't) true or beautiful. Taking an autoethnographic approach in the section that follows, John probes his own biography for signal moments of giving and getting feedback, what they taught him, and how such moments often point to formative shifts in self-understanding and life purpose. Guest contributor Mark Callahan puts CRP into the context of a broader range of investigations, examining critique as it has been practiced in arts and academic settings, including the studies-in-practice that he has engaged with his students at the University of Georgia. Finally, to conclude this round of source perspectives and to launch us into the particulars of the Critical Response Process, Liz takes us back to the concrete origins of the Process and the experiences and contexts that spurred her to bring it into being.

From Your Beginnings

Liz Lerman

It starts while you are still in the womb. People all around you are already giving you feedback, talking to you about their hopes, their concerns, and their belief in your future. You will be great. You will be beautiful. You are making my life too difficult. Wow, you moved. Oh, you are making me sick. Oh, look how strong you are.

It only increases after you are born. You start expressing yourself and someone starts doing things and saying things in response. What is the relationship between how much you cry to how much they pat you? The judgments begin to fly all around you. And yes—your behavior, your thinking, and your being are affected by the tone, style, meaning, touch, timing, sounds, and quality of everything you take in. We begin this amazing journey surrounded by opinions and judgment, inseparable from the feelings of the people giving us this information: They love us; they hate us; they want the best for us; they know more than us; they want us to do something quite particular; they want us to fend for ourselves; they want to teach us; and they want to use us as an example to themselves or others. They measure their own success by the way we act.

When a process, such as the Critical Response Process, asks you to think about your judgments and opinions, it can feel not just personal, but as something that impacts your core being. You are communicating with a part of yourself that comes from your earliest beginnings. When we examine our ancestry, we can see that these opinions and judgments are part of our inheritance. Therefore, when we adjust the way we think or act in moments of feedback, we are simultaneously moving backward and forward in time. We may not want to change because we know we are feeling the weight of our family history and cultural traditions of the past, even as we consider the way we hold our ideas in the present. These are not ordinary ideas, but rather the ethics and perceptions that make up our very nature and that anchor our core beliefs. They remind me of how my friend and colleague, indigenous scholar Bryan Brayboy, defines aesthetics: "What communities determine to be good, true, right, and beautiful." With these essentials, we are impacting the relationships we hold with those around us into the future, whether with our children, colleagues, collaborators, students, bosses, or neighbors.

That is why the Critical Response Process is so valuable. That is why it is hard to do. That is why it is a lifelong practice. That is why we, and it, fail regularly.

Living Feedback: A Short Memoir of Critique Experiences

John Borstel

People I encounter in my CRP travels occasionally ask how I got involved with teaching and facilitating this feedback method. Usually I explain that it started at Dance Exchange, the organization Liz Lerman founded in 1976. My administrative role there when I joined the staff in 1993 focused on communications, placing me in a series of deepening conversations with Liz as she was responding to the first wave of interest in the Process in the mid-1990s. At the time, CRP was "merely" the best articulated of many tools of process that Liz was fostering, as she espoused the critical value of artists sharing their knowledge and methods. Benefiting from an organizational ethos that encouraged artists and administrators alike to expand their capacities, I gradually began to develop a CRP practice. I gained experience as a facilitator, as I was occasionally pressed into service when Liz or one of the CRP-adept dancers in the company was unavailable. Having identified as a visual artist and writer rather than as a performer, I latched on to the multidisciplinary nature of CRP as a unique opportunity to be a teacher in Dance Exchange's residency work.

I gradually grew into the role. I encountered no bolt of lightning or single transformative moment in my emergence into CRP. Indeed, it's been difficult to pin down a personal origin story for my discovered vocation in this corner of the world of feedback and critique. Musing on this has left me wondering what, in my distant or more recent past, ultimately drew me to CRP. The memories evoked by the question have been illuminating.

CHILDHOOD

I'm nine years old, and I'm taking a weekly art class at the Baltimore Museum of Art. Each week, we explore a different art material. One day the medium is tissue paper collage, and the teacher says to me, "John, I want you to do a picture about something other than *Alice in Wonderland*. Isn't there something else that interests you?" Actually, there isn't; I'm pretty obsessed with Lewis Carroll's *Alice* books at that point. I fake an attempt at something else, even as I notice that (obsession being the norm at that age) the teacher is *not* redirecting the several girls in class who have been drawing, painting, and sculpting nothing but horses. I lack the words at that stage, but I know the correction is aimed at pushing me toward a "gender-appropriate" subject, because Alice is not a fitting role model for boys. I feel reprimanded at my core, judged as not quite right. Criticize my art, and you criticize me.

ADOLESCENCE

At twelve years old, I'm hanging out with my mother in the studio where she does her needlework. She asks me if I want to try one of the kits she's assembled for her classroom visits that introduce kids to embroidery: it includes a strip of burlap the size of a bookmark, lengths of colored yarn, and a fat, blunt needle. I stitch some varied-length dashes in a series of parallel lines of green and blue yarn, and hold it up for her approval. Glancing at my completed strip, she says, "Well, that's okay, but it really isn't very interesting. It's just haphazard. You can come up with something better." I am mildly shocked. Up to that point, practically all of my artistic efforts have been met with her approbation and encouragement. Feeling like I have something to prove, I make a second attempt, devoting several hours to crafting a carefully calculated series of diamonds and chevrons, which wins her distracted approval. Suddenly, my mother, the source of most of what I know about art up to that point, is holding me to a standard. Suddenly the terms of the conversation have changed. It's disorienting and somehow fiercely motivating.

HIGH SCHOOL

Attending an alternative high school program of D.C. Public Schools, I'm one of a group of students taking a regular intaglio class at the Smithsonian's National Collection of Fine Arts. The instructor, a master printmaker, mostly teaches us etching techniques and doesn't comment on content or style unless asked. But one day he's in an intense conversation with another of the students and approaches one of my prints, which is sitting next to me on the worktable. "Take this, for instance," he says, pointing to the small portrait I've made, but not acknowledging me. "It's a little abstract, a little realistic, a little like a cartoon. By being a little of everything, it ends up not being much of anything." The critique of my work doesn't hurt nearly as much as being used as a bad example, one not even worth directly engaging in the conversation. I react in kind by attempting to disappear and minimizing my future encounters with the master.

COLLEGE

Having switched my intended major at Georgetown University from art to English, I'm nonetheless in search of an artistic mentor and find one in Professor Daniel Brush. Dan's harshest criticism is silence; I notice that he saves even his negative commentary for the students whose work he respects, so I actually feel good when he tells me to give up on a piece and move on to the next. His most useful comments are often the tersest. Responding to one of my collages, he asks, "Why have you fragmented Greta Garbo when she's already fragmented?" When he remarks about another, "You have achieved the implication of color without using color," I feel triumphant.

POST-COLLEGE

In my late twenties I'm taking a course on illustration at the Corcoran School of Art. My drawing skills are below the class average and I tend to compensate with an effort at surprising content. At every class meeting there's a group crit where we pin that week's assignment to a board. The instructor makes selective comments, asks occasional questions, and opens the floor for reactions from students. True to form for a noted art school, the peer critique is untrammeled. One of my classmates executes lifelike renderings and handles media with great finesse, but I judge her work as vapid. When the assignment is to draw a still life using complementary hues, she brings in a watercolor rhapsody of three curling autumn leaves, and, invited to introduce it, enthuses about the beauty of the season. I roll my eyes and make audible noises of disdain. When the discussion turns to my piece—an overworked inking of a tortoise skull, a staple remover, and three anagram tiles—she turns on me and says, "John! Why do you always have to be so clever? Those things together are just weird." Given our complementary sensibilities, we could be learning a lot from each other, but nothing in the structure of the class or the protocol for critique supports that possibility. Crits are a sparring match. And much of the responsibility is mine: At that point I don't have the capacity to recognize how my biases, based in the imagined threat of someone with skills I lacked, were thwarting my own growth.

CAREER

In my forties, as my professional work increasingly focuses on writing, I take a series of courses at the Writer's Center in Bethesda, Maryland. Group feedback is a constant, but the structure and style of the critiques vary with the instructors. Some encourage dialogue and questions, others hold strictly to the principle of keeping silent while your work is discussed. "Your writing needs to stand on its own without your explanations or defense," we're told. When this is the rule, I try to adhere, but more than once the teacher glares at me and sternly says, "You don't get to talk." The reprimand deflates me. Because my own excitements, doubts, and inquiries are off the table, I feel disconnected from my own process, unmotivated about making revisions, deprived of the natural joy of making something.

EMERGENCE

During the same period, I'm starting to facilitate and train others in CRP. Hoping to expose myself to other modes of critique, I sign up for a series of sessions in Fieldwork for Mixed Disciplines hosted at D.C.'s Dance Place, bringing in some photography projects I've been developing. Here, too, the standard is that artists should just listen and not engage in the conversation when their work is up for discussion. But somehow the effect is different. Because we are meeting every week and a spirit of reciprocity is established as we support one another in shaping works in progress, I really deepen my investment in the rigors of my own work. For a point of comparison, I bring the same project to Dance Exchange for a session of CRP. The combination of critique modes and the information I gain from two supportive communities proves highly motivating. I submit some of the resulting work to open exhibition calls, and for the first time I have my work selected for public display.

GRAD SCHOOL

A perennial late-bloomer, I'm finally in grad school in my fifties, getting an MFA in interdisciplinary arts through the low-residency program at Goddard College in rural Vermont. The student body for the program gathers once a semester. These weeklong residencies are a combination of summer camp and seminar. My classmates include not only the expected dancers, actors, and painters, but also clowns, glassblowers, rap artists, and cartoonists. Critique, to the extent that it happens, tends to be catch-as-catch-can, either at the whim of a particular faculty member or inside the various affinity groups that form. I offer some well-received workshops and structured facilitations in CRP, but mostly I find I'm practicing the Process in one-on-one conversations. Listening. Offering observations and statements of meaning. Inviting, answering, and asking questions. I seem to gain a reputation as a valuable conversation partner, and people seek me out. I know my innate capacities are only incidental. It has everything to do with the skills I've gained through CRP for listening, reflection, and inquiry.

Personal stories have anchored the ways we have introduced CRP since its beginning. Often we ask workshop participants to contemplate questions like those Liz was asking herself when she invented CRP: "Think of a time when you had an energizing experience of feedback, or think about a person whom you trust to give you useful feedback—defining *good feedback* as the kind that leaves you so you can't wait to get back to work. What happened in these encounters that made them effective? What concrete approaches or principles were at play?" Just as most people can conjure vivid experiences of discomfort and anxiety from their memories, most people, when asked, can also relate an incident of effective feedback from their life history. The question elicits numerous values and qualities, at least some of which are embodied in CRP and addressed at some point in this book: trust, respect, focus on the work as opposed to the person, specificity, inquiry, and so on. In that way, the discussion directly fertilizes the ground on which we'll be planting CRP. Moreover, it helps people recognize that effective feedback generally has a structural, technical, or value base of some kind and casts feedback experience out of the discomfort zone and into an appreciative light.

As I hope my introduction to this essay has made clear, I had no role in the invention of CRP. Thus I long hesitated to link my own history to CRP or the general discipline of critique. But then I did, writing and sharing the narratives in the above memoir with our CRP students and certification candidates, encouraging them to excavate their own pasts for resonant feedback moments. In doing so, I discovered anew the significance of feedback in our lives. Almost always, I've found, each of the memorable experiences of feedback a person invokes marks a formative moment in their life. The time they understood they had a distinctive gift or passion. The moment when they realized they had to be the source of their own self-worth. The incident when they were directed on a path that ended up defining their life. The insight that illuminated a passage from one culture, aesthetic, or value system into another. The turning point when they realized they'd found an artistic, vocational, or spiritual home. Feedback defines our human relationships and shapes our sense of self. Feedback matters, and it matters to have effective principles to guide it.

THE BROADEST POSSIBLE INTERPRETATION OF CREATIVITY

Mark Callahan

In my capacity as a teacher and artistic director of an interdisciplinary initiative for advanced research in the arts at the University of Georgia, I encounter creative people working at different stages of learning in an array of fields. An inherent challenge of this work is to enable productive critical communication so that students can grow and collaborative teams can improve their work. Curious about the experiences of my peers, I developed a habit of asking how they "did feedback" in their respective fields and began recording some of these conversations in a podcast series as a way to share perspectives. The *Feedback* series includes interviews with professionals in art, creative writing, dance, music, theater, biology, athletics, community design, psychology, and engineering.

While informative, the conversations often raised even more questions about how we learn to give and receive feedback, what makes it effective, and how we measure success. This line of inquiry eventually led me to create a seminar course to examine critical evaluation methods in the arts with a practice-based approach for better understanding. In the seminar, students engage with contextual readings and discussions to help illuminate their own experiences with critical dialogue and participate in group feedback in varied formats, including the Critical Response Process.

From a historical perspective, the development of CRP can be viewed as part of a broader range of investigations of critique that emerged during the late twentieth century. Given the involvement of feedback in almost every aspect of an artist's training, in hindsight it is surprising that the delivery methods for such an integral part of teaching were not already under constant scrutiny and improvement. Instead, students were more likely to experience a range of inherited critique practices in settings where learning objectives were rarely, if ever, openly examined. The acquisition of feedback skills through social learning was mainly effective in reinforcing the expectations of a particular teacher, institution, or field.

Much of the scholarship on critique methods provides insights into conventional values by capturing some of the vast informal knowledge that saturates each field through stories and practical "survival" advice. These perspectives tend to be constrained by disciplinary boundaries with an emphasis on how to get more out of existing approaches. Students are envisioned as the primary beneficiaries of critique, if they are somehow able to manage the simultaneous processing of feedback, articulate defense of creative decisions, regulation of emotional sensitivity, editing and synthesis of received opinions, and temporary dismissal of their ego.

While the "how" of critique seems to be more implied than understood, its specific value to education has been widely articulated. In academic settings, critique is variously described as a platform for peer review, a means of assessment and evaluation, a training ground for professionalization, and a vehicle for practice in appreciation and criticism. Viewed collectively, the amassed information about critique methods and objectives suggests the theoretical existence of a multiuse tool that can attend to the needs of all constituents.

But in practice there is a different reality. In typical academic critique, artists are called upon to navigate a complex set of technical, psychological, and institutional conditions both within and beyond their control. Students are confronted with nonviable advice ("Don't take it personally," "Drop your ego") and false dichotomies ("Be receptive," "Be thick-skinned") that only add to the confusion of expectations. Ideally, a basic shared goal of critical feedback is authentic, personal, artistic growth—the palpable excitement of self-revelation that translates to creative actions. Unfortunately, when institutions and instructors depend upon critique to deliver multiple learning objectives without first establishing its role as a pathway to growth, the resulting environment is inconsistent at best, ranging from enlightened discourse to the domination of unhelpful opinions.

My conversations with students reveal as much useful information through examining what happens before and after feedback as in studying the critique process itself. Artists commonly experience hope, dread, anxiety, a mad rush of work, self-doubt, overconfidence, and inflated expectations for critique. Peers and teachers may be completely unaware when students self-edit work to be shared in anticipation of the kind of feedback they think they will receive. If the objectives of a critique session are unclear or not fully understood, the feedback may feel unauthentic to the artist. Post-feedback routines range from celebratory relief to cool dismissal, including some creative (and some unhealthy) practices to gain a sense of distance from the experience. Even when students excel in the stated goals of a critique and appear receptive to relevant feedback, they are often left on their own to attempt to filter commentary and try to understand what they did well.

Some of the pressure students experience relative to critique may relate to a sense of being judged and trying to meet the expectations of their chosen fields. A comparison of critique methods across disciplines can highlight ways that specific professional values are deeply embedded in different approaches to feedback. For example, the discursiveness that characterizes writers' workshops and visual arts critiques reflects an importance placed on the articulation of intent and multiple interpretations. In some performing arts fields (and athletics), feedback happens in practice settings such as rehearsals, where complex protocols of deference to master class leaders, directors, and coaches have evolved to prevent chaos (and injury) within ensembles. Creative practitioners who share their work in more than one environment notice other contrasts and limits of critique methods; they may, for instance, receive evaluations and suggested revisions that completely contradict one another, without clear rationale or a sense of priority.

I do not consider the Critical Response Process to be the all-purpose teaching tool that can supply evaluation, professional development, appreciation, and criticism in every situation. I do not think that such a tool exists in a singular form. But the principles that animate CRP are fundamental to a productive learning environment. The intentional sequencing of steps lends utility to the Process as a formative assessment method, allowing teachers and students to work together to address specific areas of strength and needs for development. Its transparent system reduces anxiety (students know what to expect) and invites participation without requiring excuse or a compromise of values. And the formality of the Process is complemented by a flexibility of application to creative work in multiple states of development, encouraging the seamless integration of reflection and critical thinking with making.

For the practice-based component of my critical evaluation methods seminar, CRP provides a format that allows us to study the dynamics of feedback from the inside. It creates a common ground for seminar participants with previous experience in critique from different disciplinary backgrounds in the arts. Over the course of the seminar, each participant has opportunities to inhabit the three key roles of CRP (artist, responder, and facilitator). It is exciting when a participant steps into a new role with a fresh point of view and demonstrates an increased awareness of how those relationships can better support one another. We pay special attention to the designated role of notetaker (or "scribe"), a duty that creates a tangible appreciation of how much communication occurs during feedback and invites the artist to focus completely on the content of discussion. The scribe is additionally charged with capturing what the artist says in moments of self-realization and the uncovering of new ideas.

The structure of the Process invites artists and facilitators to thoughtfully prepare for feedback by generating questions and addressing concerns before critical dialogue begins. For students, this is a truly productive exercise that encourages peer mentorship in an organic way and can help replace stress with focus. We immediately sense the benefits of preparation during feedback as the artist and facilitator work together to lead with the most relevant and urgent issues surrounding the work, effectively bypassing the risk of getting sidetracked by introductory statements that may be laden with extraneous background information or preemptive defenses. Following the feedback, students receive notes from the session that will support their ability to evaluate ideas, identify action items, and, most importantly, achieve a kind of second feedback by reviewing their own questions and statements.

Artists who encounter the Process find a protocol that preserves and nurtures the personal and emotional aspects of making art and participating in feedback. Their role is not to explain or defend their creative work but to share and invite inquiry. They receive direct responses and have time and space to arrive at their own creative solutions. For students who are accustomed to methods that prioritize the values of teacher, institution, or field before personal feedback, an experience of the Process can lead to questions about who is truly being served by critique.

I remain fascinated by the Critical Response Process in part because it does not aim to address or fix problems that persist in conventional modes of critique from any single field. Instead, it embraces the broadest possible interpretation of creativity and proceeds directly from the premise that the goal of feedback is to be useful to the artist. This clarity of purpose is instructive to any program that seeks to build learning objectives around the central core of sustained artistic growth.

Reimagining Feedback

Liz Lerman

I was raised classically, which means that you are either right or wrong—and mostly wrong. That is almost the definition of classicism. You prepare yourself to reach standards set long ago by other people, and then you go about meeting or bettering these expectations. Yes, there is some room for interpretation, but mostly it's working the measurements. I received this education as a ballet student from my early childhood through my teens, and I loved it. I loved working at it, and I loved the satisfaction I felt when I met the demands.

I didn't mind the corrections. It meant that others saw you and expected that you could do it. It was all built into the system of training to become a ballerina. I didn't mind being told what to do or how to do it. But I hated the yelling. I hated the fact that my teachers could use verbal assault to get at me and my body in any way they wished. They could berate me for all kinds of things that didn't feel true to me: you are lazy, you are not working hard enough, you should be able to do that by now. Even as a child I knew this was wrong. But I loved dancing, so I put up with the harangue. In fact, I built strategies for dealing with it. I would pretend that I was made of holes and the screams went through me. I practiced putting on a "listening" face accompanied by head nods. I told myself while it was happening that it was going to be worth it because someday I would be dancing on the great stages of the world. Sometimes I simply pretended I was behind a screen and just didn't listen as the words rained down on me.

Looking back, I can see that my strategies were highly creative. Without strategies like these, we wouldn't survive our schooling. The problem is that in filtering out the abusive delivery, we missed the useful substance of what the critic was telling us. Despite this eventual realization, I don't think I would have devised the Critical Response Process if I had stayed in ballet. It was when I left that part of the dance field for more contemporary forms that I began to see that my established strategies wouldn't work, in part because the feedback I was getting was changing.

In contemporary dance, there still seemed to be a right and a wrong. I just couldn't tell why or how they had been determined. And now it was not just about how high my leg could go, but also about what I was doing and communicating as I made dances for myself and others. The feedback was all over the place. I tried to listen, and in response I tried to do "what they wanted," because, after all, they were my teachers. It worked for a while. But when I began to grow up as a choreographer and truly started to have my own ideas, it became a wrestling match between what I thought I had done and what they thought they had seen. I don't think I would have made CRP, however, if this were all that was going on. I could have muscled through it.

But something else was happening at that time (the mid-1980s), and it added to my troubles. For a brief period in the history of the United States, the National Endowment for the Arts awarded fellowships to individual artists. I received one for $2,500, and as a recipient I was then sent around the country to see and report on the work of fellow applicants. Apparently, the panels that judged the applications were interested in what we had to say about each other.

Off I went with a lot of energy and enthusiasm to see the work of my colleagues, my compatriots, my competitors, and my field. I was shocked. In the simple language I would have used then, I said to myself, "I don't like this." At the time I was making intergenerational dances about documentary topics, often employing the spoken word. So where were the old people dancing? Where was the political subject matter? Where was the part where the dancers talk onstage? As I walked out into the darkness after the shows, I slowly realized that what I liked was my own work, and work that reflected back to me elements I valued within it. What was I going to make of artistic material that was so entirely different from my own?

I went back to the hotel and pulled out the report form. What was I going to say? These awards were important, a vital step for moving one's work around the country and gaining opportunities to continue making dances. I was stymied. It was important to me to be fair. There had to be other ways to think about work than simply reflecting my own values. Obviously, I had to ask myself some different questions in order to write honestly about the choreography I had witnessed. How could I come to terms with aesthetics I didn't share?

The problem compounded itself as I began to tour, and was asked more frequently to teach composition classes at universities, which meant giving feedback to people not all that much younger than I was. I noticed I had plenty to say. But based on what? I knew how to get them to make work like mine. But I wondered: What should I say or how should I ask questions that would support them to create work more like themselves?

The issue of feedback was taking its toll on me, and I fervently began to problem-solve, first by observing what I was doing. In teaching dance technique classes, I had already spent at least a decade playing with feedback systems. I had experimented with pairing students and assigning protocols for observation, comments, and questions. Starting as an effort to share some of the knowledge of the room beyond what was usually the teacher's sole privilege of noticing and commenting, these pairings allowed for a formidable amount of growth in students' technical skills and built their investment in the class and in each other. As a precursor to what would become some of the steps in CRP, I was trying desperately to engage people fully in their own progress, to become aware of their own knowledge and to learn to give it generously to others.

Other influences were at work too. Teaching at Sandy Spring Friends School in the years following my college graduation, I had learned about Reevaluation Counseling (RC), a form of therapeutic peer counseling that, at least for me, was an effective set of tools for stepping out of some of my patterns of behavior. I learned a lot from my years in RC, and specifically borrowed two approaches in my teaching and eventual ensemble practices. The first is the idea of beginning an encounter by telling your counseling partner something affirming about their being. Over the years, this was translated and further reshaped as an important aspect of CRP's step one. The second idea was paired learning, which also came to me through a custom in Jewish education called *chavruta*, when two people study together. Both RC and *chavruta* come to similar conclusions that partnering with someone, while studying or examining ourselves, seems to increase our capacity to remain focused and curious, and that helping someone else while working hard on ourselves brings about renewed purpose. This idea influenced the dialogic nature of CRP and informed some of its most effective applications.

In addition to teaching, I was now choreographing with an ensemble and managing a small nonprofit arts organization. The tasks associated with these big jobs also began to bend under the pressure I felt to bring humane systems into the workplace and to challenge ideas of leadership and even artistic authority. Countless small tragedies, blowups, breakthroughs, and beautiful moments of synchronicity called on me to develop ways of working to make our time together as a staff and company worth the effort, and to give us all opportunities to grow. Received ideas about how businesses are supposed to be run or dances supposed to be made could be reimagined in light of our dreams, our best sensibilities, and our deep-seated knowledge. Though flawed or faltering at times, our collaborative spirit, enthusiastic sharing of ideas, and participatory democracy suffused our organizational functions across the range from the dance studio to the conference room.

In this grand stew of influences, I was also reflecting on my own experiences of feedback. I asked myself why I could hear almost anything from certain people in my life. What integral element in some relationships made it possible to move through all kinds of feedback regardless of tone or language? I approached friends and colleagues with this question and heard many anecdotes that championed directness, even bluntness, but never cruelty and never brutality for its own sake. They described how these very trusted people in their lives did not use their position, their knowledge, or their authority to hurt someone with disdain, dismissal, or discouragement. I knew I wanted to figure out how to secure the essentials of that kind of relationship, even between strangers. Gradually I recognized that a feedback process would need to offer a way to filter out the very human inclination to club another person with our intellect, our knowledge, our point of view, our position. Key features of CRP grew out of this realization.

Over the first fifteen years of doing and teaching CRP, the practice was all about giving and receiving feedback. It was only later that I began to understand that we were engaging in more. The word *feedback*, though helpful, didn't necessarily cover the breadth of what was coming up in CRP sessions and in workshops. The Critical Response Process was asking me, and all of us, to consider what judgment itself is, and how in its myriad forms it affects our inner lives, our most intimate relationships, our artmaking, and our commentary on the world. With that realization, we started to get a grip on how to move these judgments, opinions, and feedback itself into inquiry, conversation, and useful knowledge. This is a kind of meddling of major proportions. It has been fascinating, difficult to do, and so emotional.

In this meddling, as I've conducted CRP workshops across the US and internationally, many people have offered distinctive words to describe this Process. Some say it's research, or inquiry, or mindfulness in action. Others have said it's a communication device or a practice for civic dialogue. I firmly believe in multiple words for the same thing, so I take pleasure in contextualizing the frameworks of CRP within these various constructs. But I also believe that some words hold many meanings, so when people began to refer to CRP with one particular word—ritual—I found a certain contentment, even though the term can be off-putting to some. Perhaps it is my years of training that imbue the idea of ritual with a sense of well-being. Preparation and repetition call on us to set aside time and space, and declare that this thing that is about to happen has importance—enough importance to require setting up a circle, acknowledging all who are present, and preparing ourselves to receive a creative gift or a perilous idea from another human being. And so we begin a ritual of giving feedback.

Thirty years after its introduction, the Critical Response Process is thriving. Part of what makes it successful is its capacity to live with both rigorous hairsplitting orthodoxy and flexible structure that promotes a vigorous diversity of practice. I am relieved to witness this, as I have a certain distaste for codification but love theme and variation. With CRP, we have the formal four-step facilitated approach to giving and receiving feedback. We have roles and responsibilities as experienced through years of practice that have taught us a few things: We can see the disasters coming. We can take time-outs to help us reconvene our ambitions and our senses. We notice that within these codes are multiple directions that one can take. We see that even within the constraints of the system, multiple possibilities enable us to move ahead with our creative and critical faculties on full alert and harnessed for purpose.

But we also see that by disaggregating the steps, the roles, and the rules, we begin to discover other uses and many divergent pathways. Over the past decades some of us have jumped into these spaces with urgency and curiosity, and more recently we hear from people out in the world about how they are experimenting with deconstructing and remixing CRP. Some of that history and news is gathered in the coming chapters of this volume.

Like anything that has been let loose into the world, some of these experiments go awry. Some work is shoddy. Some processes lack commitment or full comprehension of the principles. The Process itself meddles with our histories, and right now our histories are meddling with the Process. I was motivated from CRP's inception to find a corrective for some of the abuses of power, privilege, and influence that have been perpetrated in the guise of artistic feedback. But also from its beginnings I have been concerned about how this Process may reflect biases and assumptions that I hold, having been born in the middle of the last century and raised in a liberal household. In the last decade, within CRP circles we have witnessed how distortions of the Process can lead to pain and alienation among people of color and people living with personal and historic trauma. We are pressing deeply into CRP's effects to see if we can bring the best of its principles into supporting the present work of equity, justice, and belonging.

I am happy to see that that the variations continue, along with challenges to some of the language and practices that may accompany the Process. Enough of a global community cares about protecting the innate virtues of the original Process so that its life can be extended for years to come, even as we all push the boundaries and permeable membranes of its simple but very complex structure.

2 ROLES AND STEPS

When we lead a workshop to introduce the Critical Response Process, we often begin with conversations about the functions of critique, our experiences in giving and getting feedback, and the impetus that gave rise to the creation of CRP—topics that have been the subject of our opening chapter. After that groundwork, we briefly describe the essential three roles and four steps of the Process. Then we do CRP, usually starting with a low-stakes demonstration through a role-play using cake, before moving on to an actual work in progress by one of the participants. In doing CRP, often by taking time-outs to annotate what's happening or answer questions that come up, we begin to uncover CRP's potentials and problems, its subtext, inner workings, and the purposes and possibilities that underlie its mechanics. Often questions that arise don't have one right answer but point to a range of choices that a facilitator, artist, or responder has in a given moment to draw the most from the Process. After we've experienced CRP in this way, we move on to variations and exercises that help build skills and offer a deeper dive into the values of the Process.

This typical workshop structure unfolds CRP from its basics and practicalities to its ramifications and variations, an expansive arc that we attempt to capture in this chapter. We start with a brief description of the essentials of the Process and then expand in sections devoted to each of CRP's four steps. These begin by addressing the purpose of the step, offering examples, and exploring typical dynamics. Following these core ideas are individualized notes from each of us as authors that further shed light on the step, reflections not so different from those time-outs in which we'll respond to a question, grapple with a dilemma, or share a source of ongoing curiosity. Thus we set the scene for the wider view of CRP and its applications that constitute Part II of this book.

"Practice, Practice"

Liz Lerman

"Practice, practice."

I am not sure exactly how this phrase came to echo in my head as much as it did growing up. Even though I started taking dance classes at the age of five, I don't think my first dance teacher told me to go home and do the exercises. However, I think my mother did. In fact, I think she is the one who suggested that without practice I would get nowhere.

And so I practiced. I practiced what I could remember from class. I practiced what I saw in books. My father built a little ballet barre in every room I lived in growing up, and there were many, as we moved around a lot. I think it gave him pleasure to put the barre into the wall, and both my parents liked hearing the music coming from my bedroom as I repeated the steps over and over.

I had one teacher who told us that she could tell if we were practicing because our dance slippers would wear out faster. I used to sit and watch TV with my dad and rub the shoes on the floor at the same time—a way to cheat myself into being one of my teacher's favorites, which was important in the world of ballet.

When I took up flute for three years, the parental pleading took on a new urgency. Maybe because they could tell if it was "good" or not more easily than with the dancing, or maybe because I was a beginner and the sounds were a bit off. Regardless, with a public school flute in hand and free lessons at the library on Saturday mornings, off I went to play the flute, and the demands of practicing thirty minutes a day took hold . . . that is, until my dance teacher called the house and said that my time spent playing the flute was diluting my dancing and that it was important for me to focus on just one thing. With relief all around, I gave up the music and went back to the barre.

I mostly liked the practicing, but I wasn't practicing for the steps. I was practicing to become a dancer, and to me that had little to do with the barre. Even as a child, I knew I was aspiring to something beyond the steps. Something that would be larger than any one thing I could do with my body. Larger than any series of things I could do to capture the music or the feelings and sensations of a human being. But practice was the way to get there. It would not, as my mother said, be possible without it.

And so it is with the Critical Response Process. We need the steps to practice. Practice helps us figure out the nuances, iterations, possibilities, and problems. Working through the steps of the Process is central to the use of CRP when we do formal critique, but we don't do the Process because of the steps. Ultimately, we do the Process so we can manage our judgments in real life. We practice the Process so we can internalize its underlying values as mental and compassionate behavior. It's a form of training to achieve generative and thoughtful ways of being with our colleagues, friends, and families.

When we sit down in a CRP circle to do the four-step Process with a facilitator, we know we are preparing for an experience that requires us to be conscious, thoughtful, and aware of managing our impulses. Yes, many new understandings will occur, and innovative ideas and solutions will be formed in response to our questions. But by being in ceremony we are practicing a kind of awareness to language and to relationships that the four steps nurture. Nowhere is this more evident than when we transfer the principles of CRP out of the formal process into real life.

In practicing the steps, you hold yourself *in relation* to the values, values that can be very hard to keep. Of course, if we choose to think of CRP as a kind of ritual, that is what ritual does. It keeps you practicing what is otherwise hard to do. We need the "rules and protocols," or we will fail. And we fail in the trying as well. But the practices make it a living reminder of what we are trying to do, and when we are successful, we know that the practice is worth it.

The Critical Response Process in Brief

THE ROLES

- The *artist* offers a work in progress for review and is prepared to question that work in a dialogue with other people.
- One, a few, or many *responders*—committed to the artist's intent to make excellent work—engage in the dialogue with the artist.
- The *facilitator* initiates each step, keeps the Process on track, and works to help both artist and responders use the Process to frame useful questions and responses.

THE STEPS

The Critical Response Process takes place after a presentation of artistic work. A work can be short or long, large or small, and at any stage in its development. If the situation allows, participants sit in a circle with the facilitator positioned next to the artist.

The Core Steps

1. *Statements of Meaning*: Responders state what was engaging, interesting, stimulating, or striking in the work they have just witnessed. Discomforts, doubts, and negative opinions are withheld until the appropriate opportunities occur later in the Process.
2. *Artist as Questioner*: The artist asks questions about the work. After each question, responders answer, being mindful to stay on topic with the question. Responders may express opinions, including "negative" perspectives, as long as they are in direct response to the question asked and do not contain suggestions for changes (unless suggestions have been specifically requested by the artist).
3. *Responders Ask Questions*: Responders ask neutral questions about the work. The artist answers. Questions are neutral when they do not have an opinion embedded in them. For example, if you are discussing the lighting of a scene, "Why was it so dark?" is not a neutral question. "What ideas guided your choices about lighting?" is.
4. *Opinion Time*: Responders state opinions, subject to permission from the artist. The usual form is: "I have an opinion about ______, would you like to hear it?" The artist has the option to say no.

More Steps

A. *What's Your Next Step?* After step four, artists talk about the next steps they are planning based on information gained through the Process.

B. *Subject Matter Discussion*: Sometimes a work will generate a vital discussion about an issue of social or aesthetic controversy. An added step to discuss the issue allows the artist to receive additional useful information but avoids sidetracking the Process away from the art itself during the four core steps.

C. *Working the Work*: Sometimes a Critical Response session can move directly into labbing aspects of the work, sometimes with active participation by the responders.

A Note on Fixits

"Fixits"—that is, directive suggestions from responders for changes or additions to the work—can come up in any step of the Process. How CRP participants manage them depends on the step in which they occur, as well as additional factors such as the work's stage of development, the relationship of the responders to the work, and, most importantly, the artist's preference.

In step one, responders occasionally slide from a statement of meaning directly into a fixit: "I really like how fast you moved in that one section. I wish there had been more of that." Or, more pointedly, "Your dancing is so passionate! I think your costume should be red, not black." These expansions from meaning into suggestion are out of line for the purpose of step one, and the facilitator may intervene to suggest that the responder consider how to use the later steps of the Process to explore their idea.

In step two, the artist may ask a question that invites suggestions, such as, "What kind of icing would you enjoy on a cake like this?" Fixits are appropriate if they stay on topic with the request.

In step three, fixits sometimes appear couched in responders' attempted questions to the artist, as in, "Have you thought about doing X?" or "What do you think would happen if you did Y?" These questions are not neutral by virtue of containing suggestions. The facilitator may suggest that the responder formulate a nondirective question about the broader topic that their fixit would address, and possibly follow up in step four if the artist is interested in hearing the suggestion.

Step four is where fixits most often occur, as opinions often take the form of suggestions. It's not always clear where an opinion ends and a fixit begins. There are multiple approaches for managing them:

- Fixits are acceptable, either by the artist's preference or by the general consensus.
- Fixits can be forbidden, either by the artist's choice or because of reasons established in a context such as a specific class or a post-show discussion.
- A facilitator can add to the step four protocol by requesting that responders let artists know that when a fixit is part of an opinion, as in: "I have an opinion about your costume choice that contains a suggestion. Would you like to hear it?" The artist may then decide whether to hear both or neither.
- The responder verging on a suggestion can be directed back to step three to frame a neutral question about the topic of their suggestion. A neutral question that leads an artist to find their own solution is usually more inspiring, motivating, and illuminating than merely handing them a fixit.

The Roles

- The *artist* offers a work in progress for review and is prepared to question that work in a dialogue with other people.
- One, a few, or many *responders*—committed to the artist's intent to make excellent work—engage in the dialogue with the artist.
- The *facilitator* initiates each step, keeps the Process on track, and works to help both the artist and responders use the Process to frame useful questions and responses.

The functions and responsibilities engaged when people gather for feedback using the Critical Response Process are delineated into three roles. We recommend that anyone serious about using CRP on an ongoing basis find a way to experience each of these roles regularly. Doing so helps enlighten the dynamics and varied facets of inquiry at play, while sharpening the skills it takes to get better at the Process. It also supports reciprocity in groups using CRP on a regular basis: If you know you will eventually be in the artist's seat, you will likely be a more mindful responder, and the insights gained in either of these roles are invaluable once you assume the facilitator's position. By gaining experience as artist, responder, and facilitator, one can better manage the multiple learnings going on during any given session and more fully grasp applications of the principles of CRP outside of formal contexts. As the Process adapts, the roles adapt: in a one-on-one conversation about a work in progress using CRP principles, one or both parties may internalize the functions of a facilitator; when a group of collaborators has a CRP-infused dialogue, everyone involved may move fluidly between artist and responder roles.

Beyond the three central roles in the dialogue, two supportive positions are often called to duty. Almost always, it is invaluable to have a *notetaker* or *scribe*. A person in this role frees the artist from taking their own notes, making them more alert to the dialogue and assuring that the most meaningful aspects of their own participation are captured. When CRP is under a time constraint, as is often the case, a *timekeeper* can also be helpful, freeing the facilitator from clock-watching to concentrate more fully on the dynamics of the Process itself.

Like much about CRP, the principles underlying these roles have changed little in the thirty-year history of the Process. But as experience has added variation and nuance to our understanding of how these functions play out in practice, the language used to communicate them has evolved, as reflected in the following discussion.

ARTIST

The artist is the person (or, in collaborative instances, the persons) putting their work forward for review, fully embracing the idea that it is still in progress, still pliant and subject to change, and ready to benefit from close questioning. Although we continue to label role as "the artist" for general discussion, other words like "maker," "researcher," or "presenter" have come into play as we've watched the Process move from artistic spaces into the fields of science, management, education, and counseling. In any of these contexts, the person in the artist's seat is assuming responsibility for the work under discussion, which may mean that they are the primary author of an artistic work, the coordinator of a creative endeavor, or a representative of a group venture.

In the years since the introduction of CRP, a greater need has emerged for giving and receiving feedback in collaborative settings where at any moment anyone in the assembled collective could be the "artist" in CRP terms, as the focus of responsibility progresses in a shifting conversation. How do we use the Process to aid the necessary speed in which ideas grow, expand, get critiqued, reiterated, polished, accepted, or rejected? To complicate these dynamics even more, many of these ventures are collaborative across disciplines. Whether these are multidisciplined teams of artists devising new work together or scientists from a variety of fields trying to solve what they call "wicked problems," we've observed teams employing CRP both formally and flexibly to get work done. When a collaborative ensemble includes an instigator, a designer, an engineer, a programmer, a project manager, and an implementer, anyone might be the artist one second and a highly invested responder the next. Knowing CRP and its values helps move ideas along and can also mitigate some of the consistent issues that occur in such collaborative groups, including territorialism, the need to prove expertise, and the use of critique to wield power.

RESPONDER

Giving feedback on the work in progress, responders are invested, for the duration of the session, in the artist doing the artist's best work on the artist's own terms. This may mean temporarily setting aside a competitive perspective if the responder is a peer, or temporarily releasing the force of authority if the relationship is hierarchical.

You can learn a lot as a responder. We are convinced, having sat in on hundreds of CRP sessions, that people giving feedback function not only in reaction to the work they are reviewing but also in relation to their own ideas and thinking processes. Engaged responders can use the Process to reinvestigate their own aesthetic positions or disciplinary mindsets and even question their likes and dislikes as the dialogue moves forward. As we lead sessions, we occasionally pause to make sure that responders are following along, listening, and tracking for their own purposes ideas that come up in the discussion of someone else's work. In fact, it's possible that when we are not the maker, we can hear the broader value of feedback better and be more adept as we find our own ways to apply it.

Paloma McGregor, cofounder and artistic director of Angela's Pulse and an active CRP trainer, enlists a vivid metaphor to describe the interaction between the responders' awareness of their own perspective and the work in progress they are addressing:

> As a responder I ask myself what experiences I bring to this moment of witnessing and exchange, and how those experiences color what I'm seeing. I might notice that my aesthetic lenses are yellow, because I make yellow work with people who also make or value yellow work. Then I encounter an artist who makes blue work with people whose practice centers seeing blue in all its multiple shades and possibilities. If I put my yellow lenses on that blue work, I'm going to see green—some combination of what the work is or wants to be and what my lenses bring to my witnessing. So it's important for me to recognize that I have yellow lenses on, whether it's the long history I bring, or what's going on for me today. The steps of CRP give me a way to both value my lenses and find out more about the work, or the Process, or the opinion that's being shared with me in the moment.

Vast experience and deep knowledge of form, craft, and technique may also inform response in CRP. For teachers, mentors, bosses and other guides, setting aside authority as a responder does not mean abandoning expertise. In this way CRP is different from certain schools of artistic coaching, where inquiry is intended to draw out insights latent in the coachee, and coaches are strongly discouraged from developing questions out of their own perspectives, expertise, or curiosities. Of course CRP provides a central starting point to the artist's questions, but it doesn't end there. We want and need people's expertise. Through the sequence and filters provided by its steps, CRP helps those with expertise to suspend or engage their knowledge and directive guidance.

FACILITATOR

When CRP is practiced as formal structure, with its specific protocols for each of the steps, a facilitator is a necessity and, ideally, an asset. Encompassing dimensions of guide, coach, and traffic controller, the role calls on the person facilitating to judge many gradations, including when to intervene and when to hold back, when to adhere to the letter of the rules and when to trust the momentum of the session, how actively to support participants, and more. Because of these complexities, the role benefits from ongoing practice. But facilitators are generally more effective when they do not assume the position of an authority or expert, and the structure contains sufficient guardrails that a newcomer to CRP facilitation can be fairly secure in guiding a solid session.

Whether or not an official timekeeper has been assigned, it is ultimately the job of the facilitator to manage time in a CRP session. How long to linger in each step, when to move on to the next question or comment, when to intervene on artist or responders who may be dwelling in repetitive or secondary material—these all are judgments a facilitator makes, as they read the needs of the artist or group to shape the Process to the time allotted. For almost always, in our experience, a formal session of CRP happens under some kind of time constraint as dictated by factors such as program schedules, class periods, or reasonable expectations of an audience's attention span.

These considerations raise the question of time as it functions in the Critical Response Process. "How long does a session take?" is a common question among newcomers to CRP, and while forty minutes might be a standard target for any work of substance, the truer response almost always relies on how much time is available. When CRP finds a home in institutions as it so often does in theaters, schools, and art centers, management of the Process is governed by clock time. At least in the capitalistic West, time is commodified in such a way that respecting people means respecting the limits of their time.

But the human elements of CRP—the reflection, trust, dialogue, and measured consideration of a person's work—all emerge with their own sense of time that often defies the strictures of a schedule. Often a session of CRP goes into a kind of "zone" where the unfolding conversation, the flow from one idea to another, and the spirit of mutual spark and synthesis establishes its own experiential sense of time. We might look up at the clock and say, "Oh . . . we lost track of time," but it might be just as valid to say that we claimed time from the tyranny of the clock and, in focused absorption, gained a grasp of it that often eludes us.

Facilitators of CRP may find that they're simultaneously managing these two experiences of time—clock time and emergent time, as we often call them—and adjusting priorities to reconcile them. When we discuss these contrasting perceptions of time with participants, we hear them named in varied ways: colonial vs. indigenous, capitalistic vs. collectivistic, knowledge banking vs. liberatory pedagogy. These suggest that our experiences of time carry deep history, cultural import, and political implications (ideas explored in depth in Cristóbal Martínez's essay "The Critical Response Process: Aesthetics of Time" in chapter 5).

It is beautiful when circumstances can accommodate an open and flowing tempo, when we can let the needs of the work at hand and the people assembled determine the use of time. More often, a clock is ticking, and the facilitator is watching it.

A session of CRP typically takes place immediately after a showing of work in progress—with numerous exceptions, such as its use in collaborations (where the work may have been experienced by the participants as it developed over time), with public showings (where the feedback might be delayed until the morning following a preview, for instance), or with longer written forms (where responders might come to the session having already read the material under consideration).

If the circumstance allows, participants sit in a circle with the facilitator positioned next to the artist or artists. The circular seating arrangement promotes a sense of equal investment and power balance among those gathered and encourages a more collaborative, less oppositional relationship between artist and responders. Artist, entrepreneur, and CRP facilitator Erika R. Moore is eloquent about the power of the circle in CRP: "There's something that happens when you're in a circle. Everyone can see everyone else and there's 360 degrees of knowledge being shared. Your attention and energy moves around the circle and goes to what's inside it. The circle acknowledges the experience that everyone has, no matter their age, no matter their background, or where they come from."

Modified circles (such as double rows, gaps, or one or more people positioned outside the circle) often lead to miscommunications or missteps. At times, as with a larger audience in fixed seating or in a virtual gathering on a video conference platform, the ideal of a circle can't be met, requiring the facilitator to encourage a "circle mindset" by keeping participants engaged and aware of each other's contributions.

Once the circle is set, the Process begins.

Step One

> *Step One: Statements of Meaning.* Responders state what was engaging, interesting, stimulating, or striking in the work they have just witnessed. Discomforts, doubts, and negative opinions are withheld until the appropriate opportunities occur later in the Process.

The Critical Response Process is inquiry-based; all four steps employ questions in some way. Step one starts with a question the facilitator asks the responders, which usually takes a form like the following (with the particular words subject to endless variation): "What stood out to you? What in the work we've just experienced was notable, energizing, evocative, or provocative?" Responders address their answers to the artist. This step generally elicits a wide range of response that touches on various aspects of the art or other work under consideration.

Step one responses must be honest. It can be very helpful to make them specific. Words in the starting prompt such as "exciting," "meaningful," and "memorable" generally lead the commentary toward the appreciative or positive (but see Liz's note later in this section on the perils and benefits of naming). Be clear, though, that step one isn't about saying something affirming merely for the sake of being nice. Being nice may feel supportive, but it doesn't help the artist advance the work. Goodwill, though, is essential. Responders may remind themselves that they are present to support the artist in doing the artist's own best work. And the practice of step one has a way of nurturing goodwill among peers and colleagues, often as a long-term proposition.

Like all of CRP's steps, statements of meaning applies a particular filter. Responders withhold strong discomforts (another problematic word, so keep reading) or negative reactions to the work, until the appropriate means of communicating them arrives in the subsequent steps, each governed by its own filter. A facilitator may choose to name the filter in introducing the step, using phrasing like: "If you have strong discomforts or negative reactions about what you've experienced, we ask you to filter them out for the moment. They can be the source of valuable information to the artist, so hold on to them, and be thinking about how they might inform your involvement in the steps that follow."

What we label here as meaning can be as simple as naming what you noticed or as personal as describing your own reflections, feelings, or memories as evoked by the work. The core possibilities of step one are suggested by those words the facilitator uses: "stimulating," "notable," "memorable"—and you can always find more words to open the portals of what's meaningful. Meaning is more than what you liked or what you think is effective, though those ideas can be a path to what is meaningful. Meaning can hold interpretation, but it is more than interpretation—and often less, as work that does not strive for explicit meaning can still summon a rich response. To state personal meaning is to express back to the maker some essential experience that the work elicited. In the moment of step one, the work in progress steps beyond the artist's process of making and into the scope of being witnessed, perceived, and comprehended by others. The artist has put something forward and responders offer something back. A communication loop is completed, which sets a solid foundation for the remainder of the Process.

Here are some examples to suggest the possibilities of step one.

In response to choreography for an ensemble dance work, responders might say:

- *"It was so satisfying to watch the unison movement transitioning into patterns that were more individualized."*
- *"I noticed a lot of backward walking. It looked kind of fearless."*
- *"I loved that quirky elbow thing that got passed around."*
- *"It was fun seeing pedestrian movement set on baroque music."*

In response to solo theater work:

- *"You really took us inside the experience of a person with disabilities in a job interview. The fact that you do it as a monologue with the other character implied brought me especially close."*
- *"This has so many levels: what the interviewer is saying to you, what you are saying to them, and what's going on inside your head. I appreciated the complexity."*

In response to a documentary photo series:

- *"The emotion in these pictures is so visceral. You really must have won the trust of your subjects."*
- *"I like how you've included an image showing the aftermath of the protest, once all the people had left. It completed the story for me."*

- *"They are intriguing images that definitely make me want to know more."*

A lively round of CRP step one can offer multiple perspectives on the work in progress, including striking observations, personal resonances, and interpretive insights. But not everything spoken needs to be deep or momentous. Sometimes the step one response is simply a collection of moments, impressions, and connections that flock into significance. Like a microscope, step one can probe, magnify, and sharpen particulars; like a kaleidoscope, it can amplify and elaborate the subject; like a periscope, it can shift the perspective to highlight aspects otherwise out of view.

Several elements in a typical CRP step one function to leverage breadth and diversity of meaning. Simply assembling a group to witness will offer as many lenses for viewing the work as there are people gathered. The facilitator's categories of "exciting," "memorable," and "evocative," or invitations like "What stood out?" and "What did you notice?" can welcome different kinds of insights. When members of a group share points of reference because they study or work together, aesthetic or technical points can further enrich commentary. Diversity of response often equals plurality of meaning, including the possibility of multiple meanings for a single moment, or of even the coexistence of apparently contradictory meanings. Sometimes this plurality can exist in a single person's response.

For the artist, the experience of step one usually has several dimensions, often interacting with one another in positive ways. Frequently, the anxiety that naturally accompanies putting work forward for critique will be calmed by having it received and translated into the palpable, describable, significant experiences of others. Sometimes artistic intention is confirmed when an idea the artist was pursuing lands with comprehension, or when a nugget of inspiration that is vital for the maker proves resonant for others. Often, a viewer's observation reaches beyond the scope of artistic intention or the maker's grasp of the meaning in what they made, which can be either fulfilling or destabilizing for the artist. In either case, step one can help us see the art as having an independent existence, a life of its own, which in turn can open new paths to be explored in the future development of the work.

For all the benefit of step one responses, it can be a challenge for artists to experience them. There can be a strong impulse to dismiss the significance or deny the value of these comments. But the same discipline that applies to the responders in step one also applies to the artist: filter out the negative. For the artist, this act of filtering out their own negative internal voice, even just for the few moments in which step one is happening, becomes vital conditioning to call upon at will throughout the creative process.

In step one we are focusing on letting the artist know what was of value in the thing they made. As a responder, you may notice your discomforts, but you don't use them yet. Withholding your discomforts at the start may feel dishonest, but remember that the full story is still to unfold. Follow the steps of the Process and it will. Listening to step one responses has a notable effect on both responders and artists. For responders, step one offers a level of replay, refocus, and a chance to re-experience the work, perhaps with the fresh slants afforded by other people's perspectives. For the maker, these re-projections of the work can be set against their own internalized image of what they've made in all of its dimensions of impulse, intention, and process. In sum, the practice of statements of meaning filters out strong discomforts, placing a broadly defined idea of meaning at the forefront to enrich developing work in progress in the following forms:

- A vein of response in which rational and emotional reactions are enlightening one another
- Externalizations and interpretations of the work that offer the artist a comparison with their vision, intention, or generative experience
- An amplification of the work to precede the deeper interrogation through question and opinion, which happens later in the Process

Usually, step one promotes an atmosphere of goodwill, heightened potential, and forward momentum for the work under consideration.

The practice of step one—that act of first finding and expressing the significance in what you encounter—becomes a valuable rehearsal for countless intersections with people and experiences. If you try to find the meaning before you jump to your discomforts, you might find you like art better, enjoy living more, and coexist with fellow human beings with greater ease.

NOTES FROM LIZ LERMAN

On Meaning and Naming

Usually when I am teaching the Critical Response Process, I will stop after our first round of step one responses to check in with participants about how they experienced the few minutes we took to deliver these ideas about meaning. Having done this often, I can predict the kinds of things people will say. Typically, someone will talk about the positive spirit in the room. Some might note the many differing reactions that members of the group had in response to the work. Some will reflect about getting to experience the piece over again through other people's eyes, or how others' comments alerted them to aspects of the work they hadn't noted. And sometimes someone will say there were a lot of "compliments."

When that happens, I will take the opportunity to discuss how we characterize our experiences. Often, without realizing it, we describe an experience with a label that then determines where we file it in the retrieval systems of our brain. My concern is that when someone names the step one statements as compliments, they will promptly dismiss what just happened. The word "compliment" is so belittled in our society, so instantly thought of as an insincere remark or a fake way of being nice, that no matter how strongly you felt in the moment of experiencing a CRP step one comment, you will forget it, or delete it, or think it is unimportant if you categorize it as a compliment. We are accustomed to compliments addressing less important subjects such as clothing or possessions, which falsely suggests that the serious work of critique can only happen when we open the door to the negative.

So when I hear "compliments," I always ask the group, "What else could we call them?" To think about multiple words for the same thing is a very creative act. It allows the person who said "compliment" to retain that idea while adding to the list of file names for themselves. Others in the circle might call step one responses "personal reflections," "working examples," "generosity," "honest kindness," or "an asset inventory"—the list goes on. In fact, by taking this time-out and thinking about it, you can also re-file all of what has just been said into categories that help catalyze responses the next time you see or experience art.

Another troublesome word that often comes up in relation to step one is "positive." And here, I have to admit that my complaining self kicks in with a litany of issues I have with this word:

My problem with the word "positive" is that the negative is positive too, at least when living inside the CRP protocols.

My problem with the word "positive" is that it is always set in opposition to "negative."

My problem with the word "positive" is that it is dismissed as a kind of "icebreaker" (another word I dislike) as you supposedly wait for the "real" substance of the critique: the negative.

My problem with the word "positive" is that it doesn't have the breadth to hold the mysteries and beauty and information that always come out of step one in a CRP session, where the data rising to the surface goes far beyond the merely "positive." Taking a moment to find other ways to name this range of response helps you recognize the many kinds of connection that the work has achieved.

Assigning multiple names also helps us with our capacity to frame ideas so that others can see them in a fresh way. When I bring up this subject in relation to the "compliment" label, the reaction always suggests that I have caught people thinking in a way they wish they didn't. They are relieved to be tasked with a way out of the limitations of a singular label and are excited by the simplicity of the solution.

Applied to step one, using multiple names for the same thing is a very handy idea when opening up the space for responses. Meaning is very big. There is not one form of it, or one experience of it. If you lay out the multiple beginnings or portals, newcomers to the Process will find their way through one of them. Finding portals can be as simple as asking people what they like about a given thing. For example, if you ask people what they like about food, the answers you get are pretty interesting. "I like to make it," "I like to share it," "I like to arrange it on a plate," "I like to experiment," "I like finding it," "I like consuming it." Each of these answers includes a different portal: creativity, companionship, design, innovation, research, taste. The word "like" is merely a bridge to the idea or feeling.

And we know that if we substitute "like" for other kinds of words—what is interesting, curious, elegant, surprising, thoughtful (there is an endless supply of these words)—each one can take the viewer back to the work of art at hand and help to show it in a new light. And in time, these practices with CRP can come to be a livelier companion out in the world. These predicates become a more normal part of a person's personal vocabulary for seeing and notating experience. They change the way we actually inhabit the world.

Step One for Responders

The effects of practicing CRP on how we relate to the world—and, indeed, how we function in our own minds—has been a growing theme in my understanding of the Process in recent years. So much of the origins of CRP rest in my own needs as an artist. While I gave consideration to responders in my early years with the Process, the weight of my attention was on the artist as the primary beneficiary. I considered the circle of a CRP session as a community and trusted in the reciprocity that would happen over time as each person took on all three roles. My thinking was something like this: I will work hard for the person sitting in the artist's chair because at some point that will be me. I can bring my best self to the critique by attempting to leave competitive thoughts behind for a few minutes. Such thoughts might be a barrier to full participation; so learning to dismiss them for an hour seemed like a good thing. Thus, I knew that as I sat as a responder, the time was well spent because I was developing my conceptual skills as a form of critique while also practicing ways of being a member of a community. When the session was over and I left, I could return to my competitive sense of self as if slipping on a coat.

More recently, I have come to understand some of the particular benefits of reflection, perspective, and growth that the Process offers to responders. The possibilities start in step one as responders share their observations. For some, this alone is a big step. The hurdle of self-doubt lurks in everyone's soul. (Well, almost everyone's.) In this first step, people practice speaking from their own experience as if it matters—because it does, often in ways that are quite visible. It affects the artist, who is listening intently. It affects the way the energy moves in the group. It brings new ideas to mind for others who are sitting in the circle.

And this voicing of experience affects the speaker. Step one requires the responder to notice that they have had an experience. Until I started doing CRP, I hadn't realized how many people go through life without reflecting to themselves what kind of life they are having. They might notice their extreme likes and dislikes, but, for many, having the immediate opportunity to put into words perceptions that might otherwise remain more subterranean is a useful practice of articulation.

Responders in step one also have a chance to rethink their own judgments about the work just shared, and to enlarge their comprehension of the thing being discussed. When a group comes together over one brief event and then brings into the circle each person's awareness and history of the subject, it is a quietly exuberant form of learning.

But probably the most absorbing aspect of CRP's step one, a feature that causes both difficulty and opportunity for growth, is the idea of filtering for meaning. For the responder, this engages the impact of being able to (1) notice the negative; (2) filter the negative out of immediate comments by putting it somewhere else; and (3) continue with the Process, participating fully with enthusiasm and vigor.

Perhaps it is this threefold task of filtering that offers biggest benefit of step one as a personal practice. I often ask people about what happens to them when they begin a creative endeavor. I want to know how fast the negative slips into their consciousness. How quickly do they judge their own thoughts and actions? Usually when I raise this question, the response is laughter, followed by silence, then an answer: "It begins before I even sit down," or "The negative is instantaneous and continuous."

It is very hard to do any kind of creative work (perhaps any work at all) with a constant flow of negative, judgmental thoughts as a companion. Creativity thrives best, according to those who study it, when it affords both time for freedom and exploration and time for judgment and discernment. Most people do not give themselves enough time in that first mode—or they try to do both at the same time.

Even discomfort itself, a feeling we often recommend filtering out in step one, might call for some careful discernment. Sometimes it seems evident that the artist wants to provoke an audience in a way that causes discomfort. I have seen responders in step one tell the artist they are uncomfortable, meaning it in a way that they think confirms the artist's hopes for the work. But the artist doesn't necessarily hear it that way, so it's useful to consider how you may sometimes have to contextualize the comment, both to the artist and to yourself.

What I am advocating here is for each of us to find a way to filter out some of the judgments that occupy us so quickly at various stages of our work. I can sometimes accomplish this because I have worked at it for so long in step one of CRP sessions. And if I remember that the steps that follow will help me engage and process the critical idea I am holding at bay, then I can temporarily set that idea to the side without concern that I am dismissing something useful.

Meaning and Affirmation

Step one underwent some alteration during the early years of CRP. At first, I called it "Affirmation" and expected this first round of responses to be supportive of the artist as a person. The comments were to be directed to the artist as if they were the work. It became clear to me very quickly that I had that wrong. Within a year or two, we had transformed that step into one that focused on affirmative statements about the work itself, which brought the idea of meaning into the foreground position it carries today.

But another transformation is taking place at the time of this writing, as artists increasingly make work stemming from personal and collective trauma, that makes me want to revisit this change, going full circle back to the beginning. Perhaps now step one needs to be a time to exchange meaning to support an artist who has decided to take a hard look at difficult subjects and bring those to the surface. Often these are artists of color, and often they are taking on systems of oppression that have existed for centuries. These works are personal, unflinching in their detail, and very demanding of both artist and audience.

Asked to state the meaningful in reaction to such work, responders often begin by saying something like, "You are very brave to be making this work," or "Watching was very emotional for me because I've lived this experience too," or "I am so glad, even though it must have been hard, that you made this and gave me a way to see into your world." I have heard from some of the artists who have made such challenging works that without these kinds of statements, they would have a hard time advancing to the next steps of the Process.

So I conclude that affirmation is back, that step one does not need to choose between meaning and affirmation. There is room for both. How intentioned this will become in the years ahead, we will have to see. But supporting people who are bringing their deepest experiences to the public in the present may mean that all of us in the circle can move beyond expressing our thoughts about the work to also supporting the person who created it. It's a twenty-first-century form of caring.

NOTES FROM JOHN BORSTEL

On Observation

It's a provocative experience to look at a person's creative work knowing that your first task, once it's over, will be to deliver a step one response. You will state what has been meaningful about what you've witnessed, following the many possibilities that meaning can hold and remembering that nothing is too small to notice. Anticipation of the task calls you to a higher level of responsibility to the work and to the person. At the same time, it can be a relief to be reminded that your internal response may be multidimensional, even conflicted, and that details matter, even the details in your own reaction. Maybe most significantly, the immediate opportunity of voicing a statement of meaning stimulates your powers of observation as both a critical and a creative skill.

It is very difficult to keep observation purely objective. Though it is not a formal aspect of CRP, I sometimes ask workshop participants to look at a picture or a scene and simply name what they see. It's almost impossible to do this without imposing meaning: choosing what to name, forming a perceived connection between multiple items, or communicating the kind of identity statement or self-declaration when you cite a detail ("Look what

I noticed!") or see what is beyond the immediately obvious. And in the "name what you see" exercise, people quickly slither beyond naming to interpretation ("This means X"), deduction ("This suggests Y"), or judgments, opinions, and statements of personal significance.

Perhaps the readiness with which we slide from observation into these realms of the subjective stands as a measure of how creative it is to observe. When theorists enumerate the capacities that mark human creativity, they often place observation, a similar function, near the top of the list. It stands to reason. Observation precedes discovery, and the more refined our observation, the greater the potential to see or create something new from our perception.

Observation inevitably precedes critique as well. If feedback is the moment when the creator's work meets the discernment of a witness, observation starts with the actions of the maker and continues with the perception of the viewer. Critical discussion of a work is grounded in observation of it. That may seem obvious, but for some of us it is so easy to jump from the objective experience of looking at someone else's work to the subjective satisfaction of witnessing our own reactions to it that we may bypass the value of fully engaged observation. Engaging in focused and mindful observation takes concentration, as it is easy to be seduced into subjective sidelines, seeing someone else's work as a (negative or positive) mirror of one's own experience and preferences, looking for it to be a reflection of something we know and can name, and if it's not, being either unsatisfied with what we're seeing or assuming we're unqualified to respond to it. If the work is in our own discipline of practice, it is all the more easy to use ourselves as the measure and view the work as similar or dissimilar to what we would make, and if we are offering opinions or giving guidance, directing it toward building work that looks like our own.

Singularity in critique is easy and satisfying: Things are right or wrong, working or not; there's a fix and we can find it. But it is plurality that will ultimately serve us if we want feedback to hold a richness that meets the actual potential of the work, and if we believe that the artist should be the ultimate author of their work.

Liking "Like"

"I like how you varied the pattern." "I love the sweep of the costumes." Often enough, responders will say, "I like . . ." or "I love . . ." as lead-ins to their statements of meaning. So, what is the role of liking or loving what you've experienced? Is it acceptable to use these direct statements of affinity and affection in CRP's step one? These questions often arise in our trainings and discussions with practitioners, particularly educators. Generally we'd advise keeping "like" and "love" out of the facilitator's prompting for step one, avoiding a lead-in such as, "So, what did you like about this piece?" As to whether these words should be encouraged or discouraged in responders' statements, different practitioners argue for different approaches. The argument *for* says that "I like" is the most accessible phrasing for many responders, the readiest way into a statement of meaning; it acknowledges that step one responses are subjective by design, so why limit phrasing that identifies them as such? Moreover, not forbidding "I like" means one less aspect of the Process for facilitators to police. The argument *against* suggests that discouraging "I like" will shift the emphasis away from responders merely providing information about themselves and their preferences and toward concrete discussion of the work under consideration, allowing step one to set a decisive tone for the full Critical Response Process. Michael Despars, a California-based theater educator who uses CRP in teaching International Baccalaureate classes at the high school level, holds this point of view:

> I do not allow students to make "like" statements, but rather encourage them to use phrase like "I found this work evocative because . . ." or "It was meaningful when . . ." The use of the word "like" is subjective and does not help the performer to develop a work in progress; it is a hindrance. Instead I encourage students to really make statements about what was surprising, provocative, meaningful, because the use of these words as beginning statements encourage deeper discussion and elicit strong meaning.

A facilitator can take a middle path when the "I like" phenomenon dominates by saying, "We are hearing a lot of 'I like' statements, so let me remind you that step one isn't just about what you liked. You can state something that stood out to you, an idea or memory that the work brought to mind, or talk about a particular detail." Using "like" is a good point of entry for a statement of meaning. Getting beyond it will expand the possibilities of step one.

Step One Is Not a Sandwich

When I ask workshop participants to describe what has worked in their experiences of feedback, they will occasionally tell me about something called "the sandwich." In this practice, if you have something negative to say, you precede and follow it with a positive. It may be effective, and it can certainly sound like a sort of step-sibling to CRP's step one. But the approach and its name suggest that the negative is the "meat" in the sandwich and that the positives are the padding, the empty carbs, the puffy supermarket bread softening the blow of the tough stuff. The positive functions merely as a palliative buffer on the negative. If, as a responder, this is all you are doing with the positives in the sandwich or with the statements of meaning in step one, you may be missing the power of engaged meaning and may need to challenge yourself to be more specific, more outside your usual habits of thinking, more honest. If, as an artist, you are inclined to dismiss step one responses as mere analgesics for the toothache of critique, I invite you to relax, breathe them in, and trust in your notetaker to capture them for your future perusal and reference. More than one artist has turned to me in my facilitator's chair during step one and said, "All these comments are nice, but can we get to the real stuff?" To which I reply, "Artist, this *is* the real stuff. Everything you've heard is concrete information that can inform and support the ongoing work on your project."

Step Two

> *Step Two: Artist as Questioner.* The artist asks questions about the work. After each question, the responders answer, being mindful to stay on topic with the question. Responders may express opinions, including "negative" perspectives, as long as they are in direct response to the question asked and do not contain suggestions for changes (unless suggestions have been specifically requested by the artist).

In CRP's step two, the artist asks questions and responders answer. It sounds simple and often is. But the experience of step two is frequently colored by complicating factors bearing on the high-stakes act of submitting a work in progress to witness, consideration, and response. If the artist has worked in relative isolation up to this point, the exposure of sharing work can be a stressful moment triggering the release of pent-up energy hinging on self-worth, relationship to the group, and the viability of a new creation. If the process of developing the work has been collaborative or already exposed to assessment, stepping into CRP's structure can bring a jarring shift in perspective and a sudden recalibration of how peers and stakeholders relate to one another. Hope, vulnerability, and doubt all come to the fore as CRP arrives at step two.

We like to suggest that the artist come to CRP in a mindset that combines a readiness to question their own work, a willingness to acknowledge—even embrace—its unfinished state, and an eagerness to hear from those who have just experienced it. In this disposition the artist has much to gain by posing questions that draw on the specific moment they are in with the work, its state at the time of the showing, and the particular group of responders, be they peers, collaborators, or strangers. At the start of the Process, step one has typically cultivated the kind of openness of perspective to support the artist in getting the best out of the Process as step two brings them into direct dialogue with responders. But this ideal state of mind can be complicated by the public exposure and bouncing energy that arrives when a person places their work in front of an audience. Awed by the chance to hear from a group that is devoting its attention to the work, the response can be befuddlement, a rush of conflicting emotions, a pileup of ideas. Under those conditions, the seemingly simple invitation to form a question that you sincerely want answered can be challenging, so the facilitator may get involved in helping the artist find, sort, and shape their questions.

With this invitation to the maker to pose questions, CRP departs from many traditions of feedback in the arts. Authors in writers' workshops may be told to keep silent, because "the work should speak for itself"; students in visual art crits are often placed in a position only to defend while peers and professor are free to offer responses unchecked by any measure of the artist's own perspective; and in post-show Q&As in the performing arts, the privilege of posing the questions frequently sits only with the audience.

Indeed, the resistance to inquiry can imbue entire disciplines. In the hierarchical ranks of classical dance, music, and theater, performers with questions may be considered troublesome or insubordinate. Formal training in some art forms treats certitude as a critical part of the product. In this school of thought, if you haven't resolved questions on your own, you aren't ready to put your work forward. Seasoned in an atmosphere like this, an artist may have little practice or mental conditioning for the potential of inquiry, and it will come as no surprise if they arrive at CRP's step two at a loss for how to shape a useful question.

Being able to ask questions allows us to stand inside and outside of our work at the same time. That is the challenge, and that is the benefit of step two. Once you have asked a question, you are in a receiving position, but if the question is on point with your concerns, that position is not a passive one.

For the maker, CRP's step two is a chance to voice curiosity and gain understanding about how an audience of responders is receiving what heretofore may only have existed in the insulated space of the page, studio, or rehearsal room. Sometimes the artist is eager to jump in, with questions already front and center in their mind, merely awaiting the opportunity to be broached to an engaged group of viewers or hearers. At other times the challenge of formulating questions is a practical, concrete task that might be prompted by a facilitator saying something like, "You have the undivided attention of a group of people invested in the success of your effort; what do you would you like to know about their experience of your work?" Whether the artist is voicing the questions that they've already been asking themselves or is motivated to curiosity by the new situation of placing their work in progress in front of a group, questions can take many forms.

- *"What resonates to you in the stories told by these word-and-image combinations?"*
- *"Should the dance start with the soloist already onstage or should she make an entrance?"*
- *"If you had to give this painting a title, what title would you suggest?"*
- *"What do you think motivates the mother character to walk out?"*
- *"Where do you see the connections and disconnections in this group of photos?"*
- *"Do you recognize the melody in the sound cue that starts about halfway through the monologue? What associations do you make with it?"*
- *"How did you experience the encounter between characters from two different historical periods?"*
- *"What information did you take away from the statistics I included in the report?"*
- *"Did you perceive any changes in tempo in my performance of this movement, and if so, what effect did they have?"*
- *"Is it too long? Where did your interest flag? If I cut something, what should I cut?"*
- *"What cultural allusions did you hear in the poem?"*
- *"If found a way of adding a translation for the part of the dialogue that's in Mandarin, what do you think the effect would be?"*
- *"What's missing for you?"*

- *"I'm worried that the visuals and narration are sometimes just saying the same thing. Did you think they were redundant at any point?"*

Observe the variety of content and approaches in this short sampling. Some questions seek divergent, wide-ranging impressions about particular points or personal associations, while others request a choice between options. Some are outright bids for suggestions or guidance in the editing and crafting process. Questions may bear on the particulars of the current iteration of the work that has just been shared, or they may speculate about reactions to elements that might be added later. Among all these alternatives, there is no absolute right or wrong dictated by the protocols of CRP. Facilitators may guide artists in one direction or another based on a range of variables, including where a work is in its development, whether the showing encompassed the entire work or a short excerpt, and the degree to which an artist's larger path of progress is under consideration (as with students developing portfolios or culminating projects).

Throughout, step two allows the artist to move among various approaches for asking questions and may call on the facilitator to guide the artists to the question that will both be generative and pertinent to their concerns. An artist who poses a question too negatively may receive more confirmation or reassurance than substantial information about the challenge they are probing. On the other hand, an artist's question posed too generally may never reveal the issue the artist really needs to explore. Consider the question, "What was your response to the use of multiple languages in this piece?" in contrast to, "If you heard a language you didn't understand, did you feel alienated or excluded when the actors spoke it?" The former is open, general, and neutral; the latter may lean toward the negative but also may get at the artist's discomfort and also at the essence of the audience's experience and the power of the work. The two questions may elicit different sorts of answers and between them are further gradations of possibility. It's part of the art of facilitation to gauge the emotional state of the artist, their confidence or hesitancy in entering the question, the stage of development of the work itself, and to judge what option is appropriate to the needs of the moment.

Thus far we've been addressing step two in terms of the challenges and options for the artist inherent in the opportunity to ask a question. But a question asked implies an answer given, which is the other side of step two and the role that the responders play—subject to this limitation: responders must stay on topic with the artist's question. They temporarily suspend the full range of their concerns about the work to particularize their response to the matter that the artist has named. In step two the artist sets the strategy.

The injunction is not merely a filter for the responders. It is a contract that holds parties on both sides of the dialogue to a particular responsibility. As artist, educator, and CRP facilitator Raji Ganesan succinctly put it: "If you are the responder, it means answering the question the artist has asked, not the question you *wish* they'd asked." This means resisting the temptation to pivot to a topic that you judge to be more in need of the artist's attention, or that might simply be a shinier platform for your own intelligence. If you are the artist, your question signals that you are willing to hear any authentic answer, even if it's negative, even if it does not validate your hope or intention on the topic broached. By asking the question, you as the artist have opened the space for discussion of the topic. Positive, negative, or otherwise, to get your answer now, rather than in step four where responders' concerns can suggest the topic, is itself a validation of your priorities, your terms, and your ultimate control as the creator of the work.

This two-way contract also reminds us of a shared responsibility in forestalling the defensiveness that might shortchange learning and discovery. The responder has responsibility in staying inside the limits that the artist dictates in step two and framing questions neutrally in step three. The artist commits to their own questions with a willingness to hear the responses, implying the consent for opinions that's explicitly expressed in step four when responders are in the lead. Sometimes this calls on the artist to assume a conscious attitude of non-defensiveness.

To understand the workings of step two, imagine a visual artist who has just presented a series of paintings distinctive in numerous ways, including the fact that they are on triangular canvases. The shape has already been remarked upon in step one, and the artist wants to know more: "How did you experience the shape of my canvases?" Answers might include: "The shape was arresting; the first thing I noticed about the work." "The triangle really drew me in and focused my attention." Or even: "I think a triangle as a shape has symbolic weight . . . it made me think about the delta in mathematics, which signifies change." With the responders staying on topic, answers might also include, "The shape seemed a little gimmicky to me. I didn't see what it added." If the artist is truly invested in what step two can offer, they are ready for a response like this. (In these cases an artist may choose to do follow-up on a response they hear, asking responders to expand on what they mean by "symbolic weight" or "gimmicky." Multiple paths can branch from a step two question.)

There is another kind of answer we might hear in step two, something like: "The triangle worked for me, but the colors are what I was having trouble with. They are so drab and murky." This answer is off topic: The artist has not asked about the colors. Therefore the facilitator would need to intervene, redirecting the responder to the opportunity to explore the colors in steps three and four: "You've moved off topic from the artist's question, but hold on to your thought. You may have an opportunity in the next two steps of the Process to bring your reaction into the dialogue."

Staying on topic in step two also supports a key discipline of CRP: listening. If we as responders are committed to staying on topic with the artist's question, it means we are listening for the limits of our response, and therefore paying careful attention to the question, which will quiet the noise of our own judgments beyond the scope of the question. Everyone is learning in CRP, and the learning, listening responder will have more to offer the artist than a responder who merely surfs the wave of their own opinion.

The dynamics of inquiry exercised in steps two and three of CRP entail more than flatly stating a question and seeking its answer. Conscious of how a question may influence an answer, artists and responders may be challenged to engage in a kind of elastic thinking about the question in which they move the framework from general to specific, preliminary to follow-up, wide to narrow, and biased to neutral. To encounter art in this way is to probe its potential, grasp its implications, and grapple with where the artist ends and the art begins.

As is true throughout the Process, how active the facilitator is in step two may vary considerably depending on the context, the experience level of the artist and the group in using CRP, the state of the work under consideration, and the facilitator's own style. Typical facilitator interventions in step two include catching the artist who rambles and voices a jumble of questions, helping the artist to sort them, checking to see if a follow-up question or a refining of the question might be helpful, and redirecting responders who veer off topic.

Some facilitators practice active coaching of the artist's question during step two, with no preliminary consultation prior to the CRP session. This approach exposes struggle in the moment, which may be enlightening for both artist and responders, and can illuminate the inner workings of the

Process itself. Other facilitators like to meet in advance with the artist to help them prepare their options for step two questions. As described by Linda Chapman later in this chapter and by Jill Waterhouse in "Mentoring and Facilitating in the Visual Arts," this approach can be especially useful in artist development situations where the broader benefits of inquiry are to be cultivated as part of the larger growth of the artist.

Time doesn't always allow for the artist to get answers to all of their questions in step two. If the clock is ticking, the facilitator can invite the artist to pose remaining questions but not take time to answer them. This can cue responders to additional concerns of the artist, which may influence responders' engagement in steps three and four.

In step two, by asking questions, the artist drives the discussion of the work in progress. In the dialogue that emerges, step two can offer:

- A range of personal viewpoints and language choices that may create new distinctions or dissolve assumptions;
- An exploration into relationship between artist and audience as it functions in the case of the art in question;
- A probe into the power and challenge of the expressive choices that this artist has made; and
- A chance to expand knowledge about the subject matter or the artistic form and the terms on which it addresses its audience.

NOTES FROM LIZ LERMAN

When Questions Don't Arrive as Questions

Often our perceptions and feelings about what we are making can remain in a twisted pile of obsessive thoughts, circling back to moments of clarity or to singular problems with multiple solutions that we can't quite name. An image that comes to mind for me is a tray of jewelry in which the necklaces and earrings are caught up in a tangle. It can be fun straightening them out, unless you're in a hurry. But the focus that comes from the simple task of separating each item is a worthy investment of effort, with a clear outcome.

Also worthy is the act of sorting out the questions you might ask as an artist in step two. You discover what is connected to what, or even how to characterize the issue: Is it an earring, is the hook of the earring, or is it the length of the necklace? What's causing the tangle? After observing many CRP sessions, I see both the problems and the value that comes from working through these tangles.

Separating the overriding sense of trouble, fear, confusion, or shame, and finding the series of questions is often the first thing that happens in this step. Often an artist will talk at the beginning of step two, trudging haphazardly through various concerns as if wandering in a morass. Facilitator and responders can hear the multiple questions, and often all it takes is a simple prompt "Which of those questions do you want to ask first?" for the artist to achieve enough clarity to begin the task of sorting. That basic nudge can place the artist on a road to discovery that will enable them to return to work with concrete ideas, rather than a sense of confusion or dread. It's exciting to cut through that apprehension into a source of action that can cause a breakthrough in a project or an entire process of working.

How do you ask questions about things that are messy, problematic, unfinished, blemished? How do you decide what to ask when you have a person to ask or a group of people to talk to? Do you really want to know what they think? Do you even know what you think? What do you ask when the project is not due for weeks or months, and what do you ask when the curtain will be going up in just a few hours? When do you want actual help fixing something, and when do you want guidance to send you on a pathway to your own discovery?

Many factors are involved in what makes a question valuable. One class of questions that I often encounter among students, and among artists still finding their footing, is what I call the "art school question." These can emerge from the curriculum that student is learning or from a point of craft that an artist is hoping to master. At a basic level, these questions allow the artist to discern whether they have absorbed the principle under consideration. Such questions become really valuable, however, when the artist can discover if they are experimenting enough with the ideas that they begin to iterate new possibility as opposed to merely getting the principle right.

Questions on the theme of "Am I a good enough artist?" make themselves known under many guises, including: "Did the dance satisfy you?" "Is the story compelling?" "So, is it working?" or simply, "Is this piece good?" Such questions are difficult to answer fruitfully in the moment of a feedback session and are rarely useful. With some extra support, however, one can work to reshape these worries into purposeful inquiry.

Sometimes a facilitator can meet the "Am I good enough?" question right inside the CRP session. Often this means asking something more particular. If an artist says, "Is this work good?" the facilitator might suggest that the artist to narrow the field a bit by asking, "What would 'good' look like to you?" or "What part of 'good' are you striving for?" or even, "What is 'good' to you in this piece?" The artist might respond, for example, "This work would be good if it had a better ending." Then the facilitator can help the artist narrow in on a question about the ending.

Another approach is to open up the field for broader reflection from the responders before narrowing in. An artist's question such as "Is the middle section working?" could be restated as "In the middle section, what images or narrative are you getting?" This might allow the artist to find clearer terms on what constitutes "working," and then follow up with a more specific question, such as "What elements specifically conveyed those ideas?" or "Were there moments that were more or less effective for you?"

With "Am I good enough?" at the heart of an artist's doubt, guiding them toward answerable questions that help fill the cavern of fear that underlies their work is a true gift. Step two lets artists do just that, if they learn how to find questions that let the work itself grow as opposed to feeding the doubt and the worry.

One day, while doing a workshop in Australia with a group of participants applying CRP to their own projects, I had a kind of epiphany. I noticed that the artists were having trouble coming up with their questions. I remembered some of my earlier entreaties: Think about the concerns that keep you up at night. Consider the apologies you would make if you had to get up right now and show the work. I realized that neither of these phenomena actually emerge into thought nor live in the mind as questions. You stay up at night because you are worried and obsessed by fears and fragments that circle around ceaselessly. You apologize just before a showing because you know that aspects of the work are imperfect and you hope to preempt harsh judgment, perhaps helped by a show of humility.

So I pondered in that moment whether it would be worth actually naming the worries. Could you make a list of your worries and then actually just put "I wonder why" or some other opening phrase in front? Would that help you work on transforming the worry to inquiry? Could you enumerate all your apologies to yourself, but then dignify them by turning them into questions? We tried it. It was transformative. The artists formulated all kinds of interesting questions.

The essential fact is that questions don't arrive to the maker fully formed. Sometimes the information that fuels the inquiry doesn't feel like a question at all. You have to figure out what to focus on among the many worries, obsessions, hopes, and apologies, then evolve it into a question. And this act, too, demonstrates the transformative power of inquiry to move the questioner from helplessness into the realm of action.

NOTES FROM JOHN BORSTEL

Looking in the Mirror and Seeing the Back of Your Head

A value we might call "agency" moves to the fore in step two. This is a currently trendy word for a quality we might also call "exercising autonomy" or "taking ownership" or maybe "empowerment," with different labels being favored at various points over the history of the Process. Whatever you call it, the artist assumes a degree of control and helps to set the agenda by naming their own concerns for the work and by signaling the importance of their own process of thinking and making. In CRP, the artist's questions are sequenced before the responder's questions. Agency for the artist continues in step three with the non-defensive premise of the neutral question, and will return in step four when the artist asserts control over the influence they absorb by agreeing or disagreeing to permissioned opinion requests. With agency comes responsibility. Through the step two questions, the artist gains a considerable role in how useful, generative, and constructive the critique session will be.

For over twenty years as associate artistic director for New York Theatre Workshop (NYTW), Linda Chapman has prepared and facilitated countless formal and modified CRP dialogues on theatrical works in progress. As an aspect of NYTW's efforts to nurture and mentor emerging playwrights and directors, she is emphatic about the importance of step two:

> What's important about this conversation is that the artist is directing it. Step one statements of meaning are a helpful start. But the step two questions are really important to help artists take control of what they're doing. And if artists aren't already attuned to thinking about how they're working on the piece, they may not be ready for the conversation. We try to bring the artist along a little bit beforehand, so we outline the Process with them in advance and ask them to think about some questions. The younger artists will want to please us. Often there's this little dance, where they will ask us, "What do you think?" and we bounce it back to them, "What do *you* think?" because the feedback is not for the audience, it's not for us, the prospective producers. It's for you . . . The artist's questions are the next step of empowerment. It's learning how to be a critical thinker about yourself and about your own process.

Chapman also highlights the significance of the artist's questions relative to the other steps and as an important component in establishing guiding terms for the conversation:

> Because we want artists to have control, we've experimented with letting artists choose which steps of CRP they want to do and in what order. Sometimes artists want to respond to neutral questions before they ask their questions, or skip their own questions entirely. I find that's almost always a big zero, because without the artist's consciousness about what it is they're trying to achieve, what use is a neutral question, really? The conversation usually just flat-lines. Without the information about where the artist is looking for answers or wanting to solve very particular problems, it's hard for us as responders to understand what we are looking at. . . . Consciousness tends to relate to unconsciousness. I think the more conscious, the more determined you are about being able to see what you're doing, will just help you see what you're not doing. The unknown can only be known in relationship to what we can actually quantify. And what's great about Critical Response is that it's like looking in a mirror, but we can never see the back of our heads. And in Critical Response we're hoping that the responders will show us what the back of our heads look like.

Step Two Thinking: A Generative Practice

CRP in its essence hasn't changed much since its invention. What has changed is how we introduce it, the scope of what we're teaching people, and our understanding of why it's valuable. The evolution of our approach to step two is case in point. In the early years of teaching the Process we would just assert the directive, "Artist, ask questions," and then coach those receiving feedback through the possibilities. But working with artists who are daunted about how to use step two or hearing from teachers who want to know how to coach students on asking their questions, we recognized the need for skill builders or preparatory exercises in order to make the most of the opportunity to ask questions. Encounters like the one Liz describes above with artists in Australia have sparked an expanded practice in which we guide people into a question-formulation process. Once we identified exercises that build the skills, we came to see the value of those skills independent of CRP and even of feedback. Through this progression we've discovered the power of the artist's question as a form of generative thinking, a discovery principle, a research mindset, and a general clarifier. Helping artists ask better questions proves to serve for much more than the process of a structured critique following the guidelines of CRP.

Every creative process, at any point in the progress of work, sits somewhere on the edge between what's known and unknown. Step two's challenge to ask a question puts the maker directly on that edge. In the struggle to find a question, or to get beyond the flat "artist's statement" of what you already know, is a kind of grappling with the "dark matter" of artmaking—you know it's there, you feel its weight and substance, but you can't see it or define it. The clarifying act of forming questions from the gaps, excuses, and inadequacies that you're conditioned to suppress or feel you're supposed to overcome can shed the light that reveals value and brings clarity to the murk. Just stopping to do this work is part of the power. When you switch from forward drive into inquiry mode, the questions you stop to ask can change your brain.

So, consider the gaps (in fact, some theorists place "gap perception" the beginning of all creative impulses). Consider your excuses and apologies, your worries and doubts, your hopes and aspirations. Take stock of observations, points of process, intuitions, and motivations. These add up to quite a collection of sources. Take a sheet of paper divided into cells, boxes, or free-form shapes with space inside, labeled as follows: worries/doubts; excuses/apologies; gaps; hopes/aspirations, observations; process; intuitions; motivations. Fill in each box with current perceptions or statements. Then turn them into questions. You may find these questions useful to take into a CRP or adapted CRP situation, to spur a research process, or to pose in conversation with a helpful thought partner. You may find yourself reframing goals or intentions, or clarifying the path forward.

Critique is creative: It's in exercises like this one that CRP and its supporting practices intersect with the creative process. When we guide the Process I've described in workshops, artists invariably feel elucidated and motivated; teachers usually see it as an invaluable way for students to assess, reflect, and assume critical agency. What started as a way to get people past the impasse of how to ask a useful question in step two has proven a valuable end in itself for the purpose of generating new ideas, gaining traction and direction in a process, and regaining creative energy.

Bulking Step Two

Sometimes, as we've stressed, artists are challenged by the task of forming questions about their work. But sometimes not. In 2017, I facilitated two rounds of CRP for *p r i s m*, an opera produced by Beth Morrison Projects, then being hosted in a developmental residency at the music school of Arizona State University. The first round engaged the student soloists and chorus as the responders, giving the composer Ellen Reid and librettist Roxie Perkins a chance to warm up to the uses of CRP and receive performer feedback. The second round happened two days later when a twenty-minute excerpt of the work in progress was performed before a public audience. When, arriving at step two, I turned to the artists (now joined by stage director James Darrah) and asked if they had any questions, the librettist pulled out a printout of an entire page of questions, already dog-eared and marked up from being handed around by the collaborators. Some questions were pointed, seeking clarity about comprehension plot and text, and some were more expansive, touching on mood, emotion, and musical resonance. The combination gave the dialogue dynamic momentum, with responders raptly engaged. So keen were the collaborators to put the power of the artists' questions to use that I was quite content to let them stay in step two for about twenty-five of the forty minutes allotted for the session. Apparently the momentum continued, as Darrah reported to me that "after the session, Roxie, Ellen, and I went to dinner where we immediately took all the information from the feedback and began to discuss alterations, revisions, and new ideas." Eighteen months later, when *p r i s m* had notable success at its Los Angeles premiere and New York performances, and when it went on to win the 2019 Pulitzer Prize for music, I took some satisfaction in knowing that an artist-driven CRP session had played a role.

Step Three

> *Step Three: Responders Ask Questions.* Responders ask neutral questions about the work. The artist answers. Questions are neutral when they do not have an opinion embedded in them. For example, if you are discussing the lighting of a scene, "Why was it so dark?" is not a neutral question. "What ideas guided your choices about lighting?" is.

When defensiveness starts, learning stops. CRP's step three proposes that a neutral question can re-sequence the dynamic of attack and defense—frequently encountered in conventional critiques—into one of inquiry and emergence. Rather than a negative opinion prompting a retort or a shutdown, neutral inquiry draws out knowledge that informs, alters, or surgically narrows the focus of the responder's opinion to prepare it for sharing in step four. It can diffuse assumptions and open up an exchange for a fuller understanding of the work and its possibilities by artist and responder alike.

A neutral question is a question that does not reveal an opinion. Responders' queries may be motivated by unbiased curiosity or by a strong opinion that informs but is not exposed by the question. Either way, the artist's answer to the question allows responders to gain insight into the artist's perspective, expanding shared knowledge and understanding. Sometimes it functions as an end in itself, bringing the artist to insight and informing all participants with a deeper understanding of the artist's process, their intentions and aspirations, and what they consider resolved or unresolved in their work in progress. At other times, step three bears an integral and reciprocal relationship to step four. When inspired by a strongly held opinion, the neutral question elicits information and ideas from the artist that informs or makes unnecessary the sharing of the responder's opinion in the following step of the Process. A dialogue based in the neutral question positions the partners for a more open, mutually invested, and particularized offering of opinion. With ideal goodwill, the responder is hoping that the response to the question will inform that opinion, whether particularizing it, reformulating it, or rendering it unnecessary.

Sometimes controversial (read on) and rarely functioning as an absolute, the neutral question can be a difficult concept to put into action; inevitably, responder questions in step three don't always emerge as neutral. The facilitator may intervene if they perceive a question as biased, coaching the responder and sometimes engaging the group in working toward a more neutral alternative. This activity usually refines all participants' understanding of what makes a question more useful as an opening to dialogue and reflection. In fact, the clearest way to give examples of neutral questions is to contrast them with their biased or opinion-embedded first attempts, as below.

Biased Question	*Neutral Question*
Am I supposed to believe that the characters you are playing are mortal enemies?	*What is the relationship you want to portray between these characters?*
Do you have any idea what this song is about?	*What meanings did you want to bring to your interpretation of this song?*

Why are you using that cheesy type font in your presentation slides?	*What informed your choice of fonts?*
Why is your poetry so angry?	*Talk about the role of emotion in your poetry.*
Have you considered using more of the upstage area for some of your dance?	*How did you think about the use of stage space in choreographing this dance?*

The neutral question is both one of the most potent and most contested aspects of CRP. The neutralizing of an opinion into a bias-free question may be a challenge to grasp, and may even seem an affront to free expression and open exchange. If you value your own perspective and are invested in the artist's success, the task might feel distinctly at odds with your conviction: How can I take the opinion I feel so strongly about, the aspect that I passionately want the artist to address, and render it neutral? Won't this remove all the vitality and authenticity? And isn't this just a smoke screen on what I really think, offered in an attempt to manipulate the artist?

But when the passion and intelligence driving the opinion is channeled into the act of inquiry, neutral questions can be powerful questions. With a neutral question, you can create an opening that the artist will *want* to venture into, extending an invitation for thought and an impetus for on-the-spot research. Admittedly, this can be a radical shift for those whose roles have given them license to deliver no-holds-barred critique or administer fixits and directives. As a responder, this shift may call on you to reprogram your expectations for the situation and your role in it. It asks you to think of yourself as a partner and guide rather than an adversary or authority.

The aspiration of CRP's step three is to find a way to ask a question so that it uncovers new knowledge from the person being asked and/or informs the perspective of the person asking, before or even instead of delivering an opinion. Though not the only way to realize this aspiration, the attempt to frame the question neutrally has proven to be a valuable if sometimes problematic path. As a component of a feedback process and as a general precept for human communication, this approach has many potential benefits:

- Asking a neutral question is a way of building a relationship with the artist. It is a protocol that substitutes inquiry for time, the time that we tend to view as essential for building the kind of trusting, respectful relationship with friends and colleagues who "have our back" and keep our best interests at heart. It's not that the neutral question "fakes" a respectful relationship built on time; it *is* one because the questioner has applied sincere effort and mental focus to finding the best way to put forth the inquiry. This act of kindness makes the ensuing dialogue richer. With this generosity comes the potential for a dialogue that holds more risk by taking the artist into the unknown.

- Asking a neutral question means that the responder will hear, or should hear, what the artist is thinking about the topic area. This information is critical to the artist/responder dialogue. It might reveal that the artist has already attempted a solution the responder hopes to offer and has rejected it. It might make a responder's opinion less relevant or in need of further investigation. Or it could redirect the responder's understanding, leading to diligent but nuanced follow-up.
- Asking the neutral question forces the responder to dig a little deeper into their own patterns of preference. It can help them determine if their concern is actually an issue related to the artist's terms or if it is one that reflects the questioner's values, personal aesthetic, or training—biases that actually may have no bearing on the work under discussion.
- Asking the neutral question can help the questioner disentangle a set of issues that the piece under consideration has raised. Without the neutral framework, feedback often comes in bunches of problems in which the critic bundles multiple issues into a single, rambling query—requiring the receiver to sort and organize before being able to respond or eventually take action. Getting to neutral may require a responder to ask multiple questions, each to be answered separately. Every strand of inquiry deserves its own starting place, and that is at neutral.
- Asking the neutral question slows down the fixit process. Whether out of a creative urge, a strong belief in what makes work better, or just the sheer joy in iterating what is in front of us, the speed with which we jump to fix another's work can be astonishing. Managing this impulse and instead taking the time to locate the neutral question usually leads the artist to interesting reflection, sometimes deeper comprehension, and occasionally the grasp of a principle

that will enable them to find their own solution. If the neutral question doesn't enable the artist to reach this level of clarity, a responder can still use step four's permissioned opinion to get their point across.

In formulating and posing a neutral question as a responder, you may need to expand, contract, or shift a frame of reference to recategorize a perspective. To get to neutral, you may need to interrogate your impulse to inquire, opine, or guide and break that impulse down in your own mind before asking your question(s). If you are truly invested in the artist's success, you need to be ready to reexamine your assumptions or recognize how your categorization of a feature of the work might have limited your understanding.

In responding to a neutral question as the artist, you are welcoming the question that may throw you into a new line of thinking. It is a useful discipline to focus on the question as asked, resisting the urge to speculate on the agenda behind the question and respond instead to that. Both parties in step three are navigating the area between what's known and what's unknown, what's evident and what's assumed, what is stated and what isn't.

Neutral questions have value even when they aren't answered. As with step two, when time only allows for responses to few questions, it can still be illuminating to go around the circle and collect any that remain for later consideration by the artist. In some contexts, at some stages in a process, and with some audiences, it may even be preferable to defer answers. "We find that the best neutral questions usually can't be answered on the spot anyway," says Linda Chapman of New York Theatre Workshop's CRP sessions with emerging playwrights. "The best neutral questions need to be contemplated. Sometimes we will just skip the talking back and forth and just take as many neutral questions as we can."

For all participants in the circle, neutral inquiry and response deepen the understanding of the work and its potential. Step three elicits valuable feedback and enlists dialogue for research and generative functions, advancing rather than pausing the creative process. Thus, as you frame, facilitate, or answer a step three question, it's useful to remember that neutral formulation serves:

- To forestall defensiveness and thereby potentially open up discovery for the person answering the question.
- To condition the person asking the question with a step back from the opinion that may be motivating them.

- To inform the conversation with information that sets the stage for opinions that are particular, pointed, and relevant to the artists' concerns—or to set to rest the ones that are not useful.
- To surface new inspirations for the work or articulations that may be helpful in advancing the work.
- To identify points that need to be clarified and to explore ways to clarify.

CAUTIONS, CAVEATS, CONSCIOUSNESS

Is the neutral question the best or the only way to get at the kind of open, mutually informing, discovery-based dialogue that we're seeking in CRP's step three? In recent years, some of the sharpest minds in our circle of regular CRP facilitators (including Isaac Gómez and Bimbola Akinbola, who have contributed essays to this book) are placing the concept of the neutral question under particular scrutiny for its own possible assumptions and biases, prompting such questions as: Can any question ever truly be completely neutral? Is the urge toward neutrality an illusion of those with power, an insidious form of cultural dominance that inhibits vital exchange at a time in history and an era of artistic expression when so much is at stake? Can the effort toward neutrality betray and silence vital truths? Does every artist seeking feedback want to be prodded toward the discovery that the established orientation to step three proposes? Does every responder gain from the abstract exercise of filtering passionate experience and response through the filter of neutrality? And who decides what's neutral . . . or "neutral," as some practitioners have come to prefer?

As much as people like to become secure with CRP as a set of guidelines, as much as users welcome it as a framework for a purpose where structure may have previously been lacking, as much as newcomers tend to facilitate by policing what they perceive to be the rules of the Process, it's helpful to think of CRP more as a statement of principle than a rule book, more a contemplative exercise than a set of commandments carved in stone. Nowhere do these distinctions come more to the forefront than when we consider the workings of CRP's step three, currently influencing the authors as we consider whether more pluralistic language might supplant or accompany the "neutral question" label. (See Liz Lerman's "Preservation and Change" at the end of this exploration of step three.)

Intended functions of the neutral question are to diffuse defensiveness on the part of the artist and inspire reflection on the opinion of the responder. Remembering these principles may be more useful than enforcing an abstract litmus test of pure, perhaps impossible, neutrality; because the judgment of whether a question *functions* as useful usually comes down to the context and purpose of the moment, the utility of the question for advancing the artist's quest for meaningful feedback, and ultimately the artist's reaction to the question, as can be judged by their physical response and readiness to engage.

Our colleague Paloma McGregor, who brings to her work as a facilitator/trainer of CRP not only years of experience as an artist/educator but also the perspective of an earlier career as a journalist, emphasizes that neutrality is an *active* stance. Rather than a step back from involvement, it is a focused, engaged position that supports the revealing of truth—both about the work in question and, importantly, about the aesthetic lenses we bring to witnessing that work. Indeed, the most valuable step three question is one that is challenging, probing, and moves the conversation into discovery and exposure, with the asker and answerer engaged as partners in thought and learning. "As a journalist, I learned that there's no such thing as neutral," Paloma says. "But that's all the more reason to practice identifying and moving beyond our own histories and biases to exercise genuine curiosity—the so-called neutral question. Is any question ever truly neutral? Probably not. But let's try, anyway."

NOTES FROM LIZ LERMAN

Into the Unknown

The keen challenge of step three lies as much with the artist as with the responder. It is very interesting to watch an artist's reaction when they don't have a ready answer to a question asked in step three, to observe how their discomfort gets expressed in a rapid retelling of everything they *do* know. They will make a quick connection to *something* inherent in the inquiry and then ramble on as if answering the question. But almost everything that follows will be a description of their well-understood process up to that point, or their intentions, or what they plan to do. These factors are almost always already well known to the person speaking.

It took me a while to recognize this behavior. But once I caught on to the phenomenon, I began to think about why it happens, and then what to do about it. I was interested because it struck me that *not knowing* is supposed to be a good thing for a creative soul. So why were we artists running away from the opportunity?

One reason might be the very nature of Critical Response circles, which are often a curious combination of public and private. With their inherent vulnerability, they can feel intimate and inviting. But they are public in the sense that those in the circle—who may or may not be known to the artist—are proxies for the work's eventual audience. Perhaps this leads artists to a sensation of "I should know" as opposed to the possibilities that emerge when we don't know.

What I began to do, as an artist receiving CRP feedback, was to try to conceive of the circle as an audience that is willing me to do my best. And in that situation, I thought about trying to use their presence to actually help me dive into the unknown. With the circle conceived of as a very good listener, I practiced "thinking out loud" in front of people—as opposed to doing so alone, on a walk, or in the shower. I began to look forward with hope that a CRP session might get me into a place of unknowing and then, by deep immersion in that space, discovering something new about myself, the piece, my process, or even CRP.

Another challenge is that we simply may not know how to harness the power of group listening because we have so little practice. I have thought back to times in my life when I felt particularly "loose" and really able to spark ideas and be attuned to the potential in an encounter: In teaching situations when the room is ablaze with energy and the excitement of discovery; during certain interactive performances when the rapt attention of an audience seems to help everything click; and in excellent conversations. In every case, it's a kind of love that emanates as the ideas and experiences flow, leading to fresh ideas or a newer expression of old ideas.

What aspects of CRP could help create these kinds of conditions to allow for a deep dive to take place in step three? The first comes in the initial set-up of the Process. It is always worthwhile to reassert the point that we are gathered to help the artist do their best work—not their "almost-best work" so that I, a responder, can still be "better." When we agree to be responders, we practice letting go of the ambition we have for our own work while retaining our full intelligence for the benefit of the artist.

Secondly, we have been building a relationship with the artist in step two. By responding to their questions first, we pay attention and bring our knowledge to bear on what is on their minds. I am convinced that even if we think they are on the wrong track with their inquiry, they will not be receptive to being redirected until they at least have a chance to mention their worries and doubts. For professional critics and teachers, this waiting can be excruciating. But it is also a training for stepping back and allowing another person's ideas to take the lead.

It's not just the artist who gets to practice living in the unknown. The responders can, too, especially here in step three when they are searching for the neutral question. This is an insistent reminder to make space for the artist's growth. Rather than filling the room with what we know, or what we think to be true by the veracity of our opinion, we are instead looking for the questions that will aid the development of the art or project in question. That act is a discovery in itself, and it may require spending focused time in a space of openness.

These commitments all contribute to a setting in which the artist has the opportunity for finding the new rather than spending time within the confines of what they already know. This can be difficult, especially when we are training artists to have their missions, their artist statements, and their ideas all laundered and pressed even before they begin a project. I am advocating that the artist can have these things, but can let them go if offered a question that leads into new territory. It is so compelling when you see it happening in front of you, when you witness an artist emerging through the unknown with a passion that will get them right back to work.

Feet to the Fire

Most creativity theory suggests that when you bring two things together and ask people to make a connection, they will and can, even if the two concepts are widely divergent. This line of reasoning has occupied some of my artistic work and teaching in the past decade, as I've explored how bringing unlikely sources together can spark an idea for rehearsal, or for a section of a piece, or for individual growth.

So I suppose it wasn't too surprising to notice a kind of connection-based inquiry slowly moving into my own practice of CRP. It started in earnest as I observed artists using their answers in step three to express what they clearly knew already. At first I tried to interrupt this and let them know that this wasn't really useful. But then I began to muse about how I could "hold their feet to the fire" while still following the lead of the artist's own work and ideas. I reasoned to myself that if the artist was devoting time to talking about their intentions and convictions, then they should be asked about them.

Soon I discovered that the best way I could construct an inquiry was to listen carefully, notice where the artist's explanation did not align with my experience of the work, and then ask them to state where that part was expressed in what we had just witnessed. It was a way of bringing together the history of the artist's thinking with the work's current manifestation, and then to explore the ways in which the ideas had and had not been fulfilled. I began to note that setting things in relation to each other sparked ideas but also offered a particular way to approach neutrality. I was truly interested in what an artist had to say, and often their remarks immediately led them to new solutions.

Asking, Not Fixing

I have always been frustrated at being handed a solution to an artistic problem. I don't mind "finding" them myself through conversation and research, or trials and error. But when told exactly how to fix something, I have balked. Early in the practice of CRP, I noticed that a certain amount of critique took the form of responders offering solutions to problems that may or may not have been named by the artist. I reacted for a brief period by banning any solutions. You weren't "allowed" to do it. And almost immediately, I realized that I had cut off my own creativity. Perhaps a legitimate way to experience someone else's work *is* to think about improving it, or to think about how I, the viewer, might have addressed the same pattern or subject or need for illumination. Take away the option to share that, and suddenly some of the energy and purpose gets drained from the conversation.

This was shocking to me. I recognized that I had to solve this dilemma of offering solutions in another way. I had, by this time, already established that you could "turn discomfort to inquiry." I began to experiment with turning the fixit into inquiry too. Could I take my idea, my solution, my own form of creative activity and use it to shape a neutral question for another person, instead of just telling them what to do? As with so much else in CRP, it turns out that I could and I couldn't. It turns out there are ways to do it, and sometimes it feels impossible. It turns out the effort is worthy but sometimes it's easier and perhaps better to offer an opinion in step four making sure the responders let the artist know that the opinion includes a way to fix the problem being discussed.

It's creative to fix someone else's work. It's generous to turn that fix into inquiry. It requires some rearranging of your understanding of the fix itself. You might have to consider where and how you name and file the idea that you are having. It often means a reframing of some kind. In that reframing, a kind of molecular change occurs. And in that change, you might discover something new about your own idea that is stimulating and worthwhile.

Frequently, the artist answers the question in a way that is more interesting than the solution I had in mind. In the early days of self-isolating during the first wave of the Covid-19 pandemic, I was on a video call with a young choreographer. She needed to figure out how to present her senior project online instead of as a live performance. After showing me some rehearsal footage, she described the subject of her work—namely, why women of her age were always apologizing for taking up space with their bodies. As I watched her in her bedroom on the video call, it occurred to me that her subject matter was intensified by the environment she was in. It would be interesting to have the dancers appear in different settings within their quarantine environments as a way of both expanding the role of space in her concept and of addressing one of the challenges of online choreography. I searched for a question and asked her, "What is the relationship of your performers being in their homes to the subject matter of the dance?" She responded with some enthusiasm. And then I followed up with: "Where do you think they might be solo and where might they be occupying the same space?" Even more excited, she began to speculate about her performers being outdoors and then finishing the dance in the kitchen, where women liked to gather.

It had never occurred to me to think about either of those spaces. If I had made the suggestion "Have your dancers perform in the home spaces where they are quarantined," she might have dutifully fulfilled it but the solution would not have been as good as the one she imagined, nor would she have "owned" it. Instead, she got off the call with great joy, avid to get back to work.

NOTES FROM JOHN BORSTEL

Labbing the Neutral Question, Cultivating Non-Defensiveness

The neutral question can be both a daunting challenge to newcomers and one of the most valuable and transferable dimensions of CRP. For that reason, when teaching or facilitating the Process, we often transition into step three by saying something like, "If you are sitting with a curiosity or a concern that you're not sure how to phrase as a neutral question, please just jump in and give it a try anyway. Don't be intimidated into silence by the challenge. If the question doesn't feel neutral, we'll work on it together." It often turns out that the "neutral question clinic" occurring in such a moment is one of the most valuable points in a training. In a time-out we'll venture and debate alternatives, grapple with the concept of neutrality, and weigh in on the factors that might bring a question closer to neutral. Usually we work together to discover some of the variable, never ironclad strategies that can help us think and frame more neutrally.

Of course, this process of openly labbing a biased question into a neutral one raises issues of its own. In this kind of time-out, the responder may already have revealed an opinion in their phrasing of a question. The group has offered readings on why it isn't neutral, put forward suggestions or pointers on making it neutral, and maybe debated the merits of various alternatives. After all that parsing and processing, is it even possible for the artist simply to respond to the ultimate rehabilitated neutral question, free of the defensiveness that knowing the underlying opinion might trigger? The artist starts out vulnerable and as much as the goodwill of step one and the agency of step two can build ease and receptivity, once defensiveness is triggered it can be very difficult to quell the rushing need to explain, defend, or push back. In this situation, a facilitator might encourage the artist to bring their attention back to the revised neutral question as it was asked.

Sometimes I invite people to think of it like this: With early GPS systems, when you took a wrong turn or intentionally diverged from the path that the system had set for you, a voice would come on—robotically bland and blessedly free of reprimand—saying, "Recalibrating route." It didn't matter if you made a mistake, got lost, or thought you knew better than the system: you just picked up the journey and found your way from where you were. That is how we might hear the revised question—as an invitation to recalibrate and reset the route from that point.

The two-way contract forestalling defensiveness in step two is redoubled in step three. Just as in step two, in which the responder commits to answering only the question the artist has asked, now—ideally—the artist commits to answering the neutral question at face value, as it's been asked, undistracted by prior knowledge or speculation about what's motivating the query. The neutral question is the core of the discipline of non-defensiveness that CRP promotes. Responsibility for that non-defensiveness is equally shared between the artist and responder.

A Flexible, Fallible Guide

The task of framing an opinion into a neutral question does not lend itself to a quick-fix recipe or boiled-down "best practice" formulation. But our insistence on this point doesn't stop people from asking. Teachers, especially those with younger students, have been particularly persistent in their requests for clear examples, sentence stems, and bullet-list posters that they can share with their students as scaffolding for the mental challenge of neutral question formulation.

Rather than capitulating immediately with a distilled cheat sheet, we usually respond to the request by saying, "Let's lab some neutral questions and see what principles we can uncover." Such a lab can take numerous forms. Sometimes we pull an example from a CRP session that the group has experienced and collaborate to transform a problematic opinion, overt suggestion, or biased query into a neutral question. In another approach, we might observe the room we're in to transform our reactions about its fixtures into opinions, then biased questions, then neutral ones. Or we offer game-like structures in which participants work together to shape some preformulated opinions from fictional scenarios into neutral questions. Inevitably in all of these structures, some hilarity ensues as people confront the futility of perfection in forming the neutral question. Often there isn't consensus on whether a particular attempt is neutral or not. A group of participants will come up with multiple alternatives for a given neutral question, and we recognize that the art of the neutral question is often more a matter of finding the right alternative for the moment than discovering the single perfect expression. Eventually we are able to name a few principles that help in formulating a neutral question. With all our cautions against cheat sheets and quick fixes, here are a few:

- Try a "how" question, as in: "How did you decide to . . ." "How might you plan to . . ." "How did you view the challenge of . . ." Approach "why" with caution. "How" often points to a more exploratory, process-focused answer, whereas "Why" sometimes suggests that there's a better alternative that the artist didn't choose, prompting defensiveness. (But in avoiding "why," you may be avoiding a valuable, probing class of questions, and "whys" can as often get artists stimulated and alert as they also get them defensive.)
- Though it's technically a request rather than a question, "Talk about . . ." can be a great neutral opener into a topic. It can be broad: "Talk about your intentions for this piece." "Talk about why you are drawn to this subject matter." Or it can be quite specific: "Talk about how you chose to end the scene." "Talk about your use of red."
- Think about how you can shift the frame of reference to a more general category to make the question neutral.
- Consider the possibility of a two-part or multi-part question, starting with a larger category, as above, and moving to a more specific query, if you need to, after you've heard the response.
- Relative to this idea of naming the category, especially for students still building their vocabularies but useful to anyone, it can be

useful to name the category of aesthetic attribute or component of the artistic task in which your concern resides and pose your question about that: color, texture, staging, use of space, dynamics, composition, and so on.

- As Liz has suggested, ask about a relationship—particularly if you perceive a discrepancy between what the artist is showing in the work and what they are saying about it. "How does choice X support intention Y?"
- Finally, in the category of what *not* to do, we often discover that neutrality isn't the same as niceness. A case in point is the classic "Have you considered . . . ?" as in "Have you considered adding a prologue that allows you to give the background on the characters?" This kind of question, though it sounds polite, is usually a way of cloaking a suggestion or cozying a directive, and most decidedly is not neutral.

A list of practices, principles, and strategies like the one above can be one product of a neutral question lab, but the more meaningful outcome is to confront the complexity of the task and the plurality of alternatives and approaches, and to work through befuddlement into a state of game, flexible competence. Participants never emerge from these labs with a surefire formula. But they almost always gain greater confidence in their ability to tackle the challenge of formulating, facilitating, and teaching the neutral question.

A CONCLUDING NOTE FROM LIZ LERMAN

Preservation and Change

In other essays, I have written about how much I admire the intended structure of the Talmud and the US Constitution. One ancient, one a few centuries old, both attempting to secure preservation and adaptation within the same enduring document. I once made a dance called *613 Radical Acts of Prayer*, in which I tried to expand on the meaning of the words "radical" and "prayer." We made several versions of this work, my favorite being the one in collaboration with colleagues in Japan. That piece was in two acts:

Act One: Protect us as we preserve the original meaning of things.
Act Two: Protect us as we change the original meaning of things.

Those prayers have fresh resonance as we find ourselves in the evolving story of the neutral question at the heart of the Critical Response Process. In recent years, no aspect of CRP has caused as much struggle, consternation, and determined argument, attracting enthusiastic supporters, articulate contrarians, and thoughtful mediators in almost equal numbers.

The founding purpose of the neutral question was to protect the maker of the work, and to challenge the power structures in place for typical feedback in artistic circles. It was meant to restrain teachers, critics, directors, and high-ranking professionals accustomed to pronouncing their opinions as facts, their aesthetics as universal, and their processes as the singular path to making good art and finding success in a chosen field. Inducing people to consider their assumptions and their biases seemed essential for their own learning, and for maintaining the ongoing openness of the artmaker.

As this chapter has described, a lot of theory and practice has grown up around the discipline of "going to neutral." I find this invigorating. At the same time, that discipline is inspiring impassioned challenge and vigorous analysis among some of CRP's most ardent practitioners.

For many, the name and the practice of "neutral" implies a sly, even overt, form of White supremacy that is making people feel that they have to separate themselves from their cultures, their traditions, and their most closely held ways of being in the world. They believe that there is no such thing as neutral, and to some extent they find the injunction to search for it inauthentic and possibly even cruel. The insistence on neutrality can be used to shut people down. This presents a dilemma for the community of practice that has become central to the future of CRP.

Naming informs our experience; renaming can change it. There is always more than one way to think, act on, or label a principle. As the voices challenging "neutral" grow stronger just as this book is going to press, we find ourselves experimenting with new articulations of step three, perhaps with a less singular emphasis on the idea of neutral, perhaps dispensing with the word altogether. Here is one version of an alternative articulation:

> *Step Three: Responders Ask Questions. The Artist Answers.* In the spirit of curiosity and research, responders ask questions about the work. The sequence of CRP places inquiry before judgment, so responders with opinions are encouraged to ask questions in a way that will inform rather than express their opinions. It may be helpful to consider the possibility of an open or even neutral question, as a way to refrain from embedding an opinion in a question. Seek information. Listen carefully.

Each facilitator in each context will find their own articulation of these ideas. We'll be listening. As CRP embraces work in progress, we embrace this evolution in the expression and understanding of step three. We are excited to watch this new development unfold in the evolving expression of the values of Critical Response.

Step Four

> *Step Four: Opinion Time.* Responders state opinions, subject to permission from the artist. The usual form is: "I have an opinion about ______, would you like to hear it?" The artist has the option to say no.

Occasionally, in a formalized CRP training, someone new to the Process will call a time-out in step one and—thinking that any sort of personal viewpoint is to be withheld until step four—will say, "But aren't these opinions?" Indeed, opinion is with us every step of the way in CRP. However much we might try to finesse, manage, or reformulate it, opinion is the first position many of us jump to when experiencing new work, and it is the one we often hold onto. Our opinions, when mined, are full of information that may be of genuine value to the maker of the work under consideration. CRP allows us to sift through those opinions to find a sequence and articulation that serves the comprehension of the maker. Indeed, it's a core idea in Critical Response that those with strong opinions *not* wait until step four to bring them to the conversation. Opinions may emerge as statements of connection, resonance, and enthusiasm in step one; as honest responses bearing directly on artist's questions in step two; and as the motivator to neutral questions in step three. Step four—note, the end, not the beginning—is when a responder gets the chance, if their request is accepted, to state it on the responder's terms. Those who have employed the disciplines of the Process in an engaged and mindful way up to that point are likely to encounter an artist eager to hear the opinion.

As much as CRP asks in-progress art to be pliant, malleable, and subject to change as a condition of meaningful critique, it also makes an equal, complementary call to opinion. Your opinion is also a work in progress. Are you, the opinionated, and your opinion open to change, development, revision, dismissal, or recalibration during the course of the Process's four steps? If the artist in CRP is engaged in a research process about the value and validity of their work, so equally is the responder engaged in research into the viability of their opinion, subjecting it to the scrutiny of the thinking disciplines engaged in the first three steps. So, by the time the step explicitly focused on opinion arrives, it may have passed through a refining fire, becoming more specific, more gauged to the expressed concerns or intentions of the artist, or more contextualized within terms that are meaningful to the maker. Or it may have resolved itself past the need to be expressed, or discovered its own irrelevance.

The protocol, some would say ritual, of asking permission to state an opinion on a defined dimension or topic may strike CRP newcomers as its most arcane or stilted feature. Relative to the refining functions of the Process, it calls on the responder to narrow, categorize, or recapitulate the subject of an earlier exchange and to renew the contract with the artist who has built the interpersonal relationship through the earlier steps. With this request, the filter for step four is in the hands of the artist who has the option to say yes or no, or even, as sometimes happens, to request a little more information about the nature of the opinion before making their choice.

As much as this exchange endows the artist with agency, the request serves other functions that add value to this final step. "I have an opinion about . . ." offers a preparation for both parties in sharing the viewpoint that will follow. An opinion can be like an object thrown in our direction. Whether it smacks us in the face, sideswipes us, or lands with ease in receptive hands has a lot to do with how prepared we are for it. You prepare very differently to catch a medicine ball as opposed to a wad of crushed paper as opposed to a bouquet. You are alert in every case, but your stance, the tension in your body, and your focus all are different in each situation. If you don't know what's coming your way, your awareness pitches up to the point of hyper-alertness, anxiety, even alarm. It is much the same with opinions, and alarm is probably not the best mental or emotional state for receiving, considering, and retaining an idea.

In using the "I have an opinion" script, both responder and artist are reminded that the ideas to be shared are indeed opinion, a subjective offering rather than absolute fact. It is a kind of mindfulness practice to be required to name this thing, which may seem to you to be an urgent truth or precious insight, as, actually, an opinion.

In its own way, the step four request requires as much discipline as step three's neutral question. Often, a responder who seems ready to charge headlong into a strong opinion can stumble over the preliminary task of stating what the opinion is *about*. Just as the step four opener helps the artist prepare for listening, it can also help the responder warm up, think through, or slow down long enough to clarify their position. "I have an opinion about . . ." functions as a welcome speed bump on the road to delivering a meaningful opinion.

Sometimes in that struggle to fill in the blank of "I have an opinion about . . ." a responder gropes through something like: "I have an opinion . . . it's about . . . Well, actually, maybe it's more of a question." At this point, a deft facilitator might intervene: "Is it a question you can phrase neutrally, and shall we step back to step three?" As hard as we might try to recognize our opinions at the start and channel them into neutral questions in step three, there are times when we actually don't meet the challenge until we are faced with the need to frame the subject of an opinion. At this point the possibility of moving back and forth between steps three and four is a welcome option, and perhaps a necessity for a truly fruitful exchange.

Here are some examples of step four opinion requests:

- *"I have an opinion about your choice of music for this dance. Would you like to hear it?"*
- *"I have an opinion about how you are using different voices in your monologue. Would you like to hear it?"*
- *"I have an opinion about captioning and giving context for documentary photos. Would you like to hear it?"*
- *"I have an opinion about your choice of colors. Would you like to hear it?"*
- *"I have an opinion about your use of statistics in this report. Would you like to hear it?"*
- *"I have an opinion about your performance of this song in relation to what you said it meant to you. Would you like to hear it?"*

If the artist says yes, the responder may proceed to offer the opinion, staying on topic with the request, as multiple opinions require multiple requests. The artist may also say no, may choose to do so for a variety of reasons, and is under no obligation to say why, though artists often do. Reasons may include a sense of fullness regarding a topic, having heard enough of the person addressing them, or arriving at the saturation limit on feedback in general by the time step four is reached. It may be too soon for some opinions: The playwright currently focused on the early stages of shaping characters and dialogue may not want to be distracted at this point by the logistics of staging. It may be too late for others: The painter employing controversial imagery may be well past processing the range of reactions it elicits and has sealed a commitment to the content that brooks no further input. Saying yes or no is an exercise of agency and a means of managing the amount of influence the artist chooses to take in.

Often what goes by the name of "constructive criticism" is actually someone fixing your work in a pleasant tone of voice. Step four offers one more opportunity for fixers to consider what their offering is about. If you're sitting on a fixit, you could go back to step three, and, as described earlier, try to shape a question inspired by the solution you want to make; you could drop it; or you can bring it to step four, letting the artist know that you have a change to suggest or a process to propose for finding a solution: "I have a suggestion for how to end the poem . . ." "I have a thought about some research you might want to do to get ideas for the horse character . . ." "I have an idea for how to organize some of the fragments you've shown us . . ." always followed by: "Do you want to hear it?" In this way, an artist can know that a fixit is coming and can exercise a choice of whether to receive or reject it.

Step four encompasses the goals of critique, research, and the exposure of new knowledge in a variety of ways:

- Externalizing an experience of the work in progress that builds and expands on step one, and weighing in on the work relative to context, aesthetic value, and audience perception.
- Sharpening the focus on an aspect of the work, particularly if the responder has used step three to narrow the focus of the opinion.
- Functioning generatively either by posing a possibility or by highlighting an idea that the artist has broached earlier in the exchange.
- Clarifying, for the artist, what they value and how they are willing to be influenced.

NOTES FROM LIZ LERMAN

On Consent

As we suggest above, it's not just the work under review that is in process in a CRP session; it's your opinion as well. Ideas and opinions held immediately after viewing something may change considerably—becoming more informed, more clear, more nuanced, more resonant—as you engage in a dialogue and internally process what you will ultimately tell the maker by the end of the four steps.

When I started CRP, I was intent on finding a way for the maker to have some agency in the discussion. All those years ago, hearing the old saw,

"If you can't take the heat, get out of the kitchen," I responded, "Wait, I am the cook and I have something to say about the heat." That was my earliest version of constructing consent. Yes, I want your feedback, but I need to have some control. I discovered that the step four opinion request, and CRP's other filters, had the effect of moving the exchange from the vertical to a horizontal, altering the position of both the person making the work and the one commenting on it. This meant a shift for everyone, especially the critic, the teacher, the supervisor, the curator—making CRP a time to learn and discover for those "authorities" as well as for the maker.

Constraints on power structures reside in every step of CRP. Requiring the viewer to filter out the negative in step one, so as not to lead with the one thing that could deflate the maker from hearing anything, prevents a destructive form of bullying.

In step two, the act of staying on topic is a constraint that allows the maker to stay in consent mode, effectively saying, "I don't consent to you talking about anything you want, or pretending it's about the topic I have introduced. I want you to tell me about what I am asking." This can feel like a restraining order to someone used to being able to express opinions at will. But for others, the act of staying on topic is like a commission. It points a path to depth and specificity that may even hold negative content as the response exists in relation with the person doing the asking.

In much the same way, step three's neutral question is a form of consent. It allows for an opening and discovery for the artist while still keeping the playing field relatively free of explosions. And ideally, if the responders understand, they can defuse those potential explosions into inquiry, preparing the way for the fourth step: delivering opinions on topics that have already been discussed.

Consent is most obvious in the fourth step. The fact that the artist can say no publicly is a major divergence from most systems of feedback. When I first devised the Process, I was pretty convinced that some responders would hold off any interaction until step four and that this behavior needed some guide rails. When the artist exercises the option of saying no, the choice has an impact on the whole group. Sometimes, responders need reminding that it is okay. Saying no *and* hearing no are both part of the privilege of being in a CRP circle.

Lately I have been thinking that the "no" is shocking because we hear it so rarely in public. When a child says no to a parent, when a student says no to a teacher, when a woman says no to a man, or when a staff person says no to a faculty member—whenever these instances happen, we wonder, *Is this resistance? Madness? Bad behavior? Insubordination?* In CRP it is used rarely, but in CRP we welcome it. Of course, remember that sometimes a "no" comes from fear on the part of the artist. You can always check this by sending the entire circle back to step three and finding the question that is living within the opinion.

Being Surgical

Some people are in positions to give critiques on a regular basis. I am thinking of parents, teachers, and bosses. I have been all of those things over the years, and I have found that it's easy for me conflate critique with teaching, pontificating, laying down the law, insisting on the rules of tradition or heritage, and using theory as a leg to stand on in asserting my right to a point of view.

Willing as I am to own up to this behavior, I have observed how CRP can be a useful antidote to it. Some of its counteractive force lies in the relationship of step three to step four. Step three opens the door for dialogue, for curiosity, and for the responder to check whether their own opinion is applicable to the situation at hand. Often, parts of what one is feeling or thinking prove to be true and useful to the artist, but frequently not all aspects.

Sometimes I think of this as a shape problem. The responder has an opinion that is formed from history, aesthetics, and experience. Over time, these ideas may become a formal or theoretical perspective that gives the responder a sense of self, of order, of having a point of view and a belief system. The ideas form something akin to a shape in the mind and body; there's a wholeness to them. As true as this position is to the responder, however, it's unlikely that all of it is true for the work we are critiquing. The responder brings it all to bear, but usually only part of it matters. Broaching it to the artist in a meaningful way is another example of a responder having a chance to pull apart what matters to them and to bring the specifics of the artist's own venture to bear on the challenge.

By asking neutral questions in step three we can begin to discern what's in the artist's mind and intentions in relationship to such weighty perspective. Through probing, we can whittle down the shape of our opinion so it becomes more fitting to the case at hand. I call this being "surgical." We don't have to lay down the entire theory or even the background to our ideas. We can use step four to be explicit, clear, and pointed.

It's true, we don't get to hear our own passions, stories, or convictions, and for some that is very difficult. But if you use steps and three and four in tandem, you can deliver really useful opinions that are congruent with the artists' needs. And they will listen, they will be grateful, they will welcome the comment, and they will go back to work in the studio.

NOTES FROM JOHN BORSTEL

Opinion: Starting Point and Destination

Early in my experience of training people in the steps and values of CRP, I led a session for some teaching artists and administrators in the Washington, D.C., public schools system. When it was over, I was approached by a woman who said, "I want to thank you. I'm a very opinionated person. My staff will tell you that it sometimes gets me into trouble. With this process I feel like you've given me a tool for working with my opinions in a way that I can bring them to the conversation without alienating people." She was grateful for CRP and I was grateful for her comment, as she was able to recognize the power of CRP to help rather than hinder those with strong opinions. Being myself a person who loves holding, cultivating, and cherishing opinions, I recognized a fellow traveler.

Being myself a person with strong opinions, I also recognize that a strong opinion is often the first thing to emerge in response to witnessing a work in progress. "The problem is X." "This is trite (or hackneyed or cliché) because Y." "He needs to fix Z." These thoughts, arising fully formed in the mind of the responder, are often the first signal of connection to the work and are at the same time a rearing up of the ego in its midst. Faultfinding reminds me of who I am by asserting my taste, my preferences, my knowledge, my aesthetic, my sense of craft (and my biases, my assumptions, my delusions, and on and on).

Opinions may be a responder's first impulse, but they come last in CRP for good reason. I used to say that by putting opinion in the final steps, CRP makes opinion a destination rather than a point of departure. Maybe the reality is a bit more nuanced. The initial impulse to express opinion may be what signals you to know that you have something particular and valuable to share with the artist, but you have to be willing to subject it to comparison, scrutiny, and the possibility of change before it arrives at the destination—when and if the artist agrees to hear it. Opinion can be both a starting point *and* a destination in CRP. Liz has described how a good CRP session will hold an artist's feet to the fire. It also turns the heat on a responder's opinion, and heat acts differently on different substances. The refining fire of CRP may vaporize one opinion, while crystallizing, concentrating, or chemically transforming others.

Not Just for the Artist

Much as the protocol of step four can challenge responders, it occasionally seems to chafe at artists. From time to time, an artist will profess not to need the permission requests and protest: "Really, I'm open to any opinions, just throw them at me." Oddly, as Liz has pointed out to me, these are the folks who often seem to need the protocol most, as they are quickest to spar back at opinions once they are offered. In the absence of the dialogic frame that the opinion request provides, the I-can-take-anything artist is likely to replace it with defense and rebuttal.

I can't overstate the degree to which the opinion filter isn't just for the artist. I was coaching a fledgling facilitator in a large circle once when, arriving at step four, the artist said, "I really don't need this permission thing—let's just hear the opinions." The facilitator shot me a glance and seemed about to assent to the artist's wishes. Having never encountered this situation when *I* was facilitating, I felt some hesitation about how to proceed until I acknowledged the sudden and very physical sensation of the bottom completely dropping out of the Process and the likelihood of splashing rudderless into a sea of unmanaged opinions. I intervened, addressing the artist. "You may feel secure in accepting any opinion, but the permission procedure doesn't just serve you. It's also here to help the responders gain their footing and to help the facilitator manage the dialogue. If we don't do it, we're no longer doing the Critical Response Process." The artist conceded, and the facilitator resumed his guidance.

Flexing the "No" Muscle

As we say in the introduction to this book, the basic tenets and mechanics of CRP have changed remarkably little since the Process was introduced in 1990. But the world has changed, and the contexts in which CRP moves have shifted, leading us to new challenges for CRP and new awareness of how its principles can function. So it is with the artist response in step four. Until fairly recently, I tended to describe a "no" response to an "I have an opinion" proposal as a rare and unlikely occurrence, stating that if that responder has been fully engaged in the Process from the beginning, the artist will be eager to hear their opinion in step four. I'd occasionally even present a digital slide with a pie chart in which a sliver-thin slice represented the instances in which artists actually respond with "no." But the reckonings of the past few years have shifted my own understanding, as society gives deeper scrutiny to the role of consent in interactions across the lines of gender and power. Meanwhile, the reactions of women, artists of color, and grade-earning students have raised the question of whether all situations in which CRP happens are free of pressure for the artist to say yes, or negative consequences if the artist says no. Does the opportunity for agency represented by the artist's capacity to say yes or no have value in a context that otherwise thwarts agency? As exemplified by the role the artist plays as gatekeeper of the opinions in step four, CRP may represent the ideal of equity between artist and all responders in the feedback process. But CRP alone cannot impose that equity in situations where other forces undermine it. As Liz suggests, though, it can hold us through ritual—and nothing in the Process is more ritualistic than step four's permission protocol—to values that are otherwise hard to keep. It thereby allows us to practice and internalize those values so we can call on them in instances where we don't have an explicit structure to guide us.

Consequently, our training of CRP at this writing is evolving toward less emphasis on "yes" as inevitable and more emphasis on supporting the possibility of "no." If I am playing the artist in one of our cake demo role-plays, I may look for an opportunity to say no to an opinion, just so participants can witness and reflect on what it means to do so. When we have people do CRP on their own projects as a solo walking and talking reflection exercise, Liz enjoins us to practice saying no to at least one opinion we are formulating about that project. It's surprisingly liberating and clarifying to do so. Sometimes we'll sit in a circle, and each participant will address the person to their right, saying, "I have an opinion, would you like to hear it?" and each person gets a chance to say no. No takes practice. It takes practice to say it, and, perhaps even more, it takes practice to hear it. Like much that is worth doing, it requires rehearsal, and we are increasingly striving to build that rehearsal into the CRP experiences we construct.

I am now adding to my litany of reasons why the request for the opinion matters with reasons why the response matters, and why "no" can matter as a valid and important option. It is the assertion of equity. It allows the artist to regulate the Process to their own capacity to hear, absorb, and incorporate opinions into their larger understanding of their own work. Finally, it allows artists to manage influence in their own artistic process and growth. Influence is unavoidable, constant, and potentially constructive within the creative act, but artists need to regulate how it enters. Early in a process, we may choose which points of inspiration sources of emulation we might expose ourselves to, and when. Avoid influence altogether and you may be creating in a vacuum; allow too much influence and you risk having your originality stifled. This is a peril of too many suggestions in CRP, which may undermine the artist's ability to discover their own solutions. And it's true of any opinion. As CRP arrives at its final step, the yes or no response to opinion requests allows the artist to keep their hand on the valve that regulates influence.

II APPLICATIONS

AUTHORS' NOTE

In broadening our focus to applications of the Critical Response Process in the pages that follow, we bring in the contributions of CRP practitioners from varied fields. In doing so, the authors would like to offer a reflection on the nature of CRP variations. As people learn and deepen in their practice of CRP, we usually note that they arrive at a point where they relate less to CRP as a set of fixed guidelines and operate more on an internalized grasp of its core principles. At this stage it is often gratifying to observe them referencing their own experiences, rather than received information, to illuminate the workings of the Process. It is also at this point that CRP practitioners begin to gain the confidence to vary and adapt the Process to specific purposes. Many variations differing from the core practice of "orthodox" four-step CRP are reflected in the contributed essays to come. These include such adjustments as using only two of the steps, reordering the steps, or adding to the guidelines of the Process with additional strictures or opportunities.

The authors share these variations with the confidence that the contributors have brought together depth of experience in CRP with knowledge of the discipline in which they are making the application. We include them in this book not as endorsements for a particular variation in any and all contexts, but as encouragement to readers to experiment with the Process even as they deepen their engagement with CRP's core principles.

3 LEARNING AND TEACHING

Feedback, as Liz suggests near the beginning of this book, starts even before you are born. In its most concrete forms, it may very well peak during the periods of life when we are moving through formal educational systems: grades, quizzes, tests, term paper markups, rubrics: all measures of progress, sometimes leading into sophisticated systems of formative assessment and summative evaluation. These instructor-driven methods supposedly tell us how we are doing and allow the learner to measure and adjust performance in relation to a standard. When used effectively, they can also tell teachers how to shape and recalibrate instruction for students to improve and excel. Over and under these explicit formats are incessant signals of validation and reprimand whose effects seep far beyond mastery of the academic material into regions of self-worth and self-understanding. Feedback's role in education is formational, pervasive, and inextricable.

In any learning pursuit beyond those requiring mere comprehension of facts or rules, in any subject where questions can have more than one right answer, the role of feedback becomes more complicated and more essential. While a weekly test score can demonstrate how you are grasping the conventions and countless exceptions in American English spelling, more nuanced standards come into play when you sequence those words into comprehensible written expression: matters of style, rhetoric, and structure, as well as consideration of audience, context, and purpose. Facts can be memorized and tested with true-or-false quizzes, but the interpretation of facts involves a synthesis of human functions that demands feedback at a matching degree of complexity. Once education reaches this level, feedback methods require dialogue, reflection, and critical thinking on the part of both teachers and learners.

Feedback in artistic disciplines presents a particular range of purpose and demand. At one end of this spectrum are all the technical skills involved in getting the violin notes in tune, the actor's voice audible at the back of the room, the anatomy correct in the figure drawing—all disciplines in which trained technique and repetitive practice inform results that can be measured by objective standards, and in which feedback and redirection from an external source can significantly contribute to the refinement of craft. This technical feedback takes countless forms: the dance teacher's corrections called out over the practice-room piano, the theater director's trenchant rehearsal notes, and the moment when the art teacher takes the charcoal from the student's hand and draws directly over their work on the easel. At the other end of the continuum are individual vision, voice, inspiration, and subjective truths that mold together to form compelling art. These elements are found by the student on the student's own terms. Though to some degree unteachable, they are nameable when we encounter them, worthy of response, and are subject to influence through meaningful communication. Feedback methods at this end of the spectrum often go by the name of critique and encompass studio art crit sessions; master classes for solo instrumentalists and singers; writers' groups where eight copies of a story are marked up by eight fellow writers; and audience talk-backs on works in progress in theater laboratories.

Experiences in this realm of critique have built and broken countless artists at every stage of emergence. The memories we have cited earlier in this book attest to the power of feedback in an individual artist's life—and, in Liz's case, to the influence of those experiences on the formation of CRP. Where feedback is formalized, you can find both the traumatized casualties of ruthless and negligent approaches and joyous adherents to the rigors and rewards of structured critique. David Tinapple, professor of digital culture at Arizona State University and co-creator of the CritViz.com digital platform for group critique, writes:

> The main reason I fell in love with art school was not that I wanted to be an artist, but that I loved the unique feeling of being in a critique. Nowhere have I had more interesting, more engaging, more transformational conversations. Where else does a small group of people intentionally try to expand their capacities for honesty and openness, share unfinished work and unclear thoughts, and together negotiate what is real and what is illusion? How much better off would we be as a society if this was more common and normal?
>
> At first, critiques can be difficult, stressful, and occasionally downright painful. But most well-run critique sessions are intensely

> positive experiences. On the occasion when someone does leave a critique diminished, hurt, and discouraged, it's usually because the critique was not facilitated well. A good crit can leave me energized for days or weeks, even when the feedback I received included difficult truths. It's in critiques where I've learned the most and grown the most. Not facts, or techniques, or how to do specific things, but where I've learned how my mind works, how to build up concepts, let go of unneeded complexity, and discover my preconceptions and true intentions. It is in critique that real knowledge is constructed, tested, and refined. Not only knowledge of how to do, but knowledge of how to be.

As a professor and digital innovator, Tinapple has made peer critique central to his teaching methods. He assigns readings that address the value and pitfalls of peer feedback, and he emphasizes a balance of qualitative and quantitative methods that often surprise students and upend expectations about the definition of success in his courses. He presents a bracing ideal for the role of critique and its core function in arts learning. Its power, as he acknowledges, hinges on the Process being "well run," and the implied presence of structure and facilitation.

Alas, it is not always so. As one example, a study of the student experience in design and architecture critique sessions conducted at three universities in England revealed a host of issues (Blair 2006). Critiques intended to deliver meaningful, formative assessment crowded up to sixty students and professors into grueling daylong sessions where instructor commentary generally dominated student engagement. Students experienced high levels of anxiety and the pressure to display confidence in an atmosphere that often emphasized defense and adversarial confrontation. As a result, "students . . . are literally frozen with fear. They do not hear or remember what they have said, or what was said about their work, or even comments about other students' work."

In light of the realities revealed by such a study, there's increasing interest in optimizing the value of the critique in education, producing a growing list of books, articles, and conference proceedings to address the potentials and the problems. Some of these resources seek less to change the status quo than to offer survival guides for students, suggesting what to take in, what to disregard, and how to simply weather the storm. Others offer alternative approaches, new methods, thoughtful structures, techniques geared by particular teachers to their specialized curricula, or approaches influenced by spiritual practice and philosophical discourse. It's heartening to witness the rise of this movement, and to discover that, in many places, CRP is finding a place in it. With the structure it offers and the mindfulness it promotes, CRP is a strong fit for many contexts in which formal critique plays a role. Beyond its feedback functions, CRP offers numerous other educational benefits, including promoting observation, building verbal and conceptual vocabulary, sharpening critical thinking, and enhancing creative capacity. And when CRP is disaggregated from the four-step Process, its principles can infuse many other dimensions of pedagogy with broad impact on the classroom and studio, sometimes leading educators to shift their approaches, even their teaching philosophies, in remarkable ways. Kristin Kjølberg, associate professor in the Music Education and Music Therapy department of the Norwegian Academy of Music, describes the influence of CRP on her own teaching practice:

> The ideas underlying CRP have become a foundation in my work. I find learning and teaching to be a partnership [between] student and teacher, where both contribute to discovering new aspects, ideas, and approaches in creative ways. Where earlier I would often give a traditional lecture, for instance, in a vocal pedagogy or voice anatomy class, I may now choose an explorative work form, opening up the field by asking questions and listening carefully to the students' different contributions. In that way, we broaden the subject together, coming up with new aspects to explore and learn. I see how students discover their knowledge in other ways, and how they ask me additional questions to fill their knowledge gaps. As the teacher, I will create structures out of the students' different meanings, questions, and comments, and by listening to and respecting what the students bring to the learning situation, I recognize that I can pass on my knowledge just as much, or even more than in traditional ways of lecturing.
>
> After working with CRP for some time, students rethink and have expressed to me that they now prefer to work with their own issues, instead of having a teacher deciding what to prioritize. They say that the method gives them the freedom to develop their own ideas. Although they may not master a specific skill yet, they feel trusted to be able to figure it out.

In arts education situations, CRP functions not just as the site of significant learning but also as a strategy that students acquire to support their ongoing practice and future work in the field. For almost a decade, we have had the privilege of bringing CRP to the Yale School of Drama where Liz and colleagues lead an immersive training in the Process as part of an annual seminar week that launches the second semester for students in the three-year MFA program. The training focuses on students; instructors in Yale's comprehensive career preparation program handle feedback and critique as they choose to, based on their pedagogical approaches, the disciplines they teach, and the techniques and traditions they represent. In such a mix of influence, the dean of the school, James Bundy, considers CRP an important asset for students as they deepen their work in the program and prepare to thrive in a competitive field.

Bundy made this point clear at the end of Liz's first residency in the program, when participants gathered for a CRP session focused on the workshop itself. It had been a complicated and fractious several days, as CRP was placed within a wide range of other curricular goals and methods, led by varied guest faculty. During the feedback session, some of the students used CRP as the lightning rod for their varied disappointments in the entire seminar: The protocols of the Process felt forced and had little relationship to how they were being critiqued by their professors. Students particularly took issue with step four and why you couldn't just say what you wanted. At this point James Bundy spoke up and addressed the students. He reminded them that feedback and criticism would be constant and often intense in their professional careers, and offered that it can be highly useful to learn ways to manage it. His voice quieted the room, suggesting that he was speaking a truth that students were only just coming to comprehend. They listened. And at their graduation, two-and-a-half years later, they hung a banner behind the stage, which included words that paraphrased CRP's step four: "I have an opinion, would you like to hear it?" Clearly the Process had been a companion to them for the remainder of the program.

The contributions to this chapter, focused on CRP in educational contexts, span the range from formal to disaggregated applications; describe the many ways that the principles of the Process can inform teaching and learning; and offer numerous variations and companion practices. Anchored in the arts, they extend into the humanities and sciences, and address the implications of CRP's values for leadership, citizenship, and the development of ethical perspective. After a reflection from Liz on the nature of authority in teaching, Elizabeth Johnson Levine unfolds the four-step Process as she's imparted it to multiple waves of teen artists over two decades. She describes adaptations of language and structure for CRP that support the still-developing minds of young people as they pass through precious and perilous stages of maturation. Carlos Lopez-Real addresses the value of CRP within the social art form and ensemble values of jazz music within his work at the Guildhall School of Music in London. A contribution by classical voice professor Gerda van Zelm reflects the kind of change that CRP cultivates when introduced into a traditional conservatory world, with valuable new challenges both for the students and the institutions. Gesel Mason zeros in on the college-level dance composition studio, with numerous ideas about shortcuts and adaptations that make CRP a sustained aspect of creation-focused learning. Moving into the ramifications of CRP beyond its core feedback function, Sean Riley reports on an adaptation that highlights steps one and three of CRP to encourage autonomy and entrepreneurial thinking among young musicians. Lekelia D. Jenkins proposes adaptations of CRP for undergraduate peer review in STEM disciplines. Kathryn Prince describes how placing CRP's principles at the center of her pedagogy has increased motivation, investment, and quality among the students in her Making Shakespeare class. Liz closes the chapter with reflection on the meaning and uses of CRP for those who teach.

Taken together, these varied contributions demonstrate how the Critical Response Process is offering change to the process of teaching and learning. The change, at its most powerful, pervades institutions and the disciplines of education. The words of Kristin Kjølberg point us forward:

> CRP as a work form gives the students space to investigate many different aspects of their artistry. It can challenge us as teachers. We must dare not to have all the answers and allow perspectives beyond our own competency to come up. But watching the students' curiosity and creativity when gaining ownership of their artistic development, and to coach them along in their part, makes working as a teacher extremely meaningful.

REFERENCE

Blair, Bernadette. "At the end of a huge crit in the summer, it was 'crap'—I'd worked really hard but all she said was 'fine' and I was gutted." *Art, Design & Communication in Higher Education* 5, no. 2 (January 12, 2007), 83–95.

Interrupting Authority

Liz Lerman

CRP interrupts authority that is built on prestige, status, professional position, or hierarchy. Used in its formal structure, with the support of the protocols built into its steps and practices, it's possible for anyone to say almost anything to anybody. It takes work. If the systems are used, no matter what the circumstance, the outcomes will give people options for going back to work with enthusiasm and purpose.

I first began noticing this possibility when I brought CRP to conservatory-style arts institutions and discovered that the unquestioned expectation was that the instructor would facilitate. I hadn't thought to mention the delight of sharing facilitation duties with students, because I had assumed that educators would be so relieved to give up the part of their authority that was about classroom management that they would jump at the chance to be free. Having discovered that this was not the case, I now make sure to remind teachers that they can be fully present as responder (and teacher, as they wish; more about that later) and let others carry on the act of facilitation.

Recently, however, I noticed another way in which CRP interrupts the authority of a system, and I observed why and how it can be difficult for professors accustomed to managing the data of their classroom space. I was on one of my trips to Europe for an intensive with conservatory professors there; after a day and a half of training, the head of the school that was hosting asked to facilitate the next session. Step one went reasonably well, but when we got to the artist's questions of step two, he began to insert frameworks such as trying to uncover the artist's intentions and processes before the artist even began. This intensified during step three. I let it go at first, thinking that I was going to get to watch a useful new adaptation of the Process. But the facilitator was very heavy-handed, hijacking all of the agency an artist typically has in helping to guide a CRP session.

I stopped the Process for a time-out and asked him what he was doing and why. His response went something like this: "When left to the artist or to the responders, the information is far too random. There is a sequence to learning and thinking about art, and this Process is going all over the place." I suggested some variations that could help keep the Process on track for longer with a particular issue, but that didn't satisfy him. And then I realized that the professorial authority that CRP asked him to surrender was about controlling how the art was projected and then discussed. There should be an order to this, he clearly thought, and he owned the order—and, more importantly, the right to assert it.

Reflecting on this incident, I realize how much my own teaching has changed. How I often don't lecture, or even lead, but move around the material depending on what is coming up for the students. It doesn't mean that I don't design an experience in the classroom. I do. But once that experience has been practiced, the rest of the class moves as the needs in the room change. It's a very different form of working. CRP is a mirror of that, or perhaps I have gained my confidence in working this way from the hundreds of CRP sessions I have been a part of.

RIGOROUS NURTURE: THE CRITICAL RESPONSE PROCESS AND ADOLESCENTS

Elizabeth Johnson Levine

Adolescence: It's a time of contradictions, of being both brave and awkward, confident and confused, indignant and insecure. It's a time of extreme physical and physiological growth, and a time of defining and redefining oneself in the transition between childhood and adulthood. It's a time when the social becomes of the utmost importance: social support, intimate social connections, social pressures, and the influence of social media.

How peers perceive teens can have a strong influence on how teens see themselves. In this context, adolescence can be harsh. Extreme judgment, labeling, and comparison can lead to damaging criticism of self and others. In often-abrasive adolescent environments, teens can become guarded, negative, spiteful—even aggressively hostile, with the prevailing feeling, conscious or not, of "If I judge you first, then I won't be vulnerable to judgment. You can't get me if I get you." And yet I believe every teen, from the jaded to the jubilant, desperately wants love, acceptance, and the space and safety to explore who they are and who they might become. The Critical Response Process provides this space and safety. In an environment that is rigorously nurturing, it offers teens the opportunity to:

- Create a culture of generosity and practice extending goodwill to others
- Cultivate individual vision and voice
- Respect difference
- Develop the capacity for greater curiosity and communication

- Build skills for social agency, of good leadership, and of good followership

In short, the Critical Response Process gives teens the tools to practice engaged citizenship. I make this claim reflecting on over twenty years as a socially engaged dance artist in numerous adolescent communities, doing work in which I've placed the principles of CRP at the core of my practice. I draw on my recent experience teaching high school residencies though Jacob's Pillow Curriculum in Motion program in western Massachusetts, and in Hubbard Street Dance's education and community programs, working in some of the most challenged communities on Chicago's West Side. In these and many other short-term encounters, I've repeatedly observed how even a small dose of CRP can go a long way. Most significantly, as long-term director of Dance Exchange's Teen Exchange, a program for youth aged thirteen to eighteen, which emphasizes creative development of original performance material, I've had the opportunity to watch teens literally grow up with the Process. This essay includes quotes from personal correspondence with Teen Exchangers I encountered between 1999 and 2010, now looking back from their young adult perspective, about how CRP affected them in their teen years and how it continues to influence them today.

> "Taking a moment to notice something, really notice the details and not just 'I like this' or 'I don't like this,' is a vitally important skill. It's so much more interesting to be able to express that something is exciting or evocative or distressing or affecting, and more importantly, why. Practicing CRP is, in part, practicing that skill."
> —Sadie Leigh Rothman, current dancer/yoga instructor, Teen Exchange participant 2003 to 2008

CULTIVATING CURIOSITY: PROCESS PREREQUISITE

We start life innately curious. Toddlers explore their world through taste and touch. Small children use their budding language skills to form questions, often asking "why" in ways that confound adults. But as we grow older, learn more about right and wrong and the rewards of playing by school rules, we begin to look for answers more often than questions. We want to know how to be right, how to get the A, how to be approved and accepted. Because questions fuel the Critical Response Process, curiosity is a prerequisite for participation. In return, the Process cultivates curiosity as the act of engaging in dialogue through CRP and develops an investment and interest in the work for all parties involved.

When teens understand the steps of CRP and watch peers perform original choreography with the knowledge that they will be engaging in a dialogue of statements of meaning and questions to ask and answer, it changes the way they witness the work. Labels of "good" and "bad" give way to questions about how, why, and what. In artmaking, as in life, we can discover multiple successful ways to address creative problems. CRP develops the capacity for complex thinking beyond the standardized test system (with which our young people are all too familiar) that allows for only one correct answer.

For the emerging adolescent artist, a goal may be to develop an individual artistic voice that is distinct from that of mentors, teachers, or peers. In such situations, CRP is helpful because it assesses the work in relationship to the artist's intentions rather than an outside model or set of expectations. Articulating an individual artistic intention is developmentally appropriate in adolescence. While impulse, intuition, and the free will to explore an idea always have value in a creative process, personal intention emerges as an important mark of autonomy and a measure of progress in teen artistic development. Curiosity is essential to this articulation. What do I want to create? Why, out of all the things I could create, do I want to create this? What is my intention for what I create? How does what I have made match my intention? Does what you perceive match my intention? If not, what revisions can I make to align my intention with your experience? Is it even important that others see what I intend, or is it open to individual interpretation? How well have I met my own goals? Have we discovered something together beyond my intention that is worth pursuing or exploring? Can I change or evolve my intention?

In step two, questions from the artist, sometimes it is challenging to move a young adolescent from simply asking, "Did you like it?" or "What can I do to make it better?" to asking something along the lines of: "I'm struggling with the opening tableau and I'm curious about what you saw in the image." It is a shift from the extrinsic to intrinsic, from seeking external validation to looking inside with curiosity, from asking for solutions to fulfilling a clearer sense of one's intentions. It gives teen artists ownership over their own work, and with this comes both creative freedom and the responsibility to make choices. Navigating the responsibility of freedom, of choice-making within independence, is an essential skill of adulthood. The creation of artistic work through the use of the Process allows teens to practice and build this skill.

To engage with CRP, responders must also be curious. True curiosity about someone else's work is liberating. It provides a counterbalance to the competitive mindset that can undermine meaningful critique. To invest in someone else's success through genuine curiosity, especially knowing that they might also invest in yours, is one of the most important community-building aspects of the Process. When I set up a showing I often say, "Resist the temptation to rehearse your dance in your mind while others are performing." When we dance for each other in an environment that is present and curious, we dance better, far better than when we anxiously replay our dance over and over in our mind while waiting our turn.

Giving and getting feedback can feel unsteady and vulnerable. Although we sometimes shy away from the discomfort of vulnerability, it is essential for connection, and while teens crave independence, they also crave social connection. Curiosity and the vulnerability that comes with it are essential for any creative process, including the creative act of being a teen and becoming an adult.

> "Critical Response Process dramatically altered my sense of how I see the world. As a teaching artist, I utilize step ones on a daily basis with my students at Greene Towne Montessori School. From even a young age, this process allows for individuals to get to the heart of what is essential. As a choreographer, I frequently turn to CRP when looking for feedback from collaborators in my artistic community in Philadelphia. As an artist, I would be a different person if I had not grown up in a community that valued offering voice to all in a concise, constructive manner."
> —Talia Mason, current dancer and teaching artist, Teen Exchange participant from 2007 to 2011

LOOKING THROUGH THE LENS OF LOVE

Step One: What did you find evocative, curious, memorable, exciting, and/or meaningful about the work?

Sharing creative work, especially when we are about to get feedback on it, can be intimidating and uncomfortable, even when we know we will be supported through a structure like CRP. Creating a space of generosity is essential. Everyone (but I think particularly the teen artist who may be highly sensitive to peer perspectives) performs better when we are being watched with benevolent eyes and with kind hearts.

To express this idea, I ask the viewers to "look through the lens of love," often making a little heart with my hands and peeking through the hole. While it may sound silly, it's caught on with many teen groups, and several of my colleagues have carried on this approach to their work with teens. This is meaningful with teens involved in an ongoing process of collaborative dance composition, and I have also found it especially effective in arts integration contexts where students are required to make dances as part of an academic subject, who may be performing for peers from other classrooms and won't have the chance to revise. "Looking through the lens of love" prepares students for this moment of constructive feedback and also infuses the space with a palpable spirit of care. The students even make the heart and peek through it, sometimes even without my prompting, as a nonverbal way of saying, "I'm here for you."

Let it be understood: Evoking the idea of love need not compromise the rigor of the feedback, and it does not call for viewers to "love" everything they see. As a shorthand reminder of values that we work to build through the encounter, the phrase "look through the lens of love" is a call to respect. It says, "If I know you are looking with the best intention of support and care, then I will return that intention to you." We will focus beyond anxiety, alliances, and competition, with an agreement for mutual trust. Each participant's choice to support another elevates the entire room. Teenagers understand and seek this reciprocity, which is why I think "lens of love" catches on so readily with them. They want to be validated; they feel good when they can validate others.

In initiating the CRP session as facilitator, I almost always require everyone to participate in step one. I state this requirement at the outset, often having participants take turns in sequence around the circle. Step one lays the foundation for the Process and is instrumental in building community trust and a culture of support. Participating provides an important skill builder for the later steps. It's unfair for someone to chime in with an opinion in step four if they have not participated earlier in the Process, especially if they neglected to find and articulate a step one.

When Critical Response practitioners learn and practice step ones in the studio, its spirit of witness, focus, and generosity often seeps into other aspects of their worldview. When you carry a step one attitude, you're able to see the glass as half full, while also acknowledging the half-empty part.

> "For me, and I think a lot of kids, being a teenager was a very vulnerable time. . . . The structure of the Critical Response Process made feedback collaborative and strengthening rather than scary and

humiliating. The Process was so important in allowing all of us to feel engaged and empowered in both the making and observation of art. [It provided me] . . . the tools to grow, rather than shrink, when faced with criticism."

—Suzannah Vaughn, current Federal Grants Manager, Teen Exchange participant from 2003 to 2008

VISION, VOICE, AND LEARNING TO LISTEN

Step Two: Questions from the artist

Any generative artistic process develops the capacity to manifest one's own imagination into a creative vision. CRP supports teen artists in understanding this vision deeply, because it provides a structure whereby a teen artist can refine and clarify intentions through productive dialogue. This can help young artists embrace their unique style, build self-confidence, and form the foundation for an artistic identity. It cultivates autonomy and individuality by allowing the artist whose work is being examined to drive the Process within a structure that does not compare the work competitively or aesthetically with anyone else's.

Requiring artists and responders to practice giving words to emotions, ideas, and experiences, CRP also develops voice. It's a process of having, noticing, and articulating an experience. You don't need to be an expert to contribute to the discussion. The Process provides a structure of participation for both the seasoned faculty member who can easily identify and name technical nuance, and the younger sibling who is emotionally moved and connects personal memory to the work. In this way, the Process is democratic: The fuller the participation, the greater the chance that the voices will carry equal weight. As a facilitator, I sometimes need to pay particular attention to ensure that the conversation is not dominated by the loudest voices and that the contributions of some individuals do not intimidate others into silence. Requiring everyone to provide a comment in step one sets the groundwork; in step two I make sure at least a few people respond to each question, and I often ask, "Does anyone have an answer that differs from the responses we have already heard?" This further invites a range of responses. If one person is overtaking the conversation, I might ask, "Can we hear from some voices we haven't heard yet?" Additionally, if a technical term is used, I ask either the responder or the artist to define it. I also assess the group climate by paying attention to body language and physical positioning; I encourage participation using eye contact and nonverbal physical cueing.

Step two's challenge to pose questions about one's own work in progress can be daunting for artists at any stage of their development. Teens may require particular coaching to help them make the most of this opportunity. Typically, younger artists ask questions that narrow rather than broaden possibility, and they often choose phrasing that poses such binaries as good/not good, like/not like, it worked/it didn't. To help them draw their questions out of their own process, I often coach on Liz Lerman's principle "Turn discomfort into inquiry" using prods like "What are you uncertain of?" "What are you wondering about or less satisfied with?" to help them form questions that will elicit meaningful responses. Working with a group over an extended time, we start to collect a repertory of questions that can broaden the response, offering further options on which any artist in step two can draw: "What did it [a particular moment or image] make you think of?" "What title would you give it?" "Where did your mind go when . . . ?"

The act of critique is creative, and it's easy to imagine possibilities beyond what we've witnessed, easy for both artists and responders to get caught up in remaking the work in their heads. Artists may pose "what-ifs" for vetting by the group, and responders can slide into unsolicited fixits. When this happens, I gently try to steer the conversation back to the immediate work in progress by suggesting, "Let's respond to what we just saw."

NEUTRAL QUESTIONS, THE TEEN BRAIN, AND THE POWER OF PERSUASION

Step Three: Neutral questions from the responders

Liz Lerman says, "When defensiveness starts, learning stops." CRP is designed to keep defensiveness at bay throughout each step of the Process, but especially in the third step. Forming a neutral question can be challenging, but it opens a space for dialogue rather than argument. Step three and the structure the neutral question provides to forestall defensiveness and the emotions that come with it are particularly important for teens. Neuroscience research shows that teen brains have more receptors for oxytocin, the bonding hormone, which is why they can make such intimate social connections, but it is also linked to why they can feel more self-conscious (Nixon 2012). Studies also demonstrate that adolescent brains are governed more by the limbic system, the emotional center of the brain, than the prefrontal cortex reasoning center, which controls rational thought and the capacity to make sound judgments (Feinstein

2009). The emotional limbic system can trigger the sympathetic nervous system into a fight-or-flight response. In this physiological state, heart rate increases, digestion ceases, and peripheral vision narrows. When this happens, the body becomes literally less open to possibility.

Understanding the role of hormones and the balance between the limbic system and the prefrontal cortex in the teen brain helps us understand why the sequence of the steps in CRP is especially effective. I posit that step one in CRP soothes the limbic system, decreases anxiety, and promotes bonding. Step one thus allows the prefrontal cortex to do thoughtful work during step two. Then step three's neutral question continues to keep the limbic system from taking control. When we are not engaged in a fight-or-flight response, we can feel safe enough to extend generosity and positivity and do problem-solving.

Teens who have become proficient in forming neutral questions have observed how helpful this skill is beyond the studio. More than one teen has noted that asking a neutral question serves them far better than complaining and getting angry about parental rules. One teen in particular had asked her parents, "Can you talk about what informs your decision for a 10:00 p.m. curfew?" leading to a conversation that provided a chance for communication, connection, and understanding. Parents have the opportunity to consider and articulate the reasoning behind their parenting decisions, and teens can better understand where their parents are coming from. The neutral question allows teens and parents to hear each other without being adversarial, and can offer the possibility of collaboration and respectful compromise.

OWNING YOUR OWN OPINION

Step Four: Permissioned opinions

> "And don't even get me started on 'I have an opinion about ______, would you like to hear it?' I wish everyone in my life who had an opinion about anything would talk to me about it in that format. Not only does it force the person with an opinion to be clear and specific about what exactly their opinion concerns, but it also gives the person being offered an opinion the option to decline."
>
> —Sadie Leigh Rothman, dancer/yoga instructor, Teen Exchange participant from 2003 to 2008

John Borstel often says that in Critical Response opinions are a "destination, not a point of departure." Among its numerous merits, step four seeks consent by asking, "I have an opinion about ______, would you like to hear it?" This gives the ultimate power of choice to the artist. Hardly ever do teen artists say they don't want to hear the opinion, especially if it is from a mentor, but it allows them the control and gives the responder a greater weight of responsibility in expressing the opinion.

In general, I have found teens very receptive to working with the "script" in step four. They like the clarity of the structure as a responder, and as an artist it is empowering to have the opportunity to say "no," even when that option isn't exercised. I believe the Process allows for the artist to be more receptive to opinions, positive or negative, in step four. Frequently, though, responders become more informed through the course of a CRP session. The resulting insight leads to step four opinions that are precise in their delivery or that return us to the spirit of the statement of meaning in step one.

Step four may yield a range of opinions that quite frequently are in direct conflict with each other. The Critical Response Process is able to hold multiple perspectives in the room without one outweighing another. We are able to say, "Isn't it interesting how different people can have such different perspectives on the same situation?" This is a practice in respecting and honoring difference. Ultimately, teen artists get to filter the opinions through their own lens as they head back to the studio to get back to work.

MANAGING CONFLICT, DANCING WITH RESISTANCE

I have worked with teens in public and private schools—some high achieving, some highly challenged. I have encountered adolescents in foster care, in residential treatment facilities, in detention and homeless service centers, as well as in ballet studios and advanced placement programs where privilege is the norm. Whether I'm in a one-time encounter or a sustained engagement, whether participation is consistent or unpredictable, whether I have a chance to introduce the formal version of CRP or not, the values of the Process underpin every engagement I facilitate.

I can't overstress the importance of a "step one spirit." This outlook allows me as a facilitator to notice even small moments of success and to build on what is working. It breeds generosity and makes me more accepting of my students. Sometimes the youth I work with want to be there, but more frequently they do not. They may enter the room with palpable resistance and with preconceived notions about who I am, what dance is, and what I will be asking them to do. I could get bogged down in this negativity and what could feel like an insurmountable task of getting them onboard. However, if I can allow myself to notice the girl who made eye contact, the guy who helped quiet the room, the student in the corner who joined the conversation, I build my capacity for resilience and the strength to keep coming back to try again.

Statements of meaning also build connection and trust. I always try to greet students as they walk in the room because, among other things, it gives me an opportunity to share such statements with each individual. "I really appreciate how you helped me with the music during the last class. Let me know if you have ideas about music for what we are doing today." I try to be specific about what kids do as opposed to complimenting what they look like, but sometimes an honest comment, such as "I like your bright shirt. It's great to have that light on this cloudy day," can let a teen know that they are noticed. As in the case with any application of step one, these statements must be sincere. Teens can tell if an adult is being fake, and it will only push them further away.

Even if I don't introduce CRP, I always incorporate a way for students to practice statements of meaning in each class, even if it is not named as such. For example, in a technique class, students might watch a partner in the final phrase work and share specific moments of strong execution. If students have made and shared creative work, I ask viewing students, "What's interesting or effective? What stands out to you?" Frequently, I conclude classes with "Take 5," a structure I originally learned from theater artist and youth facilitator Julianne Franz. I ask the teen students, "What's something you will take away from today?" As a group, our challenge is to collect five short statements in response to this question. I usually don't require students to raise their hand, but rather I invite them to claim space and speak when they have something to share. A participant will offer a thought, such as "I will take away the fun I had working with new people" or "I will take away the good music." Once a statement has been made, as the facilitator I say, "Take one" as a cue, and the group acknowledges the student's statement with a unison clap. When the last statement has been shared I say, "Take five to take it away for the day," and we close class with a single unison clap.

The values of managing judgment and promoting inquiry—which are at the heart of CRP—inform my teaching practice with youth. When a student is being disruptive, rather than labeling the action as "bad behavior" (which then leads to punitive consequences), I try to ask questions about why the student is acting in such a way. Sometimes this is an internal process, and I make discoveries about how I might arrange the room differently or make changes to class content or structure that can create a space in which they can feel more safe to participate. Sometimes this process involves direct communication with the student, if I am able to pull a student aside to ask, "What's going on? Can you tell me what was happening for you when you threw your shoe at Kayla?" Having the opportunity to engage students one-on-one with genuine curiosity and questions has given me insight where previously I would have just tried to curtail the behavior. I have discovered everything from "My cat died this morning and I'm really sad" to "I have allergies and I didn't sleep well" to instances where a student was being sexually harassed by a peer.

Teens can be emotional, and they will sometimes speak their minds. Their unsolicited opinions can be inspiring and supportive, or downright hurtful. "This is boring," "Do we have to do this again?" and "I hate this music" are exclamations I have heard on more than one occasion. Hearing these comments as a facilitator with feelings and emotions of my own can get me discouraged. In such situations, I remember something I learned from Liz Lerman: "What is the neutral question they could have asked?" Reflecting on this question allows me to respond in a way that is not defensive and that can give the students further information about what we are doing and why. "Do we have to do this again?" might translate into "Can you talk about the use of repetition in our class structure?"—allowing me to respond: "Repetition is really important in dance. Dancers rehearse the same phrases multiple times so that we can train our muscle memory, get physically stronger, and work more deeply in our bodies." When I am not defensive and I can respond to opinions as questions, I am a better teacher. I am clearer, more generous, and it gives me the opportunity to investigate my own choices.

The Critical Response Process is a valuable tool for teens and for those who work with, live beside, and mentor teens. CRP's balance of structure and freedom and its capacity for building community, trust, and respect while also delving into complex terrain are well suited for the developing adolescent artist. CRP redefines good feedback as something that excites artists and makes them want to get back to work. The structure puts challenges into relief and embraces them not as obstacles but as opportunities, building the capacity for tenacity, integrity, and a strong work ethic in adolescents. The values of generosity, curiosity, inquiry, and a growth mindset can provide a springboard for teens in the studio and beyond, and for many years to come.

REFERENCES

Feinstein, Sheryl, and Eric Jensen. *Inside the Teenage Brain: Parenting a Work in Progress* (Lanham, MD: Rowman & Littlefield Education, 2009).

Nixon, Robin. "Adolescent Angst: 5 Facts About the Teen Brain." *LiveScience*, July 8, 2012. Retrieved from https://www.livescience.com/21461-teen-brain-adolescence-facts.html/.

ENGAGING THE VITAL POWER OF YOUR PEERS: CRP IN JAZZ EDUCATION

Carlos Lopez-Real

"How do I get better at doing this?" In one way or another, this is the essential question all my students in the Jazz department at London's Guildhall School of Music and Drama ask—of me and of themselves. As they come to realize that they will be asking this question for the rest of their careers, it takes on a weight over and above simply getting a good grade. I ask myself the same question in relation to supporting them.

My jazz students are striving to be effective, "self-regulated" learners. They wouldn't use that kind of pedagogical language, but they certainly grasp the need to have a strategy to sustain their continued artistic growth and learning once they leave the institution. Naturally enough, their focus becomes about self-assessment and determining how to close the gap between their perceived current performance and that to which they aspire. The self-assessment will generally happen through listening back to recordings of themselves, analyzing what they hear, and reflecting on it. It may additionally involve transcribing what they hear into musical notation. This is all hugely useful, but only part of the picture.

My students often start at Guildhall essentially wanting me to give them all the answers. Partly this is a product of the way they've previously learned: "You're doing x, y, z. You need to be doing a, b, c . . ." Partly it's the product of a certain jazz mythology, and a quest to be let in on supposed jazz secrets or tricks of the trade. Over time, the students usually develop a more sophisticated understanding of their own self-reflective capability and how to integrate this with ideas and feedback they're getting from teachers. What's often missing, however, is how to engage the vital power of their peers.

Harnessing that power is essential because jazz is an inherently social art form in which collaboration is key. Many of the greatest developments in the genre came about through sustained musical relationships, a constant learning with and from one's peers. My jazz students have plenty of opportunities for peer feedback in their coursework, and more widely within the jazz scene in London. There's a shared passion and a deepening of knowledge that comes from regularly playing together in a community of practice. However, the peer feedback they experience often amounts to little more than generalized praise ("Hey, you sounded great on that tune"), which, aside from being a nice ego massage, isn't especially useful. Lacking in detail and a sense of how to progress to next steps, it often only serves to reinforce the reliance on extrinsic motivation by many insecure artists. The opinions of others, then, are what counts, rather than developing intrinsic motivation and the associated "mastery goals," fueled by passion. I found that without a model for effective peer feedback, students didn't really have the tools for approaching potentially difficult conversations in the rehearsal room or on the bandstand. Neither did they have the tools to seek, and effectively harness, feedback from their peers as part of their overall developmental strategy. Enter the Critical Response Process.

Things just clicked when I discovered CRP through direct work with Liz Lerman. The Process resonated strongly with coaching-mentoring approaches that I'd been exploring, such as those of Jenny Rogers (2012) and John Whitmore (2009). At the heart of both CRP and these coaching approaches lies a set of values (including honesty, respect, and a desire for growth) together with the processes of dialogue and exchange. Both also contain crucial structures that prepare the artist, or coachee, to be as open to receiving (truly hearing) as possible. Clicking for me personally, however, didn't necessarily mean that it would click for my students.

I explored different ways to introduce and integrate CRP with my jazz students. One of the most successful was an extended project dedicated to exploring both CRP and video feedback with small jazz ensembles. I worked with nine different groups of students over thirty-eight sessions (around 125 hours), which gave us all a chance to explore in depth the uses of CRP in this context. This experience clarified that there's a certain "golden" period, or window, in the development of a jazz ensemble project in which CRP is most useful. Such a project would involve around six three-hour rehearsals, working towards a final performance of thirty minutes of music (comprising several shorter pieces to make up the whole 'show'). Although I generally introduced CRP fairly early in each project and had the students regularly practice the steps, it wasn't until around halfway through each project that things really took off. Some of this acceleration was the result of the students themselves becoming more adept with CRP, but largely it was the music itself developing to the point where CRP was most useful. Once they could all play the material together competently, we focused more on issues of overall shape and development through improvisations, as well as on the ebb and flow of improvised interactions between different members of the group.

After introducing the classic four-step structure of CRP, we generally focused on one student at a time being the artist. Sometimes the rhythm section (e.g., drummer, pianist, bass player) would take on the role of the artist, exploring some aspect of how they were accompanying a soloist, while the rest of the band acted as responders. At other times, when the entire ensemble needed to consider certain issues together, I would try to facilitate a looser conversation that still utilized some underlying principles and techniques of CRP. This naturally overlapped with strategies from coaching-mentoring, including focusing on open rather than closed questions (and so avoiding opinion-polling: e.g., "Should I have played louder during that section?").

The students appreciated being able to have conversations with each other about the music in a way where they felt less attacked and, consequently, less defensive. The biggest learning moment for them often happened in step two, certainly linked with their ongoing ability to self-assess. Younger students tended to be initially alienated by the formality of the classic four-step Process, whereas the postgraduates readily embraced it. Consequently, I experimented with introducing and exploring the steps in isolation (in different sessions, even) with these younger students. Many also felt that the structure of the Process disrupted the flow of the rehearsal sessions. This got easier as increasing familiarity allowed them to bounce back and forth between elements of CRP and playing the music.

Overall, CRP has provided my students with the tools to enable them to better self-assess and to better work collaboratively with each other. In this sense, it helps them in a tangible way with their question, "How do I get better at doing this?" Very striking, especially among older students, was the capacity to transfer and apply the knowledge, tools, and ethos of CRP into other areas of their lives. Their reflective diaries showed that some of them became much more aware of how they give feedback in other contexts (musical or otherwise) and how they formulate questions (both for themselves and for others). This tallies with my own personal experience. While CRP may have its origins within artistic practice, it more broadly embodies values and skills for living life.

REFERENCES

Rogers, Jenny. *Coaching Skills: A Handbook* (Berkshire: Open University Press, 2012).

Whitmore, John. *Coaching for Performance* (London: Nicholas Brealey Publishing, 2009).

DEVELOPING THE ARTISTIC VOICE

Gerda van Zelm

My first experience with the Critical Response Process was a stimulating struggle. Encountering CRP in an Innovative Conservatoire (ICON) seminar in 2012, I was forced to examine some of my ingrained habits in giving criticism as a teacher of music and voice and I was challenged to make my brain take new turns. Exercising the step one statements of meaning, I learned that staying closer to my own experience in response to a performance awakened deeper layers of understanding, appreciation, recognition, and human connection. Practicing how to ask neutral questions—non-opinionated, nonjudgmental, and nonsuggestive questions—made me realize how often as a teacher I posed questions with my own answers programmed in. At first the opportunity to give an opinion in step four seemed easy, but to think then of how we could rephrase our opinions as neutral questions proved to be a brain twister.

Full of ideas, I went back to my school intending to use CRP in my teaching. Though nervous because I felt I was not very good at it myself, I resolved to learn alongside my students, starting in the weekly performance class I teach for all my voice students. Recognizing the difficulty of asking constructive questions, we took an entire lesson on step two. Practicing the artist's questions was instructive: Wanting to know how her character portrayal registered after performing an excerpt from Mozart's *Così fan tutte*, a student asked, "Was I a good Despina?" which proved to be a dead-end question that got little response. After a fellow student helped her rephrase this as "What kind of Despina did you perceive?" the conversation flowed. In our next lively class, focused entirely on step three, students were completely committed to the task of finding the neutral questions in response to their peers. After these two preparatory lessons, we did the full CRP. We were all learners and teachers, and I was touched by the speed with which the students changed the quality of their questions and comments. I observed changes in their thinking process and noticed how liberating it was for them to realize that they would not be forced into a defensive position after performing.

> "CRP helped me to think differently onstage. It eases critique, allowing you to process feedback more readily and to apply it immediately to your singing. It has made group classes interactive by creating a triangle between the teacher as conversation leader, the students as audience, and the performing student onstage. When the first question is 'What did you receive as a public?' rather than "What did you want from my performance that you didn't get?" the class starts in an open and positive way, and the student onstage is more able to receive critical notes."
> —Chris Postuma, voice student, bachelor's degree

After this initiation, students started having a truly mature exchange of ideas about their singing. Since then, I have taken time at the beginning of each year to reintroduce and practice all the steps of CRP for the benefit of new incoming students. When there isn't time for the full CRP, I use the principles behind it. For instance, asking students to give one comment and ask one question. I am really struck by how students answer to this in a totally respectful, meaningful, and honest way.

> "As a student, working with CRP during our voice group lessons was initially very difficult, not because of the rules—which were very easy to understand and made total sense—but because I had never before examined my process of giving or asking for feedback. This lack of knowledge in how to formulate questions or to respond to another's work made for a few early lessons where I was tongue-tied. Within a few weeks it got much easier, as I gained practice in thinking differently and really knowing in advance what I wanted to get from the performance classes. In receiving feedback, CRP gave me control to accept or dismiss comments according to what would benefit me the most at that point. It put me, the performer, in the position of instigator rather than passive receiver. The possibility of asking questions and having a dialogue creates much more active participation, both from performer to audience and within the

audience itself. Using CRP changed the class into a group of active listeners who all have something to say about the performance."
—Ruth Fraser, voice student, bachelor's degree

I also began exploring how I could use CRP in voice lessons where I work one-on-one with individual students. Without someone to play the role of facilitator, I decided to go through the steps of CRP without explicitly telling the student. This gave me the opportunity to play more flexibly with the steps. Students who had experienced CRP during group classes made the connection and actively responded to the new approach. The resulting lessons took a form like the following: The student sings a piece of music. For my first response I say something like, "I can really hear that you worked on this since last week, your singing sounds easier to me," or "I can tell that you really love this piece because I hear . . ." or "I feel this piece fits your voice very well because . . ." Then I invite the student into the function of step two by asking questions like: What are your questions? What would you like to discuss? How do you want to continue now? What should our next step be? What can I help you with? Even if the student addresses issues that I find less important, or if they neglect areas of focus that we have already established, I postpone my own response and work on what the student brings up. This has allowed me to achieve a longstanding aim to work in a learner-centered way, which increases student motivation and their role in shaping their own artistry. Moving on to step three, I use neutral questions to address the issues I have with the students' performance, whether technical, musical, or interpretive: What is it that the poet wants to tell us? What do you want to tell your public? How does the composer characterize the meaning of the text? What do you feel is the technical challenge of this piece for you? What spots do you want to check? Where does it feel uncomfortable and how do you think you can solve this? Instead of giving directions, I create space for the student and myself to work from what is already there. I hear the students as they voice what they want to develop and how. By listening, I discern a lot about a student's learning processes, which helps me be a better teacher. In fact, I find I am bored in a lesson during which I do not learn something myself, and I feel very uneasy when students put me in the position of a problem fixer because I believe there is little learning in this role. When I move to step four, permissioned opinions, I try to formulate my opinion as a question again—though I don't always succeed!

My students and I have gained much in the years since introducing

CRP into my teaching. It helps students to take ownership over their learning and makes them more active as they use inquiry in their quest for excellence. It enables me to postpone my expertise and the benefits of my experience to first let students give voice to their artistic ideas, their needs, and their wishes. I feel that working with CRP helps students to develop what is most important for them: their own artistic voice.

Building on this experience, I have facilitated CRP sessions with music teachers of conservatoires and colleges in varied situations and contexts. In my own institution, the Royal Conservatoire in The Hague, CRP is part of a professional development course for teachers. I have also been invited to do CRP in Oslo (Norway), Vienna and Graz (Austria), Lübeck (Germany), and Arnhem (The Netherlands). The composition of the groups is always very diverse, including musicians of such different "blood types" as pop, jazz, and classical music, and encompassing improvisers, composers, and theory teachers of these different styles. Groups often combine those who are primarily teachers with active performers who have a teaching sideline. In this dynamic, musicians who rarely encounter each other in their institutions suddenly find themselves in a profound conversation about the core of their musicianship. In one session, a classical pianist received feedback on his performance of a short piece by Edvard Grieg from a group that included some jazz pianists. Questions came up in the CRP about the timing in the bass-line. During the coffee break that followed, four or five pianists gathered around the grand piano to continue the discussion and try out different approaches. I remember thinking, *This is what we want for our students, isn't it?*

On another occasion, I facilitated for a classical cellist who plays in many important concert halls in and beyond Europe—in fact, his fame made me somewhat nervous. When, in preparation for the session, I told him he could ask questions, he stared at me blankly. He gave a wonderful performance of an excerpt from a Bach suite. Just to listen felt like a privilege, and in step one he received a rich collection of beautiful, respectful, deeply personal responses. I felt him growing ten centimeters in his chair next to me. So I asked the circle of responders: "Do we see what is happening here? Think of what will happen to your students when you start giving them statements of meaning before giving you your—very well intended—feedback." Reflecting on his experience of step one, the musician expressed that it made him very happy because normally he would not know what people thought or felt about his playing since he had little contact with his listeners after a concert. Moving on to step two, he continued to draw a blank on the opportunity to pose his own question, but just as we were about to skip forward to step three, he suddenly thought of one: "When I play music of J.S. Bach I do not care too much about the debate on how to perform early music. How important do you think this is?" This led to a bounteous exchange of ideas about how to use results of early music research and the consequences for performance practice.

Generally, CRP is received with respect and great interest in the alternatives it offers as a way of giving critique. Musicians receiving feedback often say that despite feeling nervous about playing for their colleagues, CRP gave them a safe place to be the artist.

The question of expertise often comes up. Instructors ask themselves if they can teach well if they cannot correct students or give them the necessary information or examples. If this happens, I tell them that in CRP you can operate from your expertise from the beginning—particularly as it may help you to pose a powerful question for the student in step three—but that you postpone the fullness of your expertise until step four. I also say that even when I don't use the formal CRP because it is not appropriate for a given teaching situation, the values of the Process still help me keep track of myself regarding who is doing the work in the lesson—the student or me. Individual instrumental and vocal lessons often have the quality of a constant feedback loop, where open, nondirective questions for the student are rarely posed. Thus it's a new and challenging task for teachers to start shaping neutral questions that enable students' learning. Since this is a new approach for students as well, their first response may be not encouraging. I remind teachers that throughout all their music education, some students have never heard a real question—one that really invited them to say what they think, not what they think they are supposed to think—and that it may take a little while for students to understand that they are allowed to speak up. But students are young, they learn quickly, and they like to use the learning space we offer them. CRP is a tool that gives students ownership of their learning.

IF THE ARTIST ASKS, IT'S OUR JOB TO ANSWER: CRP IN THE COLLEGE DANCE COMPOSITION STUDIO

Gesel Mason

As a dancer in my twenties, it was a powerful and humbling experience to engage in the myriad of activities assumed by Dance Exchange company members. In addition to performing onstage (and in shipyards, museums, schools, etc.), I established a new teen program, coordinated residencies, collaborated on a solo with Liz, and taught weekly classes. The thing I didn't do was go out of my way to volunteer to lead or facilitate CRP workshops. I didn't think my ADD brain was well suited to keep track of all the rules and guidelines I perceived in the Process. I enjoyed tangents and side conversations too much. And it took so long! Basically, I was bad at it. Or so I thought. I find it amusing that now, over twenty years later, the skills I gained from participating in and witnessing CRP, as well as other Dance Exchange activities, permeate my artmaking, teaching, conversations, and collaborations. The methods and values of CRP provide a framework for listening, observing, and offering feedback that has served me well in my career.

I have used aspects of CRP for many functions: in leading choreography workshops, in providing feedback as an adjudicator for college dance festivals, and loosely as a way to frame post-show discussions. I find it particularly useful in dance composition classes where one of the primary objectives is for students, whether beginning or advanced, to practice ways to observe work and give and receive feedback.

In classes and workshops I teach, I find it important to create a safe, challenging, and courageous space to take risks, experiment, share thoughts and opinions, and try new things. To facilitate this, I start composition classes by establishing agreements, a practice inspired by Urban Bush Women as part of their approach to "Entering, Building, and Exiting" communities. The agreements are a covenant in response to the question, "What do you need from your classmates, your instructor, your environment, or the institution in order to be your most creative and productive selves?" Inevitably, students answer with references to "pushing" each other and the desire for honest feedback.

Everyone wants to know the "truth" about how others feel about or interpret their work. Yet we are also aware of how vulnerable receiving critical feedback can be. Students want to be honest but often have difficulty verbalizing feedback in a way that is useful, critical, and respectful. Some will choose silence over the possibility of hurting another's feelings. Some feel that harsh, opinionated criticism is somehow more truthful and more useful. Others simply want to know: "Was it good?" and "Did you like it?" CRP provides a framework and language that gives space to the intentions of the artist and creates a mediated dialogue between the artist and responder. As a responder, whether or not I "liked" it is essentially irrelevant.

The goal of feedback is not to "fix" the dance for the artist, but to provide feedback that allows artists to find the answers on their own. I have found that students appreciate the rigors of the Process, the thoughtfulness of the feedback, and being held accountable in how they think about and voice their opinions on choreographic work.

To introduce CRP with a formal training often requires several hours, so I have developed a few ways to employ the Process while being mindful of the time constraints of the classroom and probably to attend to my ADD. One approach is to introduce the feedback process as a series of individual steps that accumulate throughout the semester. I use an article from the Winter/Spring 2008 issue of *Contact Quarterly*, "Liz Lerman's Critical Response Process: The Core Steps and an Interview with Liz Lerman," to lay a foundation.

As an instructor, it can be tricky to balance the roles of educator, facilitator, and responder. In the beginning, I function as the facilitator of student/responder feedback and then "take off my facilitator hat" to offer my personal feedback to the work. As an educator, it feels important to provide feedback, which the class may not be prepared for or know how to give, especially in the beginning. With the facilitator hat off and the educator/responder hat on, I use feedback as an opportunity to model the type of responses often associated with each step. Sometimes I intentionally offer feedback not in line with CRP to see if the class can catch it.

I incorporate new steps as we move through the semester. Once we become familiar with each step and trust each other to respect the agreements, the class begins to facilitate itself (including me!) like a conductorless orchestra. CRP moves beyond a feedback model and becomes part of an overall framework for honest discussion and negotiation in the classroom. As an instructor, I appreciate when the responsibility of facilitating the class or workshop environment is distributed among the participants; it removes the hierarchy of me as the teacher possessing all the answers and rules. While the buck may stop with me as the educator/facilitator, the goal is to create an equitable and encouraging environment for artmaking.

Below I outline more specific ways I incorporate the steps of CRP in the classroom.

STEP ONE: STATEMENTS OF MEANING

I utilize step one on its own as the primary response to choreographic assignments at the beginning of the semester. Since these early showings tend to be in response to instructor prompts, I usually avoid extensive feedback and criticism on work that is not of students' inspiration. Step one is a way of getting the group to talk about what we saw or experienced without the pressure (and resisting the desire) to categorize the artist's offering as good or bad, right or wrong.

In addition to standard step one prompts ("What is exciting, interesting, memorable . . ."?), I often ask responders to share "what is working" about what the artist made. Another variation is to ask students to provide three words or a single statement describing what about the work stood out to them or made an impact, which offers useful practice in formulating succinct replies. As another way to manage limited time, I encourage students to share additional responses via handwritten notes to the artist. This approach can be used for any step, either during the wrap-up of that step or outside of class time. Handwritten notes are also a way for both less vocal and more verbose students to share their ideas.

STEP TWO: ARTIST AS QUESTIONER

I add the next two steps of CRP after we have shared work with each other a few times. For step two, I encourage the artist to craft questions that provide the kind of information that will help them understand their work. For instance, if an artist asks, "How did you feel about the first half?" I may ask them to be more specific, especially for people like me who like to go off on tangents: Why do they want to know the answer to that question? What about the first half is working or not for them already? What kind of question would generate more than a one-word response or a simple reply of "I liked it" or not? The question may then become: "I am curious about your reaction to xyz in the first half and the fact that I don't return to that idea in the second half." I encourage the responders to reply honestly, saying, "If the artist asks, it is our job to answer their question." However, I urge them to provide the "why" in any of their responses and to beware of prescriptive replies that attempt to solve the "problems" of the dance. To continue with the previous example, an answer might be: "I found I wasn't able to focus on the content of the second half because I kept trying to figure out how xyz was related to what I was seeing." The objective for the class is to learn how to ask for clarity or rework a statement or question into something more useful to the work.

STEP THREE: RESPONDERS ASK QUESTIONS

For step three in this composition class variation, responders ask a few questions and the artist gets to choose which they would like to address.

It is helpful, as a facilitator, to limit time for responses while still being able to hear all the questions, and it encourages artists to be selective with which queries to answer. Also as facilitator, I try to steer students away from overexplaining, justifying, or apologizing about their work or their choices. This keeps us focused on feedback about the work rather than their feelings about making the work.

We take the time to discuss the concept of a neutral question. In addition to helping students identify opinions embedded in questions, we also distinguish questions that offer information or a meaningful challenge to the artist from those that primarily serve the interest or the curiosity of the responder, such as "What did it mean when you did . . . ?" or "How did you come up with that idea?" I give the artist the option to answer such questions if they feel it is helpful or if the responder requires context for another question.

STEP FOUR: PERMISSIONED OPINIONS

My classroom version of step four follows the protocol of CRP, except occasionally, to be mindful of time, we collectively agree to opt out of prefacing opinions with the standard: "I have an opinion about ______, would you like to hear it?" If we have successfully navigated steps two and three, the class often feels the groundwork to hear opinions has been laid and asking permission can feel like lost time. It is important, however, to not dismiss the "permission" aspect of step four. Permission is not about the validity of your opinion; it's about whether the artist can be open to receiving it. Students usually say they want to hear everything. Or so they think. I ask them to carefully consider: What are you really ready to hear? Are you open to all feedback? Given time constraints, what might be most important for you to get feedback about? As a responder, permissioned opinions encourage me to formulate my thoughts, be articulate about what I want to ask, and consider the other feedback I have heard. As a facilitator in this step, I encourage opinions to be specific rather than sweeping in their scope. If we have agreed to dispense with "I have an opinion about . . ." some students will recognize the need to ask for permission if they haven't addressed their thoughts in earlier steps, and therefore their opinion may seem to come out of nowhere. As a facilitator, I also point out opinions that could have been addressed in previous steps. It is important to discuss these issues prior to forgoing the permission part of step four.

We've added other "safety measures" for this step, which help the artist to stay open at this point in the Process:

- The artist has the power to stop the feedback when they are "full."
- Responders can snap their fingers if a statement made resonates with them. This lets the artist know that others feel similarly without having the information repeated.
- Responders are encouraged to think ahead so they can keep opinions succinct and give everyone an opportunity to respond.
- Handwritten notes can provide additional feedback if we are running short on time.

VARIATIONS AND FOLLOW-UP

As we get further into the semester, I allow students to decide what type of feedback they would like to receive. Maybe they only want to ask questions. Maybe they just want to hear questions. Occasionally, as a follow-up to CRP with work at a more advanced stage, we experiment with "what if . . ." questions, based in propositions that may be impossible, outlandish, or extreme in their simplicity or demands. Inspired by my former colleague, choreographer Michelle Ellsworth—whose suggestions often pointed toward implicit truths—"what-ifs" build on information gleaned from the dialogue with the artist and responders and challenge them to defy choreographic limitations in order to upend what they think they understand about their work, or to question what the work is doing and how it is functioning. "What-if" examples include:

- What if you had to do the entire dance as a solo rather than as a group?
- What if the audience were on the ceiling?
- What if this were performed on a glacier?
- What if the dance had to be executed in one minute rather than ten?
- What if the dance were performed in a box?

Not designed to dismiss the intention of the work, "what-ifs" can challenge an artist's attachment to an idea or help them realize how or why a certain concept is essential.

Though my adaptations of CRP are flexible and fluid, they maintain the Process's rigor and consideration in observing, giving, and receiving feedback. Some students are definitely like I was in my twenties, chomping at the bit and feeling constrained by the rules of CRP. Others are grateful for the specificity and the guidelines. Of course, each class is different. Ultimately, the goal is for artists to be thoughtful in the way they offer feedback, to find agency in how they receive feedback about their work, and to be inspired and encouraged to dig deeper into their own creative processes.

REFERENCE

Lerman, Liz, John Borstel, and Nancy Stark Smith. "Liz Lerman's Critical Response Process: The Core Steps and an Interview with Liz Lerman." *Contact Quarterly* (Winter/Spring 2008), 16–20.

UNLEASHING AUTONOMY, CULTIVATING LEADERSHIP: CRP IN ADVANCED MUSIC EDUCATION

Sean Riley

"You're just a stupid American violinist, what do you know?"

These words marked my first serious conversation as a freshman at the Juilliard School with my soon-to-be closest friend. We were discussing music—the only topic anybody ever talked about—and I vividly remember becoming defensive and fighting back. It was one memorable point on a colorful journey of building relationships with my peers through feedback and response. I've seen musicians run out of rooms crying, throw large items across rehearsal spaces, and, perhaps even sadder, I've seen countless students stay silent in the refuge of a corner. As many musicians do, I started developing my own artistic identity by locking myself daily in a practice room until the building closed at midnight. But I eventually realized that if I wanted to grow as an effective and successful artist, I would need my peers and they would need me. I arrived at CRP through my experiences as a student attempting to solve a simple problem: Student musicians consistently fail to communicate in ways that might lead one another toward performance and career success.

Broadly speaking, Western classical music training is built upon a solid master-student model proven highly effective in transferring skills from one generation to the next. However, this model can engender a follower mentality that draws students into an alluring trap of complacency. They can attend lessons, practice diligently, give their yearly solo recital, then graduate with little to no exposure to the industry outside the insular halls of higher music education. Not including lessons, orchestra, chamber music, and classes, classical musicians clock roughly twenty thousand hours of work isolated in a small room to master an instrument by the time they obtain a master's degree. This essential requirement of professionalism can produce negative consequences on the way we interact and communicate with one another. Early on as a student I perceived my peers as isolated islands moving between lessons, classes, and practice rooms. If I stayed on this path, followed my schedule, and obtained good grades, I was confident I would be a great violinist. Now that I am an educator I retain my faith in the master-student model, but I also believe it can be enhanced to help students engage their natural autonomous learning styles in different ways. The drive to practice doesn't mean a student will be driven to engage in entrepreneurialism as a survival skill outside the school. Proficiency in instrumental technique does not guarantee their ability to communicate with and lead others.

I made my first real attempt to address the isolating nature of my environment in 2005 by organizing a student-driven community at Juilliard called the Underground Project. Students who wanted performance opportunities could sign up to play for each other in weekly peer-focused studio sessions. As an "underground" venture, we were not officially a part of the conservatory but we fed off our education, performing for each other in the hopes of achieving excellence.

In this continuous series of works in progress by students exercising learner autonomy, we all wanted to discuss what we heard in response. Offered the choice, almost everybody opted to receive comments after their performance and the critical feedback was impossibly unpredictable. The stream of negative listener-focused critiques was constant: "Bar 80 was very out of tune," "I play bar four like this," "I think your sound could be better there," and my personal favorite, "Why are you playing with him? His interpretation of Beethoven is terrible. You should play with me instead." Inevitably the performer raised up a shield of defense, and on rare occasions a sword in retaliation. I cannot fault the musicians giving the heavy-handed comments; like moths to a flame they would find a critique in every possible detail, a standard they held for their own art through tireless work. I thought it was entertaining at the beginning, but had to acknowledge that a random group of five or six musicians who had spent their formative years practicing by themselves were horrible at talking with each other. This quickly became my problem as the incoming flood of musician students who wanted to perform for each other evolved into a community built around peer-based performance feedback.

Motivated by autonomous drive, each of the students taking part in the Underground Project walked through the door on their own initiative, usually with high expectations of their own ability and a natural fear for making mistakes. Focused on minimizing flaws during a performance, they seemed to turn off a switch in their mind when discussing their strengths afterward, and reacted with blank, lifeless expressions to generic compliments like "Great playing," "I like your sound," and "Wow, your intonation was perfect." Granted, the lack of specificity in such comments made them appear inauthentic and insincere. By contrast, negative comments were highly specific to the millimeter of movement on a misplaced finger. I remember the content of less than five positive comments from the many performances I personally gave, but I recall in detail many of the negative criticisms directed toward me. It's a perfect storm of ineffective communication: the performer has little will to identify their artistic strengths, and their peers feel no compulsion to discuss the strong points of a performance with any sincerity or depth. Since students' training has taught them to equate artistic excellence with technical perfection, they may not even know this is an area of knowledge worthy of exploration.

I attempted to fix the communication issues by micromanaging every interaction with the little authority I held as organizer, but it was never a solution that was meant to change the community communication patterns. Several years later, recreating the Underground Project as an Artist Diploma student at the Royal College of Music in London, I encountered the same dilemma: Music students possess the astonishing ability to dash the tireless work of fellow artistic peers with a few well-intentioned words.

Recognizing the same issues at two separate institutions, I found myself at a crossroads asking: What could I do to fix communication problems among student musicians about to begin careers in the arts? I was introduced to CRP as the answer to this question.

DISCOVERING CRP

In 2014, I was a prospective PhD candidate considering the Guildhall School of Music in London as a place to research peer-learning performance education. The head of Guildhall's research division at the time, Helena Gaunt, noted my interest in artist communication methods and suggested I attend a weeklong seminar on the Critical Response Process led by Liz Lerman. By the end of the seminar's first hour, I was fully convinced of CRP's many possibilities and the practical solutions it might offer to the problems I was encountering with performer-focused generative feedback. Buoyed by Liz's encouragement to adapt the Process to our specific needs, I left the seminar ready to experiment with modified versions of CRP, starting with my new job teaching at the Trinity Laban Conservatoire of Music and Dance.

The context for this modified version of CRP was a fascinating class model provided by Trinity Laban, focused on imparting communication and leadership skills to incoming freshmen. This weekly class was the first course in a larger professional skills training program that spanned a student's entire undergraduate studies. By the conservatoire's design, each of the fifteen freshmen instrumentalists in this class would compose, rehearse, and perform a creative work using their peers as collaborators. Not allowed to use Western classical notation, the students had exactly twelve minutes to rehearse and perform their compositions on the day of the final exam at the end of the ten-week course. With no rules or guidelines on how I should guide the students to this outcome, I was able to innovate in designing the students' learning environment.

MODIFYING AND INTRODUCING CRP

With limited time in the course, I modified CRP from four steps down to two, retaining step one, statements of meaning, and step three, neutral questions. Statements of meaning have the power to bind a community of performing artists together in trust, and neutral questions are the perfect conduit through which the performer can begin to generate creative thought in public. This is an environment where sword and shield are put away.

It is important that students know right from the beginning that the topic of the course is how to lead and communicate rather than how to compose a nontraditional work. To focus the CRP elements in this subject area, I begin by having my students describe attributes of leadership and excellent communication in the arts and write these descriptions on a board. Typically, students place words such as "confidence," "presence," and "ability" in the leadership column and words like "respect," "eye contact," and "diction" in the communication column. During this process a few students may bring up their favorite concertmasters, conductors, and teachers as inspiring examples of excellence. Next, I have a student perform a simple scale and ask the class, without stipulating any specific guidelines, to provide comments on the performance. The misleadingly simple nature of the scale serves to bring out the worst in communication problems with musicians, who attack technique and thus the performer with definitive negative statements, including, inevitably, the phrase "out of tune." The performer's original initiative to play publicly is gone in a matter of seconds, replaced with defensiveness, combativeness, and the embarrassment of public rejection. The commenter feels that their expertise has been put to good use and doesn't understand that as a peer they have stopped the performer from potential generative growth within their interaction. Observing these tendencies in action provides an excellent opportunity to discuss definitive statements and their impact on the performer. This frustrating experience is easily recognized by the entire class, and it is at this point that I offer them my modified CRP as a solution. Notice that CRP isn't introduced as a way to get a good grade at the end of the course, but rather as a solution to a communication problem they have all experienced. I discuss how peer support of a performer's work in progress can differ from offering definitive conversation-ending criticism. Finally, I introduce how they will be using CRP to develop their projects. This introduction takes thirty minutes, and the remainder of the first class is spent learning the modified version of CRP.

TRAINING BY DOING

I have found that my adaptation of CRP doesn't need lengthy explanations, but rather works best by doing. I begin by referring back to the leadership and communication board that had been populated by the students, and while they are reviewing these lists I hand them their course syllabus. Each student is instructed to read a line from the syllabus aloud to the class. After a student reads a line, their peers are asked to respond with statements of meaning followed by neutral questions. All comments must be focused on the ideals of leadership and communication they recorded on the board at the beginning of the class. Once the feedback is offered, the performer sits down and the next student follows the same process until each student has presented a line.

Throughout this introductory process, I offer no feedback other than as facilitator, so the readers start off by sitting with poor posture and facing their paper as they drone on, having to read a boring document. One by one the students quickly begin to stand, move to a visible location, speak clearly, change the intonation and volume of their tone, add intentional gestures, take away filler words such as "um," "uh," and "like," and, interestingly, memorize their lines. They are actively seeking to communicate with each other effectively on their own. The students learn equally through statements of meaning and neutral questions. When three or four of their peers state that they found it meaningful that somebody stood up to communicate to them, the rest of the class then knows that standing up on their turn will be effective; when a well-stated neutral question about posture gets the performer talking about how they hadn't thought about it but that they would do it differently now and this is how, the next performers begin to address posture as a part of their presentation.

When all students have finished, we observe how their performances transformed from the first student to the last. It's important that they note that my input was only to keep the exercise on track, that as peers they developed community leadership and communication standards through merely reading a line. The focus is less on improving the individual performance than on establishing a collectively generated growth standard that consistently raises the bar for everyone. This is streamlined by dispensing of step two in CRP, Artist as Questioner. A socially constructed dynamic emerges by taking the sole responsibility of developing community communication standards away from the individual and placing it in the hands of the peer community, with the understanding that the teacher in the room is in fact just a facilitator (whose job is quickly becoming obsolete). Finally, I have the students repeat the exact same process of reading a single line with the second page of the syllabus, and the training is finished. Each student now understands how the process works, the impact they have on each other as peers using healthy communication patterns, and the knowledge that they will be using this method to develop their personal performance projects in the coming weeks.

THE PERFORMANCE PROJECT

Now that the students have been introduced to CRP and trained in its modified format, it's time to begin applying it to their art. The assignment to compose, lead, and perform a new work, within strict time limits and without use of Western notation, is a tall order for incoming students, one that pushes them to rely on each other for input and creative inspiration. Starting at the second class, I assign two students per meeting to present their projects. The selected students present their work in varying stages of preparedness. In the early weeks, students usually just talk through their projects or experiment to see what the instruments can do. After a project is presented, the participants offer statements of meaning and neutral questions to start the flow of ideas from the presenter in a guided manner.

However, the scope of this process now includes issues such as how they rehearse with their peers, their time management, the clarity of their composition, and their leadership in organizing the instrumentation before they even begin. Following these modified CRP sessions, which last thirty minutes each, I spend the remainder of the class introducing different methods of non-Western classical composition techniques such as body percussion and graphic notation.

After a few weeks of CRP, my role in the classroom quickly becomes irrelevant and the ongoing joke among faculty is that I place myself behind the piano, occasionally raising my voice to chastise students for the phrasing of their neutral questions. However, the results of the process are no joke. Applying two steps from CRP, my students develop leadership responses for their performance community. They teach themselves that organizing musicians in the room is important for quality of sound and presentation; that the volume of each instrument type has to be addressed or the sound will be chaotic; that allowing too many questions can cause a group of musicians to lose focus on the task at hand; that overly complicated compositions take more time to train; that speaking too softly sometimes leads to more confident musicians attempting to take over as rehearsal leader; that the emotion with which you present instructions affects how your peers respond musically; and that coming prepared means success.

In practice, final projects have employed a wide range of approaches. One student brought in his computer with an additional electronic component that he had made himself. When he instructed his peers to hold hands, they completed an electric current and a bell sounded continuously. When they let go, it stopped. Through each silence, students were directed to improvise solos built off the tone of the bells. Another student rolled a game die over a matrix of images that directed sections of musicians to interact with each other in different styles of music, keys, sounds, and beat patterns. A jazz student had everybody put their instruments aside and created a complex body percussion work inspired by minimalism. A particularly shy violinist had everybody download a free synthesizer app onto their smartphones. She then sectioned musicians into parts of the room with instructions on what to play and when to play. Finally, she stood in the middle of the room and improvised a solo on her violin off of the smartphone orchestra. Through such variations, it has become clear that a group of freshmen can begin communicating with and leading each other, with CRP paving the path to their success.

IMPLICATIONS OF CRP

The Critical Response Process offers an antidote to the teacher-versus-classroom, autonomy-draining environment common in advanced music education. CRP creates a connection between students that transcends their work. When your peers tell you that your life's work has meaning, the resulting bond allows for the free flowing of critical ideas and begins the process of creating an effective artistic community in which the individual's voice has worth. Successful adaptation of CRP leads students toward meaningful student autonomy while simultaneously equipping them with the communication tools that this autonomy requires.

Having seen its potential through the experiences I've related in this article, it is only natural that I began using CRP as the cornerstone for much of my teaching and problem-solving within and outside the music industry. As a concert violinist building a teaching studio, I use CRP to equip my violin students with effective communication tools aimed at networking with conductors, managers, venues, teachers, and fellow musicians. Over a period of time using CRP, my students will develop into a community that will hold a library of knowledge passed down orally, enabling them to bring unique entrepreneurial projects to the table and emboldening them with the tools to turn these projects into reality.

I've always found it frustrating that student dancers, actors, and musicians can be a part of the same organization but gravitate toward individual art projects while struggling to establish ongoing collaborative arrangements. CRP can create student communities that train cross-disciplinary art students how to interact with each other and lead to sustained collaborations. To address the communication issues that I encountered in the Underground Project, the values of CRP could be introduced as a communication standard by seeding them first with a smaller group. To take the idea a step further, a conservatory could require the Trinity Laban Conservatoire class structure, incorporating modified CRP, as a yearly laboratory, setting communication and leadership training as the cornerstones of their educational philosophy. Concepts such as artist citizenry could be written on the board instead of words like "communication" and "leadership," creating an entirely new model that doesn't require the complete reworking of Western classical music education to guide students toward artistic practices that impact local and global communities. Autonomy is the key. CRP unleashes autonomy and, with the right set of parameters, has a lasting impact on the artists we are training now.

AN ADAPTATION OF CRP FOR PEER REVIEW IN SMALL SEMINAR COURSES IN STEM

Lekelia D. Jenkins

As a young scientist, I prided myself on giving strong, insightful critiques that did not point out petty flaws, but instead revealed methodological weaknesses, over-generalizations, and unsubstantiated conclusions. Following forms of scientific peer review learned in academia, I discovered that such observations did not transfer well to other sectors. On one occasion, as a new government employee, I attended a scientific talk on aquaculture (fish farming) and offered feedback following my typical laser-precise technique. This time, instead of the nods of accord I was used to receiving, the audience stiffened and quieted. My office colleagues studiously avoided eye contact and barely spoke to me for the rest of the afternoon. Then, to my surprise, one of them said, "So I guess you really don't like aquaculture." My sharp critique, intended to improve future research, instead led my colleague to think that I despised the whole area of study. It dawned on me that no matter how objective and dispassionate, my critiques sliced deep and exposed the presenter in ways that could be uncomfortable, even painful.

When I became a professor, I wanted my students to learn a better way. Having encountered the Critical Response Process though dance studies at the American Dance Festival, I decided to adapt it for use in two interdisciplinary courses I teach: Case Study Research: Design and Methods, and Project Design for Conservation and Community Development. My students, often from STEM (science, technology, engineering, mathematics) fields, are required to do a final presentation or paper as the basis of a summative assessment for the course as a whole. In preparation for this, the students give a presentation on the work in progress and receive feedback from the other students and me on both the content and the presentation style.

Limited time (fifteen minutes at most for student presentations and feedback) meant we needed to condense CRP for this formative assessment; the different natures of science and art influenced some shifts in sequence and emphasis. The meaning and purpose of scientific presentations are often more explicitly prescribed than in art, making step one of CRP less expansive when applied to science. In science, the meanings of "works" (presentations, papers, posters) are often explicitly stated with objectives and conclusions. It is the researchers' responsibility to make appropriate generalizations about their research and identify limitations, affording less opportunity for the audience to ascribe meaning. Given these challenges, I shortened the Process to reduce the required time and removed step one as an explicit step about meaning. This adapted use of CRP as a formative assessment generally takes the following form:

1. *Review of rubric.*
   Together, presenting and responding students review a comprehensive grading rubric that I provide for the final summative assignment. This identifies aspects of the presentation that are most important and places boundaries on what should and should not be considered, preventing responders from creating new criteria and assuring that presenters will not be held accountable for evaluation criteria of which they were unaware.
2. *Presenter shares caveats and asks the audience to focus on specific areas in which they would like feedback.*
   This step serves in lieu of CRP step two, Artist as Questioner, although the presenter does have the opportunity to ask follow-up questions in response to comments given by the audience after the presentations.
3. *Presentation of work.*
4. *Clarifying questions from responders.*
   This step is analogous to CRP step three in that the questions should simply be requests for more detail about information already presented in order to clarify intended meaning. The questions at this stage should not offer opinions or introduce new themes or topics.
5. *Presenter's follow-up questions allowed from this point forward.*
6. *Positive comments.*
   Responders offer comments on things that worked about the presentation. This step holds some of the value of CRP step one, but is more explicitly positive. If the students are unaccustomed to giving positive feedback, I will model this step by highlighting strengths about the presentation or I will ask students to consider what worked for each point of evaluation on the grading rubric. If, as sometimes happens, students move from these positive points to what needs improvement, I ask them to hold these thoughts until the next step.
7. *Things to improve, relative to focus areas identified by the presenter.*
   In the final step of my modified CRP, the audience can offer

suggestions for elements that need improvement, with a focus on the specific areas for which the presenter asked for feedback in the second step of this process. If the student whom I interrupted in the previous step does not readily volunteer their thoughts, this can indicate that the student now feels censured and hesitant to share. In order to address this, I explicitly invite that student to share their thoughts on improvements.

8. *Instructor/facilitator commentary.*
   I hold my comments until the end, in order to keep the space student-focused rather than teacher-focused. To build confidence in the advice of peers, I highlight the points of agreement I have with students and explicitly name them and credit them for the ideas.

In comparing their formative assessment presentations of their works in progress to their final summative assessment presentations, I observe that many students put the feedback they received into practice, especially with the visual and informational components of the presentations. Students can address these two aspects more readily than their oral presentation skills.

With peer review of written work, because generally the students are giving feedback outside of class without a facilitator, I use a further simplified process: (1) review the grading rubric, (2) read the paper, (3) offer positive comments, and (4) identify things to improve. The reviewers are graded on the alignment of their feedback with this process in addition to its substance and constructiveness. The author is required in their final summative written paper assignment to include the reviewers' comments as well as a letter detailing what changes they made in response or defending their decision not to make changes. This letter of response factors into the grade for the summative assessment.

I have received positive feedback from my students that this modified CRP approach for oral presentations is indeed helpful without being harmful. According to one student, Leigh-Ann Tower:

> Having my peers provide live feedback in a structured manner . . . provided transparency and . . . lessened a potential personal bias when receiving and providing feedback. Although other classes had opportunities for peer critique, they were often informal, unstructured, and randomly selected . . . [which added] pressure and anxiety to not only the presenter, but the audience.

Further evidence of the utility of this adaptation of CRP is that the model is spreading. One of my former students, Michel A. Riquelme Sanderson, who completed a PhD in education, has begun to use this approach in the classes he teaches. He wrote:

> I think asking for feedback on elements/aspects of the presentation that I want is personally way more helpful, enriching and constructive than listening to random ideas that perhaps are not needed, that I already know I need to work on, or that would not help improve my presentation. I have used this approach in a small seminar with other graduate students resulting in less wasted time, as we have a clear goal or objective when reviewing documents or presentations. It has helped us create a mindset of acceptance for feedback and be open to receive comments as a learning/reflective opportunity for our work.

Reflecting back on my stint as a government employee, I recognized that my traditional approach to STEM critique was not the norm for this group and neither was CRP. As CRP moves beyond the arts into STEM, this will often be the case. Now I have learned that even outside the structure of my classroom, I can model more sensitive approaches to giving feedback. I make sure to ask the presenter if they would like to receive feedback on a certain topic, sharing the meaningful aspects of the presentation in addition to my thoughts on improvements. In this way, CRP can spread both formally within the confines of classrooms and informally through peer-to-peer learning.

TOWARD A CRP PEDAGOGY

Kathryn Prince

Learning about the Critical Response Process completely transformed my teaching. I don't just mean that I offer feedback differently now, though this was the first stage of the transformation. Every aspect of my pedagogy has been affected. I've always been interested in trying things that might improve some aspect of the classroom experience for my students and for me, ideas I've picked up in my reading or through workshops. With the methods I tried before CRP, I saw some small improvements in student success, course evaluations, and my own sense of how things were going. With the introduction of CRP, those changes were huge: my teaching felt much easier, yet I could see from the creativity and quality of my students' final projects and the depths of their insights in the accompanying reflection papers how much more they had learned. Some students whom I've taught in other courses suddenly flourished and produced amazing work for the first time. The pervasive improvement compelled me to write a letter to my department chair explaining that the high class average wasn't due to grade inflation, and he agreed that the large proportion of A and A+ grades was entirely justified. The students were proud of their work. On top of that, I received my university's Excellence in Education award and was selected to become my faculty's first-ever vice dean of Student Experience, two developments I attribute entirely to my adoption of what I now call a CRP pedagogy, or CRPP. When I hear professors complaining about unmotivated, passive, disengaged students, about having to do heavy lifting or spoon-feeding, about learning outcomes and grading grids and the general box-tickingness of teaching these days, I want to tell them that an approach grounded in CRPP could change everything.

I teach in a theater department with a BA program that engages students in practice, theory, and history, and my expertise is firmly in the latter category. With that focus, my teaching emphasizes lectures, readings, and essays in contrast to the practice-oriented teaching of most of my theater colleagues who impart skills through hands-on activities. The courses I teach are mandatory, so while some students might be interested in the course material for its own sake, none of them are really there by choice, which can have a deadening effect on motivation, especially for those who would rather be learning about theater through direct practice of craft. Many of my pedagogical experiments have been aimed at leveling the playing field between my courses and the practical ones in my department while chasing the holy trinity of intrinsic motivation: the autonomy, mastery, and purpose described so vividly in Daniel Pink's *Drive: The Surprising Truth About What Motivates Us* (2009) and analyzed in the numerous studies underpinning his book. Outmoded systems of external reward and punishment should be replaced, Pink suggests, by a system of intrinsic motivation achieved by harnessing "the desire to direct our own lives" (autonomy), "the urge to make progress and get better at something that matters" (mastery), and "the yearning to do what we do in the service of something larger than ourselves" (purpose) (218). Focusing on mastery as the most achievable of these forces within an academic grading system, I worked over the years on developing better ways of showing students a lofty goal and then encouraging them to trust that we would reach it, step by step. Lots of pedagogical research, some captured in Karl Kapp's *The Gamification of Learning and Instruction* (2012), supports this approach. For me, this involved incremental assignments with detailed instructions, which the students seemed to appreciate. The comments on my course evaluations spoke in various ways about trust: students could see that I wanted them to succeed, that I provided the tools for them to do so, and that I was fair in my grading. I was conscientiously using all of their positive feedback over the years to construct increasingly elaborate systems for communicating my expectations, but it took CRP to make me see that these had become so explicit that the best my students could possibly strive for would be to meet them, point by tediously precise point.

Meanwhile, I had been incorporating CRP into my graduate courses as a way of structuring peer-to-peer and informal feedback following an inspiring workshop at the National Arts Centre led by John Borstel. Based on my experience at the NAC, I began requiring that graduate students respond to each other's work-in-progress presentations using the steps of CRP rather than jumping straight into a free-for-all of criticism and suggestions. This resulted in not only a more supportive classroom environment but also stronger student projects, judging from the changes discernible from early drafts to final submissions. Seeing how wonderfully CRP worked at the graduate level, and seeing, too, that our undergraduates are often called on to respond to each other's creative work in progress without having the tools to do so, I decided to build CRP into a new undergraduate course that I was designing from the ground up, called Making Shakespeare. Immediately, I hit a huge roadblock: My detailed instructions, my grading grids, my focus on clear expectations and incremental, explicit mastery made nonsense of CRP and were made nonsensical by it. Was I really going to tell every student, in step one of CRP, that "what strikes me about your project is how well you have followed my instructions and produced exactly what I was expecting to see"? I had been unwittingly promoting a very problematic way of teaching, and had been rewarded for it with fairly happy, fairly successful students. I certainly didn't want them to become less happy and less successful!

Eventually, I adapted CRP to promote autonomy and purpose without sacrificing mastery, and also, crucially, without losing the trust that my more prescriptive approach had promoted. I was able to not only teach CRP to the students in my class but also have them practice it on each other in a way that felt authentic, supportive, and genuinely useful.

To ensure that students would discover some of the many ways in which

Shakespeare has been adapted and interpreted into various forms over the centuries, then use that knowledge to make something of their own in response to these examples, I structured the course in two halves. During the first six weeks, we focused on the explicit course content—ten of Shakespeare's plays and various responses to them through theater, film, television, visual art, critical and creative prose, poetry, and more—knowing that this material supplied the fuel that students would use to generate their own projects in the remaining six weeks. This changed everything about the classroom dynamic, because suddenly students had both extrinsic and intrinsic motivation: the students wanted to learn about Shakespeare because this would serve them, not in some abstract way that general knowledge does, or on an exam, but specifically in relation to a project over which they would have complete autonomy. I never had the feeling, as I sometimes did in previous theater history courses, that this was some kind of semester-long train journey during which I was frantically shoveling coal into the engine while the students enjoyed the ride, trusting that I would do the work to get us to the destination I'd chosen.

I imposed no conditions on these projects, except to require that students complete all sections of a proposal document before starting. I retained the notion of clear instructions, because these would provide the scaffolding allowing the students to feel secure about taking a creative risk. If they followed the steps toward a complete proposal, they would begin the second half of the course with a success (and a substantial part of their grade) already in hand. The instructions were:

> Your project plan outlines what you hope to achieve and how you plan to achieve it. Your plan should be approved, perhaps with some suggested modifications, before you move on to the project itself. You can meet with me as many times as you wish, both before and after submitting the proposal. In order for me to approve your proposal, please include:
>
> - *Outcome*: the project outcome (5 points, ~500 words)
> - *Context*: at least four comparators (precedents or otherwise) within the material covered in class, in the online material, or through your own research/spectatorship (20 points, ~2,000 words)
> - *Feasibility*: your existing expertise (5 points, ~250 words)
> - *Growth*: your knowledge gaps and learning plan (5 points, ~250 words)
> - *Timetable*: a detailed plan of work allocating the 60–80 hours this

project should take (5 points, in a table), week by week between now and the deadline

Worth 40 percent of the final grade, the proposal was the highest-value assignment because I wanted to encourage students to imagine taking a risk and then to think through how they would go about achieving it. This incorporated the ambitious goal and incremental learning that were features of my previous teaching, but with a huge difference: the students, not I, decided on both the goal and the steps toward it. They had to fulfill the learning outcomes of the course, but in doing so they could spend their time acquiring and improving whatever skills and knowledge they recognized as valuable.

By citing a wide range of examples of "making Shakespeare" during the first half of the course, I helped students situate their possible projects within this context and showed them a range of approaches that, I hoped, might resonate with them and lead to new ideas. The traces of my lecture on *Star Trek*'s debt to Shakespeare, for example, are discernible in one student's mash-up between another cult television show, *The Office*, and *Measure for Measure*, and also in another student's futuristic *Tempest* adaptation for children that has nothing to do with either space exploration or television. Clear traces of the material that we covered in class are present in all of the projects that students produced—some individually, others in self-selected groups, some with outside help from friends who just wanted to be part of something cool. The projects covered a wide range of approaches, including digital adaptations (*A Midsummer Night's Video Game* and *Richard III* as an iPhone game using geocaching); psychotherapeutic approaches (Shakespeare's characters in rehab or on the analyst's couch); recreational ventures (a cruise, an amusement park, and cocktail tutorials); performance projects (incorporating puppetry, object theater, and immersive theater approaches); and interpretations in photography, painting, cookbooks, illustration, and games of various descriptions.

Some projects didn't live up to their creators' aspirations, but the students had an opportunity to reframe and pivot during a CRP session a couple of weeks before the due date and to do damage control with the final reflection if necessary. The CRP session was tremendously useful because it held students accountable for the various shortcomings they saw in their projects, at a stage when it was still possible to address them. It offered the opportunity not only to hear responses in line with that goal, but also, as an integral part of the review process, to seek out the suggestions that would be especially welcome. Suggestions are not an inevitable component of CRP, and in other contexts might even be counterproductive, but since these students shared an understanding of the overall course objectives and had developed a strong relationship of trust by this point in the semester it seemed useful to encourage cooperative problem-solving. Many students offered practical solutions to some of the challenges surrounding the execution phase of these projects, especially by sharing their own experiences with particular software, apps, and devices. I was thrilled that one unanticipated effect of using CRP in this course was a significantly enhanced body of shared knowledge. Part of the reason that these suggestions were so valuable, aside from their potential to solve problems, is that they provided fodder for the students' post-creation reflection assignment.

The project itself was worth exactly as much as the CRP session and the reflection, 20 percent each, emphasizing that in this course the finished product is not the only place in which students' learning is manifested. If the particular goal of a student's project ultimately proved elusive, the ideas discussed during CRP nevertheless pointed toward insights that could be articulated in the reflection document.

I adapted CRP for my class in a few ways born of necessity. With thirty-six students in the course, a CRP involving everyone at once would have been both interminable and overwhelming. Instead, I facilitated two smaller CRP sessions (and would have preferred four, had the logistics of timetabling permitted), using the students' proposals to get a clear sense of how certain projects might speak to others. The instructions on the syllabus were:

> *Critical Response Process*
> Your grade for this assignment will be evenly divided between your work as creator and as respondent. We will follow the Critical Response Process, which is thoroughly outlined in the online course materials. Your presentation as a creator should take no more than five minutes, and should demonstrate the proposed outcome of the project, its current status, and any obstacles or challenges you're facing. As part of CRP, you should come prepared with 2–3 questions that you'd like to ask your classmates about your own project, perhaps areas that are giving you trouble or that require a choice you're unsure about. Part of the final project involves reflecting on and responding to these comments. In order to help with this, and for me to grade you on your role as respondent, I'll ask you to e-mail me one or two suggestions

about each student's presentation, which I'll compile and forward to the creators without attribution. Please preface each suggestion with either "In response to your question about . . ." or "If it would help to hear a suggestion about . . ." reflecting steps two and four of the CRP.

I determined at the outset to limit my role in the feedback sessions strictly to facilitation; refraining from participating in the response proved to be the hardest part about using CRP. The alchemy of CRP resides in its recalibration of the typical relationship between the creator and the critic. Instead of passively enduring critique, the creator participating in CRP helps drive the dialogue, and is explicitly empowered to request, guide, and even decline to hear the opinions of respondents. Even the hint of a suggestion from a respondent who will ultimately be grading the project unbalances that process. While respecting the alchemy of CRP and the agency of the creator, I also wanted to make sure that each student did receive my feedback, especially when I could see a project going off the rails: to do otherwise seemed a dereliction of duty. The solution I found was to keep a tight rein on my verbal and nonverbal signaling during CRP, but to add my anonymous contributions to the email containing the written remarks of their classmates.

After the CRP sessions, it was no surprise to discover that the projects submitted in April were almost without exception somewhat different from those pitched in February. Every student who came to my office in a panic about some aspect of their plan left knowing that all of this would be great material for the reflection document, reinforcing the lessons learned during the students' CRP sessions. The creative process is messy, and I wanted this messiness to have a place in my pedagogy. Because the stakes for the project and the reflection were equal, students could learn from the messiness: a few students, channeling Donald Rumsfeld via David Hare's play *Stuff Happens* (2004), articulated their reflections in terms of their ability to react to known knowns, known unknowns, and unknown unknowns. CRP, with its distinct steps for requesting response about specific issues (which we might classify as the creator's known unknowns) and for receiving whatever input the respondents wished to contribute (some unknown unknowns) provides a framework for dealing with ideas that could throw a project off track or point it in the direction of even greater achievement. I saw, thirty-six times, students empowered through CRP to transform unknowns into opportunities.

Whether through Hare and Rumsfeld or otherwise, all students came to terms with the gap between their aspirations and their achievement before they received any comments from me. Not all the unknowns led in productive directions. Some students were surprised that their projects were even better than they had anticipated, and each of them decided, independently of me, how things had turned out. The instructions for the reflection were:

> You will submit your final project and, one week later, your reflection on the creative process. The parameters of the project itself will have been defined by you in your project proposal, and your reflection is a chance to consider what went well, what didn't, and why. Your grade in this course is only partly contingent on the successful achievement of that outcome—it is entirely possible to do well on the reflection, even if your outcome only partially achieves your stated objectives. Your reflection should include the following sections, for a total of 3,000 words:
>
> - A description of the project outcome in its final state as presented
> - A comparison of the outcome to the outcome described in your proposal
> - A reflection of what went well, and less well, tied to your plan of work
> - An articulation of what you learned (about yourself, about Shakespeare, about the tools and methods you employed) during the project

The students had already proven, in their proposals, that they had learned some things about Shakespeare in the first half of the course. I was surprised and thrilled to read, in many of these reflections, how much deeper their connection to Shakespeare had become through the process of making. Some of this was due to a course design that let students' intrinsic motivation drive their projects, but a larger share of that success was the result of their direct experience with CRP: if they learned to expect and even value unknown unknowns, that's a powerful lesson. They tried things, failed, and recovered; they mastered new tools, developed their skills, and saw a creative project through from inception to reflection. Along the way, they learned that Shakespeare could mean something to them.

In light of this experiment, I'm currently revamping all of my courses to reflect what I now know about CRPP. Based on my entirely positive experience in Making Shakespeare, I will be focusing on what I consider the basic tenets of CRPP: in a CRPP-led course, students choose their own projects based on a well-informed sense of the possibilities and identify their own criteria for success; they learn to give and receive meaningful feedback; they adjust their work in progress as a result of this feedback and reflect on the results. As a consequence, students exert autonomy, work toward mastery, and feel purpose: they possess the three components of intrinsic motivation. CRPP does not preclude external motivations, such as academic grades, or additional goals, such as learning outcomes; used effectively, it complements them. I offer this not as a set of principles or guidelines, but only as a summary of what I have learned so far.

My biggest challenge as I move forward with CRPP will be to think through its implications beyond my own classroom. I know that CRPP can enhance both student achievement and student satisfaction. My task will be to demonstrate CRPP's potential to colleagues who may not be accustomed to thinking of themselves as supporters of creative work in progress, and that will mean some creative work of my own as I maneuver around institutional obstacles. Luckily I know the most effective way of getting support for challenging creative work, so I'll be setting up some CRP training and inviting participants to help me develop an outreach project for professors interested in experimenting with CRP or CRPP at the University of Ottawa.

ACKNOWLEDGMENTS

Huge thanks to the National Arts Centre English Theatre team—especially Judi Pearl, Sarah Garton Stanley, and Jillian Keiley—for inviting me to learn about CRP; to John Borstel for being an inspiring teacher; and to the Making Shakespeare students who trusted me to experiment: Christopher Beharry, Monica Bradford-Lea, Joshua Carroll, Kayla Clarke, Sam Coggin, Aly Dandach, Kevin Da Ponte, Taylor Efford, Meagan Gilson, Curtis Gough, Caterina Fiorindi, Even Gilchrist, Rochelle Hilderman, BillySue Johnston, Brittany Johnston, Julie Landriault, Eva Major, Annie Martin, Christine Mathieu, Cullen McGrail, Justin Merpaw, Rachel Moore, Mikaela Morrell, Dillon Orr, Franco Pang, Hilary Peck, Paul Piekoszewski, Emily Reid, Scarlett Rowley, Mathieu Roy, Heidi Spicer, Olivia Tilley, William Verreault Milner, Bryce Vieira, Annick Welsh, and Margot Willner-Fraser.

REFERENCES

Hare, David. *Stuff Happens* (New York: Farrar, Straus and Giroux, 2004).

Kapp, Karl M. *The Gamification of Learning and Instruction: Game-based Methods and Strategies for Learning and Instruction* (San Francisco: John Wiley & Sons, 2012).
Pink, Daniel H. *Drive: The Surprising Truth About What Motivates Us* (New York: Riverhead Books, 2009).

You Are the Teacher

Liz Lerman

It's hard for those of us who teach to stay in relationship with all of the steps of CRP. As I have heard from instructors over and over:

- *"I am being paid for my opinions, so I should give them."*
- *"Students have to understand the mistakes they are making and it's my job to inform them."*
- *"There isn't enough time to ask questions."*
- *"Sometimes there is nothing good there, and we just have to tear it apart and start over."*
- *"I will not be doing right by my students if I turn them out into the world without their knowing ______."*

I am sympathetic to these thoughts. I have them myself. With that in mind, I dedicate the following ideas to all of us who teach and struggle to do justice to our knowledge while helping to shape the resources, habits, and work of our students.

Some of how we navigate between our knowledge and our students' needs depends on the goals at any given moment. We may be giving information that has a right and a wrong. We may be encouraging students' capacities to be thoughtful, creative, useful, active, amazing artists, scientists, leaders, and human beings. We may be doing both at the same time and everything in between. Critical Response can be a very useful partner as we move between many roles, all wrapped up in the profession of teaching.

As we steer this course, it may be helpful to remember a few things: First of all, you are the teacher, and you can always be the teacher. If that means giving your opinion freely, whenever and however, that's fine. Personally, I myself have discovered it isn't always effective to do so. But it is your prerogative.

Second, you are the teacher, and you can always announce when you are going to give some straight-out opinions, thoughts, lectures, ways of working, stories, or whatever forms your insight takes as you disseminate what you know. I believe this can come at any time, directed to any person. It just goes better if I tell them it's about to happen. Even my own daughter appreciated it when I had the foresight to tell her I was going into "parent" mode.

Third, you are the teacher, which means you can step back and let others in the room convey their knowledge. You can support their ideas with your own knowledge at carefully selected times and places, to add to or subtract from what has been said.

Fourth, you are the teacher, but that doesn't mean you have to know everything all the time. The fear I most often hear from teachers is the possibility that they will be in a position of not knowing the answer to something, or not knowing how to proceed in a given moment. I believe that CRP helps us through those moments and gives us skills for handling them.

When you *do* think you know, when you have what you believe is the clarifying opinion, the decisive redirection, or the viable fixit, the principles of CRP offer several options on how to act.

You might start by asking yourself whether your opinion is fixed, and why. As teachers, perhaps as teachers who have taught for a very long time, we may believe that the best of what we profess to our students is immutable. But it is worth considering whether the fundamental idea or approach may be unreliable in this particular moment in time, wrong for the person in front of us doing the work, out of date, or otherwise worth questioning. When I have checked in with myself, I find this reflection is renewing, illuminating, and often makes it possible for me to deliver the opinion in a surgical manner, more particular to the situation at hand.

One way to do that reflection is to apply the key principle of CRP's step three and try to turn the opinion into a neutral question. Just the attempt will automatically hold my assumptions up to the light. What might emerge, actually, is a series of questions that this student needs to address, not just one. Perhaps the student has been asking about one thing but needs to be taken to a different source of inquiry. Perhaps the student has understood some of what we have been studying, but has missed other details. Perhaps I'll even laugh at my own constant rants, which are preventing me from seeing what this person in front of me is trying to do or say. Forming the neutral question might prod me to remember that this could be the first time the student has thought of some fragile idea, and even if I have seen it before and know its most likely outcome, they don't. A question might aid their journey better than pointing out how it is going to end.

Yes, this can take a long time. And we don't always have a long time. In some cases, I approach this dilemma in another way: Instead of using critique to teach, I actually teach. Sometimes, in my desire to get a student to try something or to see something differently, it occurs to me that they have not been exposed to the right tools, or that they have forgotten the possibilities that lie in knowledge attained earlier in their student lives.

The simple directive I suggest for moments like this is: Turn fixits into curriculum. Instead of imposing a solution in the context of a critique, I try to teach to the problem the next time we are together. Much as we transform an opinion into a neutral question, here we find the principle behind the fixit and turn it into a structure for experiential learning.

This means the whole class might go to work on the problem that has arisen in one student's work. For instance, a student shows a dance piece and has, to my mind, mixed up how she wants the audience's eye to follow the various elements of her choreography. It occurs to me that she hasn't actually thought about foreground and background. Maybe she doesn't know where in the space, in this particular moment, most of the audience will direct their attention. Or maybe she doesn't know or hasn't experimented with various ways to guide a viewer's focus. I can, in this case, give her an opinion. I could ask her a question. Or, I can get everyone in the class up and experimenting with some tasks that will lead her to some ownership of her own struggle. Essentially, I am mirroring the neutral question by putting it into action.

This is a lot of work. It is sometimes easier, and necessary, to just name and solve the problem. And often the students are grateful, relieved, and jump up and go to work. I am not suggesting that we alter all of our processes. I am, however, offering that CRP can be a way of critiquing in its formal four-step format and that its principles can point us to action in various modes of teaching, bringing us to discovery as we attempt something we may be doing for the first time.

Many of us who teach have over our lifetimes frequently been in settings where we are set up to be the smartest person in the room—at least with regard to a particular subject. We have been granted authority by our institutions, students, or disciplines to be looked upon as the one who knows. And that is fine. It is often true. But I think this status can lead us to some patterns of thought and action that can be debilitating to those around us and even to ourselves. I see it when I frequently observe the person who carries the authority of tenure or expertise in a circle of CRP responders and who waits until step four to deliver an opinion without participating in the earlier steps of the Process.

I fear that this behavior occurs in part because the person waiting till step four doesn't feel that there is much to learn or discover in the first three steps. It comes from a belief that the ideas held are valuable above all else, and can't be mutated in any way. It suggests that getting to know the artist and their work, in this particular context, doesn't carry as much weight as giving the opinion in its original intent.

My observation, when this happens, is that the artist will discard the opinion as soon as they are free of the person. That means the minute they are out the door, out of that person's course, out of that school. The opinion might have contained a good idea, a useful perspective, a valuable principle, but it will likely go unused. Without the respect and curiosity that drives the preceding steps, I fear that the artist, maker, colleague, child that is in the artist's chair will not be able to hear the opinion. And I fear that the person giving it will remain as unchanged as the idea itself. That is not my idea of education, learning, or discovery.

Sometimes, when this happens, I ask the opinion giver to go back into step three and try to ask a question. I do this because I believe every opinion can be turned into a neutral question. And I do this because people practiced in delivering their opinions without question don't recognize the ideas they carry in any other form except as an opinion. And they don't want to do the work that is required to transform that opinion into some other form that might make it useful or easier for the listener to hear. Sometimes when I ask the opinion giver to go back to step three and try to form their opinion into a question, I am met with resistance. "Why?" they ask. Because (1) you will be heard better in step four; (2) you might discover something that makes your opinion shift ever so slightly; (3) you might discover you don't have to deliver your opinion; and (4) you get your own moment of transformation as you turn your opinion over, like turning over the soil. Something might be inside it that you didn't realize was there.

Of course, these rationales can create their own resistance. If you must work to keep an open mind, you might prefer to let the idea go unexplored. If you discern that your opinion is actually not needed, you might feel superfluous, and disengage. If turning over the opinion means that you might shift your ideas publicly or be seen making your own discovery, you might risk your reputation as an expert. But CRP does not diminish expertise. Used with care, CRP gives expertise a fresh platform, a new welcome, and an exhilarating opportunity to deepen.

Once, I asked someone who waited for step four why he didn't work on bringing his opinion to bear on the earlier steps. "The only way she will hear me is if I tell her the truth," he responded. (His truth was the singular truth, obviously.) "And I could tell she was missing the boat by the questions she asked. She didn't understand anything because she missed the whole point." (Clearly, he knew the point of her piece better than she did.)

I have suggested that artist's questions in step two often come not as questions but as worries, doubts, and obsessions. Similarly, for people used to giving their opinion at will, ideas come as absolutes not particularly susceptible to expression in any other form. So it requires a lot of work to turn expertise into inquiry that takes the form of a neutral question, or to take it apart enough to use some of it as an answer to step two or even the formulation of meaning in step one. Now, after all these years, I can see that the steps of CRP, when engaged as a constant practice, can move people from acting or speaking on aesthetic as absolutes, to a place where questioning those ideas can be a consistent partner to the conversation.

4 ARTISTRY AND INSTITUTIONS

"It starts with the art." We've sometimes used this catchphrase to anchor CRP learners in the primary purpose of the Process and to encourage them to consider the work in progress itself as the focus of a given critique: All the functions of CRP—statements, questions, responses, and opinions—are extensions of that work in its present state as the artist has put it forward and the responders have witnessed it. Yes, the artist may gain knowledge that advances their inspiration and craft in ways that transcend the work in question. Yes, the discourse of a CRP session may move to social, aesthetic, or technical implications that expand the value of the dialogue. Yes, suppositions and what-ifs may enter the conversation to speculate about broader possibilities. And yes—as the administrator of an artist residency resource organization once said—CRP can transform critiques into a learning experience for all participants. But the fulcrum from which all these possibilities arc is a palpable, discernable *something* that can be experienced in the now as a representative of the artist's developing, still iterating, potential-packed, energizingly unfinished process.

This centrality for the work may be a reason why CRP is so versatile, why it can function equally well in middle schools as in PhD programs, in self-organizing writers' groups as in plenary sessions at association conferences. The concrete nature of the work in progress, captured at one moment in its development, allows the particulars of CRP to scale up or down and locate the discourse level appropriate to the group gathered.

"It starts with the art" can also be understood as a statement of the origins and purpose of CRP, which emerged into being out of the challenges of how to give and get feedback as they were presenting themselves at the end of the twentieth century. It has thrived in informal and institutional settings that give central concern to the cultivation of new art and the support of emerging artists through the gestation of their work. CRP often enters the cultures of such institutions for the express purpose of nurturing the work in their incubator, then settles in for other purposes—functions such as employee annual review, board/staff relations, meeting facilitation, coaching, and mentoring. Regular practice of formal CRP for its original purpose of feedback on work in progress often constitutes a rehearsal and proving ground for the broader application of the Process's disaggregated principles.

New York Theatre Workshop offers a revealing case study for the applications of CRP to cultivate artistic work, support artists' growth, and extend impact to other dimensions of an institution. This nonprofit producing theater company, which has sent numerous productions on to Broadway and the Tony Awards recognition, places artists at the heart of its mission. Says associate artistic director Linda Chapman, "At New York Theatre Workshop the artist comes first, before product, before any one project that they may be working on." With extensive programs for nurturing artists and cultivating new plays, script-in-progress readings with talkbacks had been central from the group's start in 1979, but also problematic. "We were very unsatisfied with 'what did you like, what didn't you like,' the kind of standard feedback form that we were using in the early days. People stated their opinions, they sometimes grandstanded, and the conversations never developed. The room would be like an oil slick—you'd have all kinds of stuff floating around, but it was never focused and never got to the heart of the issue. We'd get sidetracked with people's personal preferences, it and didn't really address what the artists themselves were trying to do."

Encountering Liz in a demonstration of CRP at New York's Dance Theatre Workshop proved to be a revelation for Chapman and artistic director James Nicola. "We were both really impressed and moved by the focus on the artists." After engaging Liz and colleagues to lead a training on their own turf, New York Theatre Workshop soon adopted CRP as their primary mode for feedback sessions, anchored in its Mondays @ 3 weekly work-in-progress reading series for invited audiences. With the commitment to artist autonomy, CRP is treated as a flexible offering rather than a requirement. "It's not mandatory," says Chapman, "because obviously Critical Response is for the artist. We do a little prep to share the four steps with them before the reading happens. Most people want to use it. We always give them options, the opportunity to use CRP as it's useful for them in the moment. For very early works, sometimes just step one statements of meaning are enough. Or artists may want to get answers to particular questions they have, but might not be ready for neutral questions or opinions." As Workshop-affiliated artists gain more exposure and experience with the Process, the benefits of CRP accrue. "As artists become more attuned and can ask their own good questions, I think that's where you get into a deep, deep conversation. Taking the step two question seriously is where the deeper conversation comes from. Then the neutral questions can start getting at what the dark and unknown area is."

New York Theatre Workshop applies CRP in varied other programs including summer residencies at Dartmouth College, which offer intensive developmental support to six theatrical works in progress, and their 2050 Fellows program, which provides a creative laboratory to an annual cohort of early career artists. Both contexts include showings that that employ the principles of CRP. The function of these encounters, Chapman emphasizes, is always to support the artist. "At New York Theatre Workshop a central relationship with the artist is the most important element. Critical Response is an emanation of that value. It gives the artist that central position."

In a different artistic discipline on another shore, the London Sinfonietta incorporated CRP within its Blue Touch Paper program, which commissioned composers to create new orchestral works through collaboration with artists from other forms including performance art, puppetry, digital media, and poetry. Named for the fuse used to set off a firework, this program was designed to initiate extraordinary projects based on the observation that new music thrives and reaches far wider audiences when it involves other art forms. Blue Touch Paper used CRP-based audience feedback sessions to address a particular gap in the development process for contemporary concert music, as described by London Sinfonietta chief executive and artistic director Andrew Burke: "In dance and theatre, new work is made and evolves over time as part of the process of rehearsing it with artists who will perform it. In literature, a work evolves in the relationship between author and editor. With new music, there is a huge responsibility on composers to get their new work 'right' by themselves, without many (nor sometimes any) feedback loops—formal or informal—in the process of creation."

Because so little precedent exists for dialogue and iteration in the development of concert music, the commissioned composers were at first wary about the prospect of audience feedback about unfinished work. "Almost without exception, every composer involved was resistant. Some were uncertain because they had so little previous experience of *any* kind of serious audience feedback about their work, let alone one organized through a curated conversation. Others feared that the process would remove their artistic autonomy.

"Afterwards they were just as universally positive about the effect it had on their thinking. The Process proved to be supportive and liberating, reminding me of how Liz describes the objective of CRP: to motivate artists to keep working on their art. The process certainly released new energy in each of the composers."

As often happens, after CRP entered the London Sinfonietta's culture as a way of giving feedback to artistic works in progress, it was then applied to other institutional purposes, as Burke reports: "For myself, I have even tried the Critical Response Process in the London Sinfonietta office meetings—running my plans for forthcoming artistic seasons past my team. I knew I would be sensitive about my plans, but trusted the Process to help me and give space for my team to feed back in a way that was new—and constructive—for us all."

"It starts with the art" also suggests that art may not be where the applications of CRP end. Over CRP's history we've watched the proliferation of the Process in disciplines beyond the cultural sector: a liberal arts college adopts CRP as the format for midcourse faculty review; a social science working group uses CRP to advance participatory research projects; a digital gaming startup employs CRP to streamline communication between programmers and designers; a high school applies CRP in teaching about microaggression; and corporations and city governments seek out CRP to improve internal and public-facing communications. CRP is a prime exhibit in demonstrating the value of arts-based disciplines in wider and more varied spheres, as unique features of artistic practice have informed the initial design and ongoing development of CRP. These include: acceptance of work in progress as a state of becoming; audience consciousness and awareness that a work anchors, conveys, and transmits a relationship with a public or user; originality as a core value; and critique as a well-established (if sometimes problematic) feature of training. Some of these conditions may exist in other fields, but nowhere do they exist in such proliferation or constant interaction as in the arts.

After an opening essay in which Liz reflects on the varied ways that caring may be expressed in CRP, contributed essays in this chapter demonstrate some of the ways that the Process has been applied in institutional contexts to support the development of artistic work and individual artistic practice. Jill Waterhouse describes applications of CRP at Women's Arts Resources of Minnesota as part of its Mentor Program to support emerging artists. Reporting on the development of new operas at American Lyric Theater, Lawrence Edelson describes how CRP informs both public performance and artist cultivation. Writing from the perspective of an independent interdisciplinary artist, Rebekah West describes cross-cultural challenges and successes in applying CRP to photography learning and musical collaboration. CJay Philip addresses the pervasive implications of CRP to diverse dimensions of her work as a creator, mentor, and artistic director of Baltimore's Dance & Bmore. Liz closes the chapter with practical guidance on how anyone, artist or otherwise, might use CRP as a mode of personal reflection. While this collection reflects art as the home domain of CRP, we're confident that the principles that animate this work with individual practitioners and institutions are applicable beyond the arts.

In summarizing the benefits of CRP for artists and the institutions that support them, few have been as eloquent as Helena Gaunt. Currently principal of Royal Welsh College of Music and Drama, Gaunt was a strong advocate for CRP in her role as chair of the Innovative Conservatoire (ICON). She invited Liz to introduce CRP to conservatory educators throughout the UK and Europe at the group's international gatherings. Reflecting on work that sought to support emerging artists in balancing the best in the heritage of the classical arts, including traditional master-student pedagogy, with the innovation and purpose to meet a contemporary world, Gaunt describes the values of CRP as they function both for the artist and the institution supporting them:

> First and foremost, CRP starts with a principle of generosity and deep respect for whoever the artist is, believing that they are best placed to find the answers for their work and absolutely desiring that they should do their best work. And I think there's a very important principle in step one about the extraordinary diversity of possibilities of meaning in work, and the value for everyone of exploring that diversity of meaning. CRP supports the artist's ownership of work and helps the group support that ownership, particularly through the very important principle of placing inquiry before judgment. Turning judgment into inquiry is valuable for a creative process, and equally is critical to our well-being as human beings together. The Process builds connections between people and enables all voices to be heard and valued. Finally, the Process is open-ended. When we're finished, the artist is left with all kinds of possibilities, and their choice of what to do.

Critiquing and Caring

Liz Lerman

The conflation of good critique with pain has occupied my curiosity since the inception of the Critical Response Process. My personal experience told me that most of the emotional pain associated with getting feedback or criticism could be avoided. Without having to waste all of that time pulling oneself up out of the depression, fear, and panic that the critique had bestowed upon me, I could go to work with a new charge, with glee, with hope. So why insist on the pain?

It comes up in just about every CRP training I do: People do not trust critique without the pain. They associate "real" criticism with emotional suffering. This makes them distrust any information that comes in without all those bad feelings. Of course, even with CRP, responder comments can bring some pain. But it's not the pain of abuse or doing battle with your most insecure self. For me it's more like, "Oh no, I still have not solved this," or "Damn, I will never get this," or "Oh no . . . so much more work ahead." It reminds me of the challenges of the work, and it's a little bit sad. But it is not trauma-inducing, and it does not send me into the depths of despair.

Lately I have been in several large gatherings where people are discussing the nature and cultivation of creativity. When the question of feedback emerges, someone inevitably tells a story about a teacher who said, "You will never be an artist," or "This is not the way it's done," or "You think that is a tree?" Almost everyone present can relate a similar experience and associate it with the crushing of their creative selves, their capacities, and even their willingness to try yet again.

In devising CRP, I suppose that at some level I was attempting to counteract the destructive force of this kind of commentary. I knew that basic in the premise for a good feedback experience needed to be the artist's readiness to hear critique and a willingness to continue developing the work, coupled with the responder/critic/teacher's support of the artist doing their best work on their own terms. Features of the Process support that premise: the opening step with its focus on meaning and connection, and the protocols for artist agency, neutral inquiry, and consent.

When these structures are followed, those giving feedback can drop the position or authority of their knowledge, and, by doing so, give better, more immediate and useful critiques. The resulting experience, it turns out, often feels like caring. And in this new environment, even the blunt and direct, which can emerge from steps two, three, and four, feels like caring too. This kind of "blunt caring"—which some might call "tough love"—is about making the Process work as intended. If in step two, for example, someone asks a question about a particular part of their piece that a responder doesn't like or has issues with, it is incumbent upon the responder to say so. It might feel difficult or clumsy, but it has to be said. If not, CRP is failing to do its job.

CRP attends to the emotional nature of the feedback experience without being subservient to it. Nestled within the rigor of the Process, along with the caring, are ways not to over-nurture. Caring exists in CRP by calling on us to filter out the arrogance, cruelty, and authority from our giving structures, as well to be honest when confronted with the need to answer a question or give a permissioned opinion that might be characterized as negative. This probably requires most of us to work at something in our own being that's conditioned by that deep association of critique with pain. CRP gives us the opportunity to do this work.

MENTORING AND FACILITATING IN THE VISUAL ARTS: CRP AT WOMEN'S ART RESOURCES OF MINNESOTA

Jill Waterhouse

When the moment comes for feedback, the visual arts present unique needs and opportunities. Unlike dance or performance, where the action is in the moment and is reliant on memory once it's under discussion, in the visual arts, the audience evaluates objects that are available for detailed inspection, scrutiny, and analysis.

They can be viewed and reviewed in all their glory—or failure—up close and personal. This gives the artists and their viewers a distinct advantage in some ways, but also a higher level of responsibility and accountability to each other: For the audience, the aesthetic minutiae and the overall creative vision of each object can be observed and expounded upon, with each comment expanding the vocabulary and comprehension of all the other participants. Conversely, any aspects of the work noted as potential flaws become exquisitely visible once pointed out.

CRP AND THE WARM MENTOR PROGRAM

I am a visual artist, mentor, and facilitator who has had a "love affair" with the Critical Response Process for over twenty-five years. I first learned about CRP through my involvement with Women's Art Resources of Minnesota (WARM), where we began applying this revolutionary way of critiquing art in the mid-1990s within our Mentor Program. This two-year mentorship pairs a seasoned artist/mentor with a protégée who is in the earlier stages of her art career, with a focus on developing skills, vision, business acumen, and confidence, all through community with other artists.

Protégées meet monthly with their mentors and are also encouraged to develop small groups within the protégée circle to expand their learning from each other. Mentors also conduct specialized workshops such as "How to Write an Artist Statement," as well as trainings, like the one I do for the Critical Response Process. All of this mentoring, teaching, and training builds toward the final exhibition, in which the mentors and protégées have the opportunity to show their work together, offering a final "teachable moment" on how to prepare for, mount, promote, and open an exhibit.

Generally, in the WARM Mentor Program, we provide training in the Process early in the second year, with actual Critical Response sessions beginning shortly thereafter. By then, most protégées know and trust their mentors, as well as the other mentors and protégées in the group. They are also working toward developing a body of work for the final show and are eager to have their art critiqued in preparation for the exhibit.

Most of this work tends to be in its final stages. Though we welcome work in progress, most artists opt to show work that is finished or close to it, in part due to the later timing of the CRP sessions, but also because showing an unfinished work—a new baby—is often a scary or risky prospect, and/or some artists are not yet prepared for input. CRP, then, helps to inform the presentation of work for the exhibit and guides the artist in determining her next steps forward with this or another body of work as she emerges from the program. As a culmination of everything the protégée has experienced and produced in the program, the session confirms what she has accomplished and what it means to an audience. CRP is also a way for artists to integrate the work into their consciousness, to understand what they have just made.

MY ROLE AS MENTOR IN CRP

As one of the WARM CRP facilitators—and as a mentor—my practice begins with a phone discussion with each artist to explain what Critical Response is, what their role will be, and how we will move through the process of getting them ready for their first CRP session. I place a strong emphasis on preparation because, after years of doing this, I have found that the better prepared artists are, the more they can "go with the flow and work with whatever shows up." A lack of preparation, on the other hand, can leave an artist fretting inwardly, rather than really listening and responding to those who have committed an afternoon or evening to their work.

I begin the preparation by establishing an understanding of how CRP works and the key role the artist plays in it, emphasizing the responsibility—to themselves and their audience—that the Process accords to artists. I follow up by sending them documents that review what I've just covered, as well as a probing questionnaire designed to help them mentally prepare for their CRP and to address what they might want to get from the Process. This probes motivation, aspiration, gaps, and challenges and includes pointed prompts for considering their CRP step two questions.

Next, I meet with the artists to go into more detail about the Process, answer any questions or concerns they have, and review the work they plan to submit for the critique. I also review my facilitation style to assure them I will be there to support and guide as needed, as well as keep the dialogue on track and on schedule.

From this conversation, I work with them to develop their specific questions for step two of CRP. I explain that the questions are key to setting the tone and level of their audience's inquiry. I always suggest that they start with their most important questions and move down the scale from there. This is counterintuitive to most artists who want to build up to their biggest question. But I've found in the CRP format that the audience can get stuck in the minutiae and never arrive at the core issues if the artists start with technical concerns, for example, hoping to expand toward the "real meaning" of their work.

With this in mind, artists spend the next few weeks working with me to finalize their step two questions to address the core of what they need or want to know about their work. I also advocate that they follow the discipline of step three of the Process and make their artist's questions neutral. As a mentor in the Process, I am teaching the artists about the nature of the neutral question, which they will better recognize, understand, and utilize if they know how to ask it. In addition, artists are often tempted to pose questions that lead their audience in a positive or negative direction; and my goal here is to get the audience to respond to the real inquiry, not the artists' biases for or against their own work.

Though I always encourage artists to spend time seriously considering what they really want to learn from their audience, I also tell them to be prepared to throw those questions out, if the first step—or any other—takes them in a different, but important, direction of inquiry.

From an outsider's point of view, it might seem strange that artists don't already know what their questions are. But it's important to realize that they rarely have the opportunity to pose questions directly to an audience, particularly in a structured format designed to move them toward their best work. That is an anomaly, not the norm, and is one of the core values and strengths of the Critical Response Process.

MY ROLE AS FACILITATOR

The way I facilitate CRP has changed over time—becoming more fluid, less rigid, and using a lot more humor, as I have become more comfortable with the Process and with myself as a facilitator. One of my tricks to put people at ease—with what for them is often a new structure for critiquing art—is to give a chocolate bar to the first person who fumbles through a neutral question. I say, "Thank you for breaking the ice, and for giving everyone a chance to learn." It always earns a laugh, and it provides some relief for the person on the receiving end.

The biggest challenge as a facilitator is not to insert yourself too much into the Process, except to get the ball rolling or to redirect the dialogue as needed to keep both the artist and audience focused on the task before them. I have seen firsthand what can happen when this principle is not followed. A facilitator can start to dictate rather than lead the Process and can enforce a rigidity that doesn't allow the artist or the audience to get what they need or want out of the critique.

For myself, I adhere to the spirit of the Process, with a firm belief that it is important to learn the four steps—the "rules of the road"—but also to bend them, when appropriate, to meet the needs of the artist. So, I am open to some flexible movement between the steps if the artist wants to review an earlier comment or question, to get further information or insight. This is also true for the audience, as long as what they are asking for will benefit the artist and they agree to their area of inquiry.

I tend to discourage fixits from responders and bids for suggestions from artists, preferring to rely on the use of the neutral question to explore concerns about the work. Fixits are especially problematic in the visual arts because participants can examine the work in such detail, making it easier for everyone to suddenly focus in on one component and start contributing suggestions, potentially derailing the flow of the Process. Further, the artist may lose ownership of that part of the piece, as they are often only able to see the suggested fix, rather than being coached or led via neutral questions toward their own creative solution. I do make an exception and allow artists to ask for suggestions if they have already spent significant time trying to resolve the aesthetic problem and understand the artistic risks in accepting a fixit.

I am consistently amazed by the wisdom and insight brought forth from the audience through the careful delineation and use of the Process. One of the beauties of CRP in the visual arts is that the audience can move in for a closer inspection and make their own assessment based on the work now immediately in front of them. CRP teaches the viewer to separate personal style, opinion, prejudice, and bias from the insight that arises out of accumulated experience. The viewers have the opportunity to chime in with different points of view and indicate the evidence within the art before them. Sometimes the tragic flaw for one is the brilliant discovery for another. This leaves the artist to choose which variation on the theme is "most true" for them.

CRP IN ACTION

One of the most poignant examples of CRP's impact happened in a session I facilitated for two protégées, one of whom was absolutely terrified by the prospect of having her work critiqued. Unbeknownst to me, the night before her critique, she had torn apart large sections of her mosaic pieces in an attempt to destroy what she saw as the evidence of her failure. Meeting with the two prior to the start of the session, I could immediately see that something was very wrong for the mosaic artist. She told me she didn't want to do her session—she felt sick and wanted nothing more than to go home. Now.

Confident about the high quality of her remaining work, and knowing in my heart that she would lose out on an important opportunity, I gently asked her if she would consider staying through the first CRP session, just to see how it went. Assured that she could still opt out at any point, she agreed.

During that first session, she witnessed how much valuable feedback her fellow protégée was receiving, and agreed to go forward with her own CRP session. As always, I sat next to her so that I would know if she was feeling emotional or in distress, with the rest of the group gathered in an equal and intimate circle around us. As the statements of meaning poured over her, I could feel her body begin to shake. I looked over and saw that the effect was positive, but that she was getting overwhelmed. So we took a small break and started again. One of the viewers in attendance happened to be a well-known and highly respected mosaic artist in the Twin Cities. She was completely taken with this artist's work, and she very specifically spelled out what she admired about the artist's vision, technique, and mastery of the medium. That critical acclaim finally set the protégée free from the fear that had been holding her back, and she went on to have an energizing critique. I found out years later that after this CRP session, her work and her career skyrocketed. She began exhibiting in art fairs, became a respected artist and leader in the field, and began making a living off of her work.

CONCLUSION

Over the years, I have watched mentors and protégées alike grow into a kind of familiarity and ease with the Process. More importantly, they develop stronger critical thinking skills and the ability to apply those skills with more precise and insightful language to the work of their fellow artists.

In the end, all artists need and want to hear meaningful responses to their work. Most of us do not make art with the intention of hiding it away in a closet, and we grow through the experience of shaping the work and understanding its impact. And though the Critical Response Process is not the only way to critique visual art, it is the most powerful and productive method I have had the opportunity to utilize.

It is from that vantage point that my experiences and insights as an artist, audience member, and facilitator resonate and flow. This is what, for me, makes Critical Response "heavy artillery" in the artists' arsenal to help advance their work and their thinking. It is also what guides and directs how I think about and facilitate the Critical Response Process.

As an artist, mentor, and CRP facilitator, I have witnessed my own transformation in my abilities to understand and articulate the work before me—whether my own, my protégée's, or that of an artist whose work I am viewing in a gallery or museum. Through CRP, I can honestly say I have become a much better and much smarter practitioner in all aspects of my career as an artist, and, because its principles touch on more than just art, in my life as well.

NOTE

Prior to the publication of this book, WARM ceased operations, an institutional casualty of the Covid-19 pandemic.

PROCESS AND ETHOS: CRP FOR NEW OPERAS AT AMERICAN LYRIC THEATER

Lawrence Edelson

"Why don't you just tell them the truth?"

This question was recently asked of me by an aspiring dramaturge in our Composer Librettist Development Program (CLDP) at American Lyric Theater (ALT). We were discussing a scene from an opera that was being workshopped, and she was frustrated because she felt I was not expressing what I really thought about the work, and because I was holding her back from expressing her opinion as well. My response was very much informed by the work I have done using the Critical Response Process over the past ten years at ALT: "Because their truth may be different from mine or yours, and their truth is the truth that matters."

Artistic truth isn't absolute or binary. Yes, one can make an observation that a narrative does not make sense, or that the vocal writing for a character is in a part of the range that makes it difficult for the singer's text to be understood. But what if the writers are intentionally making the narrative confusing, or if the high tessitura of the vocal writing is meant to create a sense of tension that is more important to the writers than comprehension of the words? Understanding what guides artists' decisions is critical to those mentoring them. We must take the time to get inside their process and to respect that their approach may be different from our own.

When developing new works, we need to be able to discuss that work in a meaningful way. This means being able to talk about what is working, what is not, and why. But respect for the artist must be at the forefront of that process. CRP not only provides us with a framework rooted in respect to use in formal workshops and readings at ALT, but has also informed the way in which we support artists across our programs.

At ALT, our workshop process includes both private and public readings of operas at all stages of their development. These include libretto readings (just the text of an opera); piano vocal readings (a concert of an opera score performed by singers, a pianist, and a conductor); and orchestral readings (a concert of an opera performed by singers with a full orchestra and a conductor). These workshops focus on the vision of the composer and librettist without staging, to ensure that they are able to communicate that vision directly through their work. At this point, we want to be able to explore what is inherent in the score and libretto, not what a stage director will bring to the work as an interpretive partner. This can make our workshops and our public readings very exposed.

The readings are all preceded by extensive private workshop periods in our studio, but the public showcases of work in progress are an invaluable tool for the writers—in great part because of our use of CRP. Inviting an audience into this Process can be counterproductive if it is not well moderated and if all involved do not fully embrace it. I have found that it is particularly helpful to integrate stakeholders (co-commissioners, funders, board members, members of the artistic team) and the public audience fully as responders. It is also very helpful to have other members of our CLDP among the responders—supportive colleagues trained in CRP, who provide a model for the Process in real time. We usually include performers in the public CRP talk-back, but we also have a separate session with just the performers—still utilizing CRP—in order to dive deeper into their discoveries.

Of course, members of a public audience love to tell you what they think—but free-form talk-back sessions can be a disaster, often revealing more about attendees than about the piece being discussed or alienating the artists in ways that impede the development process. CRP really helps focus the discussion on the piece and the creators' intent. You can't force people to obey the rules, but I have found that strong facilitation, interlaced with a bit of humor, is very helpful for keeping things on track. It is also very important to let the audience know that step four, opinion time, is coming. When the audience knows that they will have a chance to express their opinion (with permission), they tend to more readily embrace the Process. There will always be some people who resist the protocol, but this is why it is so helpful to have experienced CRP practitioners among the responders—people who understand and embrace the Process as role models for those who are new to the experience.

We also video-record our CRP sessions. Often, the amount of information shared in a session can be overwhelming for artists. They've just shared their work with the public for the first time, and then they engage in rich and thought-provoking discussion about that work. It can be emotional, and it can be exhausting. Many artists like to review the sessions to make sure they heard everything that was being discussed. One artist told me that he also liked to study his physical reactions in the video as the work was being discussed, as well as the reactions of his collaborator. These video recordings are also invaluable at demonstrating the important role of CRP to other artistic partners and funders.

Two key things have enabled the successful implementation of CRP at ALT. First, we familiarize the artists with the Process very early in their residency with us—well before they are workshopping operas in which they are deeply invested. New artists attend workshops of artists who are already in residence with us and witness how the Process works. They are able to see that the creators remain in control of the dialogue—that they feel safe and respected. Second, I very consciously embed the values of CRP as I teach classes in the first year of our program, modeling, for instance, how the use of the neutral question prevents me from imposing my opinion when it is not valuable.

CRP isn't simply a process for me, but rather an ethos by which I hope to truly serve each artist. The Process has made me more sensitive and more careful in my choice of words while talking to artists, and it has helped me guide some of our more strongly opinionated faculty. These incredible mentors are leading artists in the opera field who sometimes have the temptation to tell other artists how to "fix" work. Using CRP principles—even when not formally using the Process—has encouraged faculty to embrace a less corrective approach. In private sessions, artists with whom I've developed a strong personal relationship might ask for criticism that is more direct or more blunt. If they ask directly, I will offer it, but I wait until it is invited.

Our use of CRP at ALT has never limited our ability to be critical or helpful. It has simply emphasized the artist over the mentor, providing a framework grounded in respect of the artist's vision.

AN ACCOMMODATING BLUEPRINT: MULTIDISCIPLINARY PERSPECTIVES ON CRP

Rebekah West

As facilitator, promoter, artist, and provocateur, I have applied the Critical Response Process in the United States, Australia, and France to new compositions in dance, writing, photography, music, and interdisciplinary art incorporating media and performance. This trajectory has revealed invaluable opportunities to explore variations and diverse permutations of CRP, enacting its values where the full Process was not possible. CRP has its own flexible cultural language, which can be tailored through understanding the nature of *investment* and encountering group difficulties as opportunities. As I'll relate here, CRP questions almost triggered a mutiny in a French photo club; and under creative pressure, three musical collaborators and I put CRP and our egos to the test in a tiny, medieval French chapel.

What does it mean to be "invested"?

Liz Lerman and John Borstel's first book about CRP (2003) guides the preparation phase for the Process's three roles, specifically suggesting:

The artist be "invested in continuing to work on the piece you are showing and open to the possibility that you might change it."

And for the responders to be "invested in the potential for the artist to do his/her best work" (31).

So, in cultures outside my own, whether by geography or discipline, I ask myself: *How can I apply this method where the cultural assumptions it relies upon, such as the implied value of developing the potential of individual expression by individual choices, don't exist—or at least not in the ways I've imagined?*

CULTURAL DIFFERENCES AS OPPORTUNITIES: TWO CRP STORIES FROM FRANCE

I'll relate two short stories about my French experiences with CRP: the first with a group of French photographers, and the second with British and American visiting musicians. I'm engaged in a multiyear French artist residency through the *Carte des compétences et talents* to "exercise the professional artistic activity of my choice in order to make a significant or lasting contribution to France's cultural prestige and to that of my own country." There's freedom to create and pressure to culturally relate there, certainly.

Photography

The French tend to make decisions via group consensus, on everything from shopping to event planning. French education is steeped in teachers providing correct answers that students can later produce. In these and other ways, in my experience, French people tend to follow tradition and convention. In CRP, the artist makes decisions and American education encourages more self-reflective thinking, individual ideas, and innovation.

When I began to introduce CRP to *L'Atelier Photo*, a village-wide group of shutterbugs ranging in experience from casual to professional, there was a loud wave of discontent. Why wasn't I, the teacher/professional, the only person critiquing? How could I be trusted if the first thing I did was ask individuals to answer a reflective question with no correct answer?

In response to the chaos, I asked the photo club to clarify: They wanted a one-hour lecture with slides, a group discussion of correct answers, and for me to judge their work. I did my best to comply while gently introducing my value and experience with individual expression.

I came prepared with a twenty-image slideshow of French photographer Henri Cartier-Bresson, and I used the images to teach a lesson in diagonals, leading lines, perspective, and composition. I deliberately chose images imbued with powerful meaning.

In responding to these images at my invitation, they began by describing: "The wall has barbed wire on it and stretches into the distance as far as we can see. The children are obviously curious about the wall and what's on the other side."

With encouragement, they remarked on the deliberate use of composition: "Several kids are playing, but the wall is the largest element in the photograph. It divides the image in half and must have more weight to it than we first imagined."

Through this process of discovery they came to realize that it must be a picture not of a wall, but of the Berlin Wall; from then on, they naturally found meaning.

They said, "It's incredible that children are trying to see what's on the other side. There are no adults, so the children can be curious. They're quite aware of the wall as separating them from something. Their playing is so normal against the abnormal presence of this warlike barrier."

We progressed from describing aesthetic attributes to what those choices conveyed; we had been able to naturally achieve CRP's step one through a process of discovery.

Next, in order to aim toward step two, I took the technical concepts into the field for experiential exercises. I listened for questions, whether from or to the artist, and encouraged them. Though I had a goal, it was easygoing.

I heard: "I see the diagonal. Where did you shoot that?" Or, closer to step two artist questions: "Do you see what I did there with composition? Does the focus land on this subject? Do you think this image shows leading lines better than this one?"

Due mainly to my limited French, but also in keeping with their convivial approach, I did not guide questions to be more neutral, but simply encouraged them to ask.

The next meeting, we moved rapidly from their comfort zone to the method: "Oh, look at how you got diagonal and line of energy in the same image," to "Wow, this makes me think of the death of my husband. He used to stand just like that, the light hitting his eyes."

That last blurted statement moved everyone, and its raw statement of meaning went a long way toward understanding and completing step one. That's progress.

There wasn't group consensus on improving one person's photography, but changes in the quality of images overall were evident, sometimes brilliant.

Through this elongated dialogue over months, between cultures, and across educational structures, I believe that this adaptation affirmed the integrity of CRP's statements of meaning, questions, and opinions and served to elevate artistic work.

Music: CRP as a Collaborative Compositional Device

The mayor of the tiny medieval village where I live and work has given me sole access to a deconsecrated sixteenth-century octagonal chapel to use for musical and photographic elements of my project. I have felt an affinity with this space since discovering its acoustics several years ago now, and I care for it as a musical sacred space.

In the summer of 2015, two musicians from the UK and one from the US came to my village to compose and record new music together in "my" resonant chapel. A French air-traffic controller strike, a frequent occurrence, delayed the musicians' arrival from the UK, and our nine-day plan was compressed to seven. We had not worked together before.

In the chapel, we flew through two days of sound and phrase discovery. As we moved from experimentation into a compressed composition phase, we didn't have a similar musical language to save us: we each kept notes and regarded the purpose of rehearsal differently, and we didn't have a single leader, musical style, or aesthetic. Due to the arrival delay, we'd missed cultural events that were supposed to center our pieces and we only had two days to finish and learn this new music well enough to record it.

One of the honest transitions that happen in a creative process is when egos break down. Our transition? We were scared we couldn't pull it off. But the revelation revealed, again, our commitment to and investment in the project's success.

And because I recognized the value of this investment, CRP principles came to mind. I suggested we shape our compositional method to find the integrity of each piece. Though one musician was not keen on this route, we agreed to give it a go.

We talked over meaning by recalling words and phrases from rehearsal and gave opinions, both permissioned and freely offered, making a combination of steps one and four, which we wrote on index cards.

Then, utilizing the spirit of steps two and three, we looked for "creative questions" to focus our compositional decisions. In the end, we chose one question for each piece:

> *How do we maintain the pulse?*
> "Maintain" directed us to keep a pulse going through silence, transitions, and across instruments. With a single core question, there was room for experimentation and musical viewpoint with a crosscheck for decisions.
>
> *What does this piece mean in this space?*
> In the rush, there had been a tendency to revert to writing music from our heads rather than respond directly to the chapel's resonance. This question made us aware of the space and of listening.
>
> *What nuance can we bring to the surface?*
> In a resonant space, too many harmonics can muddy the sound. This question implies a delicacy or clarity to notes, tones, and melodic lines, or a winnowing down of instrumentation so that a clear voice could float to the top.

These questions effectively became our new method for composing; high stakes and commitment to the process got us through. I continued using the index cards throughout the mixing and mastering process for the CD.

CRP: AN ACCOMMODATING BLUEPRINT

As a participant in one of my writers' workshops in Australia stated, "CRP has to be delivered to a willing audience: closed minds and sensitive personalities will not succeed (or even try), whereas participants who value this Process and who are open to discovery will benefit greatly."

Even if the Process doesn't unfold exactly the way you imagined, the formulation of questions, backing off of fixits and conclusions, and expressing meaning combine to reduce insecurities, nourish creative problem-solving, strengthen confidence, and reveal tough obstacles not as rigid problems but as rich with questions and possibilities.

In fact, as the most demanding and confusing obstacles arise, remember that this method of critique gives its biggest dose of support there.

Expect to discover pathways and connections that dignify each participant and the creative process they face.

The essential element of investment can emerge for a participant in any role of CRP. Investment evokes excellence, magnetizes successes, and creates an empathic connection between people, which can reveal our visions and assumptions, what we are protecting, and the possibility and freedom of taking responsibility for our opinions.

There's a grace to this Process regardless of discipline, educational background, cultural conventions, or even language. The rigor of CRP as a whole is truly inspiring; when faced with cultural or disciplinary obstacles, its living blueprint of principles and values will consistently shine through.

REFERENCE

Lerman, Liz, and John Borstel. *Liz Lerman's Critical Response Process: A Method for Getting Useful Feedback on Anything You Make, from Dance to Dessert* (Takoma Park, MD: Liz Lerman Dance Exchange, 2003).

GETTING WHERE WE NEED TO BE: CRP IN ORGANIZATION, COLLABORATION, AND PRODUCTION AT DANCE & BMORE

CJay Philip

For me, the Critical Response Process is a reliable springboard. Whether I'm using the traditional four steps or my own homemade recipe, beginning from some point inside CRP helps me get closer to where I'm trying to go.

I first became familiar with CRP in 2014 at an introduction to the Process hosted by the Greater Baltimore Culture Alliance and led by Liz Lerman and John Borstel. Curious, I applied to participate in the weekend intensive that followed. I spent most of the first day with a headache as I tried to figure out exactly what CRP was. Once I let go of the boxes I was trying to fit it into, I found myself learning about the Process with enjoyment and a sense of experimentation. Several years later, I am still discovering and experimenting with CRP in my work as a choreographer, arts educator, artistic director, and collaborator.

For most of my career—spent on Broadway and regional theater both onstage and in creative teams—other artists and colleagues have looked to me for advice and artistic feedback. Why, I don't know. To be honest, the New Yorker in me has been pretty blunt, even harsh at times with my feedback, focusing mainly on "how things should be done—if you want to do them right." But asserting that kind of authority, I've discovered, can wind up stifling other peoples' ideas. My life and perspective have undergone quite a transformation, and I'm grateful I found CRP along the way.

CRP has made room for respectful dialogue and innovation throughout my practice but centered in my work with Dance & Bmore, a multidisciplinary ensemble creating socially conscious work. The musicians, dancers, and theater-makers in the company range from sixteen to seventy-five years old. We're constantly seeking feedback from each other as well as from the people in our community programs whose life experiences are decades and zip codes apart. Our five Dance & Bmore programs engage parents and their toddlers, caregivers with aging parents, and tweens and teens in between. Every year, we reach thousands of people from North, South, East, and West Baltimore and beyond. With such a range of perspectives, preferences, communities, and cultures to navigate, it's important to me that everyone in our creative community feels respected, heard, and receptive to multiple creative approaches and ideas. CRP helps make that possible.

I find CRP to be very malleable and use it in a variety of creative settings. It shows up in our formal procedures, gets tapped on the spot in community encounters, and works its way into the fabric of some of our biggest projects.

One of our regular applications of CRP started a few years ago, when I attempted to lead a dialogue with teaching artists in my company immediately following a less-than-great class. With no set structure for how to handle these sessions, I found myself meandering through a feedback session that played out in an awkward mix of insecurity and false humility, and my shortsighted questions only seemed to make it worse. Yuck. . . I can still taste it. When I got home I immediately started typing a new plan for how to approach feedback for the next class, and that plan started with the Critical Response Process.

A few days later I returned to meet with the teaching artists with this homemade combination of CRP and "special sauce," resulting in one of the best feedback sessions I had ever had with this group. My questions had clarity and confidence that was not there days before, and their answers followed suit. No more stumbling and insecure comments. Folks were quick to respond and were very vocal. The energy and body language of the group completely changed, and we laughed and encouraged one another as we wrapped up, looking forward to coming back together for the next class.

Woot! Mission accomplished, and in record time.

My new recipe incorporated a standardized set of four artist questions addressing issues that come up in most classes, as well as optional neutral questions that address particular frustrations of mine without me giving anybody the "side-eye." The new model added a fifth step: "Shoutouts and Shine," where instructors give praise and props to each other for victories large and small. "CRP Special Sauce" was a hit and is now a standard part of the Dance & Bmore teaching artists' tool kit.

My work as an advisor and mentor frequently takes me into settings beyond my home turf, and I often bring CRP along with me. I recently had the opportunity to give feedback to several dance teams and coaches in Baltimore City high schools. This is a competitive dance context where feedback often sounds like the unfiltered voice of a drill sergeant or frustrated dance mom. For the coaches, having a dance advisor come to see their unfinished, unpolished work creates a lot of stress. In that heightened tension, my statements of meaning about their choreography and their dancers proved incredibly disarming, and I found it fascinating to see how surprised students were to be asked probing questions about their choreography and creative content. Each group was so grateful to be guided through the four steps and given a safe space to share their concerns without fear of judgment before their final adjudication. As one of a few advisors, I felt fortunate to have CRP as a tool to make the experience much more fruitful and bonding, and I felt good about giving them CRP as an approach they could continue to use.

CRP has also found a multifaceted place in the long-term arc of a major project where my roles as playwright, choreographer, artistic director, educator, and youth mentor intersect. *Voices of Carmen* (VOC), Dance & Bmore's teen program, centered on a musical theater adaptation of the opera *Carmen* set in a high school, premiered in Baltimore in July 2019. When we announced the project in June 2018 we began a yearlong journey to collect and compile feedback from several sources. The initial group of responders was my Carmen Youth Council, comprised of a half dozen performers I've worked with since their childhood. They had often sought my advice about pursuing the arts, but in this scenario I was seeking their input on my work as author of the script and songs of a new musical. During most of our exchanges, I found myself playing the role of artist *and* facilitator.

The first statements of meaning were about the concept of a show designed to examine escalating conflicts within a classic opera and relate them to escalating conflicts in teen dating today. The step ones I got from my Youth Council gave me the confidence to move forward with the project. To them the idea made sense and the content was relevant to what they had witnessed among their peers. It actually scared me a little to hear their honest thoughts about intimate partner abuse and breakups-gone-bad that sometimes lead to school violence.

My step two artist's questions focused on the songs, the music, lyrics, and new arrangements of George Bizet's classics mixed with R&B, pop, and rap. I'm big on converting concerns into questions in step two, and my biggest concern was: is the material *dated*? My music producer husband and I got lots of feedback on the music in lots of ways. The initial head nod to the beat was a good one, finger snaps, the long "Okaayy" was a sign of resonance. We also asked the teens straight out and in less direct ways how they were experiencing the sound and styles of music. Our most memorable comment came from our lead rapper. Listening to my demo of his song with a big smile, he said, "Aight, it's got that '90s flow . . ." Bwaahhaaa. We laughed for ten minutes and tried to use that phrase in a sentence every day for a week. "Yo, it's got that '90s flow." His comment was meant as a compliment, but it also made me feel pretty old. LOL.

To expand our feedback circle, we hosted a Facebook Live listening party of a half dozen songs from VOC performed to tracks in a house-party setting. For this event, two Youth Council members acted as CRP facilitators for the twenty or so people in attendance and dozens more watching online. They mainly stuck with steps one and two of the Process. My one-on-one post-party conversations were also steeped in CRP, sometimes without the person's knowledge.

By January 2019, with the help of the Carmen Youth Council, I devised yet another hybrid feedback model for our first staged workshop performance, a Martin Luther King Day presentation and conversation about nonviolent communication. Immediately following the performance, I opened up the response to the audience with statements of meaning, and with so many proud parents, friends, and fans, validations abounded. I then moved to step two, asking questions from my perspective as writer/director. For this audience (and for the sake of time), I decided to forego framing step three as "neutral," but I did suggest that questions stay focused on the Process or the project overall. In doing so, I was actually asking for questions on behalf of both the performers and myself as writer/director. I know . . . sneaky.

After a break, we invited back only those who wanted to take a deeper dive to circle up with the performers for a more intimate discussion about the characters, conflicts, and participants' own successes and failures with conflict. Each circle of ten to fifteen people was facilitated by two teens while I hovered around like an eavesdropping neighbor. Those smaller circles were thoughtful and probing as the teens guided the conversations with a wisdom beyond their years that left both responders and artists inspired and hopeful.

In June 2019 we began full-company rehearsal with forty cast members and a twelve-piece band, all of them fourteen to twenty-one years old. This project had "work in progress" tattooed on her arm, and the rehearsal process was a daily exercise in feedback between the cast, musicians, and a creative team of youth and adults whose responsibilities included costumes, lighting, set design, props, and videography.

Around the same time, thankfully, I had just begun the CRP certification program administered by Liz and John along with seven other incredibly talented and capable facilitator/artists who truly feed my soul with every encounter. *Voices of Carmen* became my practicum for multidimensional application of CRP, and for five weeks the flow of feedback within the VOC production was like a superhighway with onramps, exits, overpasses, and traffic . . . so much traffic. Each week added another lane of communication with community conversations, social media posts, news, and radio interviews about this new contemporary production of *Carmen*. It was a whirlwind.

Every performance was followed by a form of CRP, some more fruitful than others. The inconsistent results frustrated me. Some audiences seemed unaccustomed to being asked on the spot to express their thoughts and feelings about a show. I wondered if my questions were helpful or just boxing people in and making them feel stuck. They looked stuck. In an effort to free up the flow of feedback that bottlenecked with some audiences, I turned to my CRP certification cohort for guidance. The advice I got was helpful: start with a turn-and-talk or pair-share. Invite audience members to turn to someone next to them to share statements of meaning, and maybe even include an aspect of the show to discuss, like themes, music, or characters. After two minutes of each person offering first impressions out and hearing someone else's, then ask for communal step ones, now that some of the mental congestion has begun to move. That was a useful tip that helped reopen the highways.

After five weeks of production the show closed and all but three of the teens moved on to other activities. That summer Dance & Bmore was assigned Bloomberg Arts interns who worked closely with the creative team behind the scenes as stage managers and production assistants. Every day for two more weeks, they met me at my office-studio. Compared to the constant barrage of questions and activity related to *Voices of Carmen* from fifty-two teens and eight staff, it felt like the difference between rush hour in New York City and a lakeside drive in the Poconos. We sat quietly and eased into our day, took long lunches, sipped cool beverages, and just talked. I could feel my blood pressure dropping with every breath. Heck, I could *take* a breath.

With this change in energy, feedback took on a retrospective, contemplative focus. Jaylin, Nasya, and Nyema were a joy to me, and those two quiet weeks with them became one of my most memorable and meaningful moments of the summer of 2019. We talked about all kinds of things: family, natural hair, and *my* teen years. We laughed and built a much deeper connection than we had experienced during the five weeks of *Carmen*, and through this connection I once again became the student. I was asking deep, reflective questions about what we just experienced: the show we produced, the program, its impact on the students, the community, and anything else that came to mind. Another teaching artist was taking notes and I asked the girls if I could record our conversations to help me remember and make adjustments to the program based on their feedback. They agreed.

What happened next was incredible to me as we literally stayed in a perpetual state of CRP step two for ten days—with me as the artist. My interns answered any question I had. By this point they'd seen almost all aspects of the program and of me on my good days and bad. These three eleventh graders were holding so much information in their heads, and I really wanted to know what they saw and thought from their point of view. "Help me understand something," I asked. "Sometimes when I give direction that seems pretty clearly communicated, there is a pause or silence. Why is that?" Asked for a specific example, I named an encounter that had happened with one of the interns during production. She responded by telling me exactly why she paused and what was going through her head in the silence. I was really surprised by her answer and looked to the other two to see if they have ever felt the same. They confirmed it with conviction and I was dumbfounded. I must have sounded like a two-year-old to them for the next few minutes, asking, "Why?" and again, "But why?" They painstakingly unpacked and uncovered a sentiment they assured me was common among teens today. One by one they offered personal examples and scenarios of silence, anxiety, and fear.

I had worked with young people for decades and thought I was pretty good at it. I even thought I knew how their minds worked and that I was able to get the best out of them. Wow, was I ignorant. My conversation with these young ladies changed everything. I realized I didn't even know what I didn't know about teens today, but what I *now* know has forever changed the way I interact, teach, and direct young people.

As I returned to Baltimore School for the Arts in September 2019 to teach tenth-grade Interdisciplinary Collaboration, not a class went by that was not impacted by the honest, brave feedback I received from my summer interns.

I've traveled quite a distance from being that blunt New Yorker, and I'm grateful for every step of the journey. No matter how awkward and high-speed or quiet and calm, starting with CRP gets me where I want to be.

CRP on Yourself

Liz Lerman

I can't remember the first time I tried doing CRP on myself. I think it was probably part of the long untangling process we each undergo as we try to remove the critics from our imagination. We might become aware of this when we realize we are carrying a voice of a parent with us into certain situations, and that is no longer valid. In my case, that I had the major dance critic of the *Washington Post* in rehearsals with me. He came uninvited into my head and remained stubbornly present, sometimes at the worst possible moment.

I had also begun to notice that if we had a visitor in the rehearsal space, I would find myself seeing the work through their eyes. It's not that we talked about it. It's that I had a capacity to weave an amazing story of what I thought they were thinking based on either my own anxiety, or things I actually could imagine this person saying since I knew them. On good days I found this exercise useful. It was a way of putting myself in someone else's aesthetics or point of view and then look at what we were constructing. On bad days it was just another way to beat myself up for my incapacities, poor judgment, or ridiculous ideas.

It turns out that using CRP on yourself can attain the best of what you want with an outside presence in your work. And doing it on yourself is a nice form of self-study and self-practice. You get to review the values of each step, which already requires vigilance. And you get to this on your own, in your own time, and with your own questions driving the inquiry. In fact, I think doing CRP on yourself is a kind of mindfulness in action. And with a bit of reflection, you can figure out more about what you are working on, and more about the values of CRP in a living, ongoing way.

So how does it work? I usually do it when walking, or at least in a studio where I can pace. And when I teach it I do it as a form of Walk and Talk, a tool that gets you talking nonstop out loud but within a certain time frame (say, one or two minutes per question) or spatial frame (three or four times across the room and back).

I begin with an opportunity to talk about the project at hand. Starting with the principle of step one, I immediately ask myself to talk about what is meaningful, *and* I have to filter out the negative. I can notice what's not working and even name it, but I cannot dwell on it. That act alone is good practice for experiencing the pleasure and necessity of time in our imaginations without judgment.

Over the years of teaching this solo variation of CRP and asking people how they found meaning in their own works in progress, I have found a few recurring themes. One is that people go back to the origin. Why did I decide to do this in the first place? What was interesting then, and why? Sometimes that alone is revelatory. Other times people can find the meaning in the distance already traveled from the early work. Many people use this opportunity to think about impact in both small and big ways. For those that are tired and bogged down in the mud of making a project, just doing this first step can provide refuge, a moment of inspiration, and certainly a reminder of why we decided to create this in the first place.

Pursuing step two of CRP on yourself means you get to ask questions and then answer them. And you get to stay on topic. You can't let your mind wander to other problems, such as wondering how you are going to pay for this, unless you asked yourself that question. It shifts focus onto the particulars, even if you are in the phase of a project where focusing is difficult.

The third step of CRP is the most complex to do on oneself, but for me the most fun. Here you get to bring to mind anyone you want to take a look at your work. The person can be someone you know or not, someone living or not, someone you feel is a friend, or maybe someone with whom you have a challenging relationship. Your task is to have them ask you questions, and then you answer them. You can politely ask them to keep the questions neutral. This is actually quite an important practice. If this is a person whose opinions you know well, getting your imaginary version of them to ask a neutral question can be quite empowering.

In the fourth and last step comes the opportunity for you to give yourself an opinion, still with that "I have an opinion about . . ." request preceding it. These opinions can be your own, or belong to one of the voices you've brought into your head. You can decide which ones you want to listen to and which you want to dismiss. It is exciting, difficult, and often quite clarifying to practice saying no to at least one opinion. It is an exercise of agency in relation to influence.

Doing the Critical Response Process on yourself is also a good way to synthesize what the Process does. We often use it at the end of the first day of training so people can review the steps, experience the Process, and even begin the act of stepping back and facilitating. But whenever you use it, remember that you can disaggregate the steps, focus on one part of it, and use the whole framework as a way to further train yourself in CRP's underlying principles.

5 COMMUNITIES AND CHANGE

From its very start, the Critical Response Process was a framework for change. CRP began as an antidote to voids, malpractices, and misaligned expectations that were undermining attempts at feedback in the arts, especially at their intersections with education and community life. In doing so, CRP challenged authority and offered a corrective to the sometime negative effects of such forces as hierarchy, competition, and aesthetic elitism. As a gentle manifesto, CRP's initial one-page handout of basic instructions brought a structure of values to bear on the free-for-all misrule that had prevailed in many feedback sessions and sought to democratize the weight of power in institutionally based critique. CRP's core values offered a countermovement to the entrenched habits of "We have always done it this way," and the occasionally oppressive power of professors and critics, based on a few essential premises: that human connection between artist and audience is a fruitful place to begin critique; that an artist can be supported in a non-defensive position related to their work; that placing inquiry before judgment might illuminate or even redirect the path of forming an opinion; and that a person in a position to hear opinions might actually have a say in what opinions they hear.

Among the most active early adapters of CRP were artists and organizations focused on social change, progressive community impact, and cultural equity. From the annual summer gatherings of Alternate ROOTS—one of two incubation sites where the Process was first tested—CRP spread through grassroots organizations like Jump-Start Performance Company in San Antonio, Intermedia Arts in Minneapolis, and Workspace for Choreographers in Sperryville, Virginia, and via numerous artist/educator/activists who helped to disseminate CRP's change-making ethos. As part of a burgeoning movement to create access to arts participation, CRP offered a way to engage constructively with the public and nurture collaboration among arts practitioners. Presentations by Liz and colleagues at national arts service organizations soon followed, spreading word of the Process through the networks of the Association of Performing Arts Presenters, Theatre Communications Group, OPERA America, Dance/USA, and others. Incubation programs for new performance work such as New York Theatre Workshop and American Lyric Theater embraced CRP as a core method. Eventually, CRP found its way to some of the most tradition-minded and hierarchically invested institutions in the arts ecology, including symphony orchestras and conservatories, which were recognizing their need to alter their paradigms, or at least augment their approaches, in order to help their forms, institutions, and artists survive.

Driving some of this interest was one of the significant changes that CRP proposes: a shift in the power dynamics of how feedback is given and received. This power realignment fits as one dimension of Liz's career-long inquiry into the dominance of hierarchical structures and the potential of horizontal systems and perceptions as an alternative—a central idea in her book *Hiking the Horizontal*. In a hierarchical world of arts cultivation and education, dominant models include one-directional flow of knowledge from master to student, competition pitting artists against each other for limited resources and knowledge, and the vesting of authority and expertise in such cultural gatekeepers as professors, producers, curators, and critics. CRP's alternative mode adjusts the balance toward a communal sharing of meaning relative to authoritative delivery of information, nonhierarchical knowledge-building relative to the policing of knowledge access, reciprocity relative to competition, and mutual influence relative to the exercise of institutional authority.

Some artist/activists point to the power shift CRP offers as an important dimension of its value in art-and-community contexts. Brian Francoise, a teaching theater artist and facilitator based in Baltimore, observes its affinity with other revolutionary approaches:

> When playing the role of either artist, responder or facilitator, you have to *give* to get. CRP lifts up the artist to become their best self. I don't believe it's an exaggeration to suggest that participation in CRP requires selfless acts of love. It is an antidote to any culture that is unconsciously invested in self-righteousness and aggrandizing individual egos. CRP is about considerations of where power should reside. Very often resistance to CRP is about losing power. It reminds me of what is at the heart of Augusto Boal's Theatre of the Oppressed, another adaptive and malleable tool: the belief that people are "experts

in their own lives." As in Boal's approach, the *core* values of CRP are ultimately self-determination and self-authorship.

As more people have recognized CRP's potential for shifting power and supporting self-authorship, the Process has increasingly proven its practical value in fields outside the arts. In the same community—where CRP practice got a boost from partnerships with the Greater Baltimore Cultural Alliance and University of Maryland, Baltimore County—the Process was adopted by Baltimore Participatory Action Research (B'PAR). This interdisciplinary group of graduate students in the humanities and social sciences initiates projects employing the principles of participatory action research (PAR). As described by participant and Towson University professor of art education Diane Kuthy, this approach honors the self-determination of communities "committed to the interconnected ideals that expertise is shared and valued in its various forms and that people most affected by a problem ought to drive and participate in research equitably . . . knowledge is not only legitimized by the academy, but is also democratized and shared in a variety of forms." B'PAR's embrace of CRP both recognized the power-shifting potential of the Process, and the need to set a context that supported that potential. Describing how the group introduced CRP, Kuthy writes:

> Our aim was to foster a non-hierarchical environment, so we decided not to invite participants with pre-existing power differentials such as professors. Graduate students/artists presented a variety of research projects in various stages of completion for feedback, including work related to critical race theory, rhetoric, and digital arts. As they experienced the creative power of collaborative problem solving, several new participants decided to join our learning group. The process was flexible and promoted deep listening as well as interdisciplinary learning because the artists, responders, and facilitators engaged several diverse perspectives. Participants left confident, inspired, and energized to use CRP as a tool to strengthen our diverse research interests.
>
> For our second workshop, we invited several professors and community partners to learn alongside graduate students. As it turns out, the Critical Response Process is an excellent tool to begin to consider ethically who and what expertise is in the room and to practice a non-hierarchical method of knowledge building—both core components of PAR. I can personally testify that the professors

who participated experienced my work differently, or perhaps I heard their feedback differently. I experienced their feedback as one of the multiple voices affirming my ability to creatively solve problems as a researcher. The protocols and their purposes in Critical Response Process are transparent to the group, which empowers audience members (responders) to be stakeholders with real and equitable responsibility.

As B'PAR's story of a two-phase introduction demonstrates, CRP's capacity for enacting change by shifting power lies only partly in its innate features of structure and substance. The remainder lies in how it is introduced, facilitated, and deployed. That *how* factor is one of the important focuses of this chapter, which Liz opens with a reflection on consent, power, and privilege as they emerge in the practice of CRP. In the contributor articles that follow, Rachel Miller Jacobs reflects on CRP in the practice of Mennonite worship, where it can impact the relationship between belief and action within the humility, collectivism, and pacifism of Mennonite consciousness. Bimbola Akinbola and Cassie Meador, writing from the perspective of Dance Exchange as an origin site for CRP, describe the embedded applications of the Process in a community-based project with a racial equity focus. With a view to the institutional level, Charles C. Smith, Kevin A. Ormsby, and Shula Strassfeld address CRP as a tool for cultivating equity and plurality among cultural organizations in Ontario, Canada, while Phil Stoesz brings a focus to the individual sphere, reflecting on the use of CRP for personal growth and change. The chapter ends on a note of adaptation, warning, and future-focus with two contributions: Isaac Gómez describes his Civic Dramaturgy variation on CRP as used as an antiracism tool in public discussion of work by artists of color. Then Cristóbal Martínez critiques the time structure he observes in the application of CRP, with reference to the practice of *Resolana* in northern New Mexico mestizo communities. Proposing alternative relationships to place and time for CRP in the future, he provides a final guest contribution to the book by bringing a welcome spirit of feedback to bear on the Critical Response Process itself. In the essay that follows, Liz responds to Martínez carrying forward his theme of CRP-as-ceremony to conclude the book.

During the few years when this book was under development, the momentum of movements for justice and equity burgeoned during the administration of a president who was monumental in his penchant for bullying, disregard for dialogue, and intolerance for any critique of his own words and actions. Change has always been a motivator for CRP, so while these conditions can't be said to have placed the Process in a new light, they did bring into the foreground particular functions and challenges in the practice of CRP. They highlight how the forces of White supremacy, sexism, and other forms of oppression are pervasive in our shared heritage and the workings of contemporary society. These forces are inevitably reflected in the experiences or life histories of any group of people gathered for the purpose of giving feedback, whether or not the work under discussion overtly references issues of oppression—an awareness that all practitioners of CRP must embrace.

Increasingly, we who are organizers and trainers of the Critical Response Process have recognized how the power-balancing features of the Process constantly intersect with power structures that are entrenched in institutions and implicit in society, often operating in ways unseen and unspoken to some while obvious and insidious to others. We operate now with a constant recognition: While step one can potently support the sharing of meaning among a group and give voice and witness to multiple truths, the inequities of our society mean that people do not all bring equal risks or equal expectations of being understood to the act of sharing meaning. While step two activates the virtues of self-reflection, it cannot force the balance between those who are willing to question themselves and those who aren't, or between those for whom self-reflection is a privilege and those who may suffer risk by exposing it. While step three promotes neutral inquiry as a way to gain perspective, navigate assumptions, and cultivate non-defensiveness, we must make a distinction between asking a neutral question and assuming a neutral stance on an issue of ethics or justice. While step four activates consent into the process of giving and getting opinions, allowing us to exercise agency and manage influence, we must recognize that the stakes and risks of requesting, granting, or withholding consent are rarely equal.

The pace of change accelerates, and we expect the next few years will bring new insights, variations, challenges, and applications to the practice of the Critical Response Process.

REFERENCE

Lerman, Liz. *Hiking the Horizontal: Field Notes from a Choreographer* (Middletown, CT: Wesleyan University Press, 2011).

CRP in a Time of Reckoning

Liz Lerman

I never thought the little thing that I made and sent out as a one-page photocopy would turn into the Critical Response Process as a thing; a big thing in the hands of many across the globe. I made it in a different time of my own life, in a different time in our national history, and a different time in how we all work together through our institutions, our organizations, our social media, and our relationships. The Process has proven flexible: like me, a kind of shape-shifter with a certain through line of need, integrity, respect, and collaboration—and an utter belief in the power of art and artistic practices to be filled with awe, purpose, utility, tedious repetition, and restful resilience. Critical Response came along for the ride. It never became my central piece of work. It never took over my life. It was and is a lovely companion sometimes demanding individual attention and often just a very comfortable tool that I put to use constantly and in varying situations.

But now, since the election of 2016, the emergence of Black Lives Matter, the ongoing conversation around racism and Whiteness, and the surprising strength of the #metoo world, Critical Response has come into its own again, with fresh purpose and renewed meaning. Critical Response practices a form of consent. In addressing the person sitting in the artist's chair, you don't get to say anything at any time in any tone and with any words you want. You work at giving for its own sake, and you work at giving in order to build a healthy relationship. Not only are you asking permission to give an opinion, you are also asked to name the category of that remark so that the person receiving it can prepare. CRP gives us practice in how powerful asking for and receiving consent can be. And how the very idea of consent is a democratic ideal made into a verb.

Critical Response cuts through privilege. It always has, and that is why the resistance to it has been strongest among those who feel they have to most to lose. It might be a beloved teacher, or an important artistic director, or a manager who considers themself as progressive and right in their ethical beliefs. But they still feel it is their place to get to say what they think immediately and with all the force that their position secures for them. They get to "shoot from the hip," though that's a form of honesty that only benefits those in power; everyone else has to be careful.

I have been the person with that kind of power from time to time, so I know how it feels from the inside. But I also know—first as someone who has received critique in that form for years, and then as someone who has tried to develop a different path—that automatically criticizing from a place of power gives a critique that is muscle-bound, inflexible, and often useless to the maker who is busy trying to find something unique to themselves, to the moment, to the needs at hand. Individuals and institutions who are vested with power through a variety of actions and historic systems become the arbiters of ideas, imagination, and aesthetics. CRP can immediately liberate these wonderful attributes. And the beauty of it is that it liberates for the giver as well as the receiver. Our judgments are a part of who we are. We live within that reflective place with a constancy whether we are aware or not. Critical Response gives us simple but difficult tools to remain in the moment with truth and our expertise in motion. CRP positions critique as living in a horizontal world where privilege exists but does not have to come into play when we share our knowledge, comprehension, or beliefs about what matters. This is true whether we are discussing the aesthetics of time or cleaning up a room to the wonders of our imaginations.

OUT OF THE SHADOW SIDE OF NICENESS: CRP IN A MENNONITE SEMINARY WORSHIP LAB

Rachel Miller Jacobs

I originally came to the Critical Response Process from the perspective of an educator in a specific religious and cultural context: I am a professor at Anabaptist Mennonite Biblical Seminary (AMBS) in Elkhart, Indiana. Early Anabaptists were part of the Radical Reformation; their central tenets included (among others) the separation of church and state and believer's baptism. Menno Simons, from whom Mennonites take their name, was an influential sixteenth-century Anabaptist leader who particularly emphasized pacifism as central to understanding the gospel. Many of his followers, seeking religious and political freedom, immigrated to the United States and Canada; twentieth-century missionaries from both North American and European Mennonite communities spread Anabaptism in the Global South, which is where the majority of Mennonites now live and worship.

As part of the Free Church tradition, Anabaptist Mennonites neither perform a set liturgy (for example, the mass) nor delegate the creation of worship resources to a few experts (for example, *The Book of Common*

Prayer). Recognizing that learning about worship involves not only knowledge of the history or tradition but also the creation of original worship resources for use in congregational life, I established a worship lab in the AMBS curriculum as a way to engage and refine those resources. In that context, CRP was just what I needed: it is simple to teach yet meaty in its impact, promotes active learning, and is tailor-made for creative products like the calls to worship words, visual installations, dramatic scripture readings, rituals, and song sets I asked my students to develop. In the worship lab, students bring and perform the worship draft for that week (communion "script," pastoral prayer, etc.). Following each performance, I lead the group through the four steps of CRP; after the lab, students revise their drafts and submit them for a more formal assessment.

In the years since I began using CRP, class responses have generally been positive; as one of my students said, CRP "feels natural." While this fit is pedagogical, it is also surely theological. CRP helps those of us in the Anabaptist Mennonite stream inhabit important convictions about what it means to be a Christian, the nature of the church, and our communal approach to worship. It also delivers an unexpected gift, one I noticed only with experience and over time: it calls us to account for several aspects of our collective shadow around agency in community.

One key Anabaptist Mennonite conviction is that we cannot truly know Christ unless we follow Christ in life. Christianity with an Anabaptist coloration emphasizes lifestyle: of course beliefs matter, but unless they issue in changed behavior, they are of little consequence. CRP's emphasis on ongoing practice helps us concretize that commitment to performance. In CRP, we bring our actual work product (not our convictions about what it should be) and expect that the act of creation (or imagination) is only the beginning. Because CRP is a process, it fits with an Anabaptist Mennonite emphasis on "following in life" and extends that emphasis from our spiritual into our creative lives.

Another key Anabaptist Mennonite principle is that the church is a community rather than a collection of individuals. CRP's communal structure helps us enact our conviction that it is not enough to have a great idea or to create something on our own: we actually need the feedback and assistance of others to bring it to fruition. Educational contexts, including Mennonite ones, have traditionally given the teacher alone the responsibility for assessing work. CRP, in contrast, puts teacher voices in conversation with other voices in ways that more accurately reflect our shared convictions about power and authority, the individual and the community.

In addition to helping us enact key convictions about community, CRP also helps us unlearn two patterns that are part of the Anabaptist Mennonite collective shadow around community life: false humility and passivity/passive aggressiveness. Because our tradition emphasizes the importance of humility, it is sometimes difficult for us to bring our work forward. "God gave me this" or "I was doing the dishes yesterday and this idea just sort of occurred to me, but I don't know" are extreme examples of things students have said as a preface to what they (reluctantly) presented in class. It is possible that this reluctance grows out of Anabaptism's complicated relationship with culture and the arts. But I believe it is also a result of our struggles with assertiveness and agency. In the very act of bringing work forward, CRP asks us as makers/creators to release the false humility that hides our responsibility for our work. CRP's obligation to ask a question (step two) reinforces the reality that we (and not someone else) made a thing and invites us to give up being the limp recipient of someone else's opinion.

In addition to the struggles with agency born of an emphasis on humility, our historic commitment to peace has cultivated a kind of niceness that makes it hard to engage the work of others in a substantive way. CRP short-circuits the temptation of the group gathered around the maker/creator to fall into avoidance ("That was interesting," "Great," or another vague comment) or the passive aggressiveness that is the shadow side of niceness ("In my [very important] congregation, we do it this way [and you should too]"). Instead, we begin our interactions with statements of meaning in which we speak truthfully and transparently (step one), and then go on to ask neutral questions that take seriously the work of others without taking it over (step three).

Having made something, brought it into the community, and committed ourselves to ongoing work, we still need to decide what to pick up and what to lay down. Anabaptist Mennonites have tended both to be suspicious of the way majorities gather impetus from sheer numbers and to mistrust top-down, expert-dominated decision-making. CRP's emphasis on taking the time to pay careful attention to the work in progress, and to gather information from all concerned, resonates with an Anabaptist Mennonite understanding of discernment. Rather than voting on whether we "like" something, or asking an authoritarian voice to deliver a critique from on high, everyone in the circle is responsible to fully enter into the evaluative process. CRP also pushes us to do something that is harder for us to do: to hand over the decision-making to the one who has the most authority to make it. Choosing next steps or hearing and following through on opinions are the responsibilities of the maker/creator alone. Recognizing this requires us to claim the authority that it is ours as makers/creators and release the authority that belongs to others as members of the groups gathered around the makers/creators. CRP short-circuits the tediousness of endless rumination and invites creators/makers to know their limits and articulate them clearly, and the people gathered around them to respect not only the maker's/creator's limits but their own as well (step four).

Because most Anabaptist Mennonite congregations have an organizational structure that is more flat than hierarchical, CRP is also helpful to congregational worship leaders in two ways: it helps us claim leadership identity and authority (I am the maker) while simultaneously helping us hone our capacity for collaboration (there are other makers, too, and we are working together). In the past few years, I have been recommending to my students and to the congregations for whom I do worship workshops that they structure their worship committees as CRP-style practice groups. I think this structure helps them cultivate the skills of current participants and encourages them to keep inviting new (and likely inexperienced) partners to join them. This way of working at developing resources for congregational worship, as well as reflecting on worship planning and leading, allows congregations to grow the number of skilled practitioners who are available to them and to develop worship practices that better reflect the breadth and richness of our spiritual path.

LEARNING A CITY, RESISTING ERASURE: CRP IN COMMUNITY AND COLLABORATIVE PROCESS

Bimbola Akinbola and Cassie Meador

The task of surfacing and articulating the life of the Critical Response Process within Dance Exchange could easily encompass an entire book. Founded by Liz Lerman in 1976, Dance Exchange was home base for the practice and propagation of CRP after its introduction in the early 1990s. Surveys we have conducted of staff, artists, and partners point to the ways Dance Exchange has remained an incubator for the cultivation and evolution of the values, principles, and practices connected to CRP in the years since Liz passed leadership of the organization to a new generation in 2011. They also attest to how the Process creates the conditions for collaboration across a broad range of perspectives as we navigate new understandings in any context where people are in process together. The full spectrum of CRP within Dance Exchange ranges from supporting organizational strategic planning to feedback within the creation of new performance work, encompassing both formal uses of the four-step Process and embedded applications of its principles. In this essay, we will give particular focus to the complex ways the values and practices of CRP impact Dance Exchange's function beyond the formal structure, and across wide sectors and community contexts, using a specific multiyear project as our point of reference.

As coauthors, we cannot do this without being aware and attuned to each of our identities and experiences. We come to this work together with a shared commitment to artmaking as a way to counter racism and White supremacy, cultivating the conditions to be present to the realities of our world. We are curious about how our individual identities and experiences, and the capacities these have shaped, can inform how we respond and the action we take: Cassie as a White woman, choreographer, and the current executive artistic director of Dance Exchange, invested in the ways artmaking can confront and counter White conditioning within systems of racism; and Bimbola as a Black woman, an educator, and resident scholar and partnering artist at Dance Exchange, invested in artmaking as a site of liberation for communities of color. Relative to the project described in this essay, Cassie was co-artistic director and Bimbola was documenting scholar.

BRICKS AND BONES

At both administrative and programmatic levels, the conscious application of the Critical Response Process has offered a training ground for the practices that guide Dance Exchange's work. These practices include: the naming of what is working and meaningful, forming questions about what we are making, and engaging in a spirit of curiosity and discovery that leads to a practice of developing neutral questions from our opinions. In reflecting on these practices, our intention is to consider how CRP expands our capacities and provides us with the sustenance and tools to be in process with our world, and to recognize the work in progress that is always unfolding in and before us. The Process supports ways to work from the deep knowledge and experience of each individual in a given group gathered to create something new, and can also create safe conditions for not knowing. Connecting to what we know and opening ourselves up to what we may not know allows for expanded perspectives and visibility of what can often be obscured because of the bias of our conditioning or limits of our experience. We are particularly invested in how the Critical Response Process might help us recognize and address the ways that privilege and power can diminish the possibility for deeper levels of understanding and creative potential within our lives. The practices and values connected to the Process offer the opportunity to slow down, question, and engage with our opinions, valuing and allowing multiple perspectives to live alongside and influence each other. To examine the ways these practices and values live within our community collaborations, we will reflect on a project that took place between 2012 and 2015, *Bricks and Bones: A performance series in response to the erasure of black lives and communities in Dallas, and the movements to recover, rebuild and honor those lost histories. Bricks and Bones* was co-designed and co-directed by Cassie Meador and Paloma McGregor. Paloma, a Black woman, is a Caribbean-born, New York–based choreographer and arts leader, cofounder and artistic director of Angela's Pulse, and founder of Dancing While Black. Paloma has spent more than a decade centering Black voices through collaborative, "community-specific" performance projects. She brought to the project her antiracist organizing in dance, which is steeped in Urban Bush Women's Entering, Building and Exiting Community methodology, and the People's Institute for Survival and Beyond Understanding & Undoing Racism® and community-organizing principles. These practices supported and made possible our ability as a multiracial team to build more equitable partnerships with community stakeholders.

Step One: Statements of Meaning

The process of creating *Bricks and Bones* occurred over a three-year period and began with a commission from Lauren Embrey, the president and CEO of the Embrey Family Foundation, a Dallas-based philanthropic organization that focuses on the arts, human rights, gender equity, racial equity, and social justice. Embrey attended Dance Exchange's Annual Summer Institute in 2012 and was inspired by Dance Exchange's use of community-centered creative practices, and tools like CRP, to bring people together to contend with complex social issues across difference.

During this same summer, Dance Exchange was encouraged and moved by an invitation from MK Abadoo, a choreographer and cultural organizer also steeped in the justice-making traditions of Urban Bush Women and the People's Institute for Survival and Beyond, to attend the upcoming Facing Race Conference in Baltimore. When Lauren reconnected with Cassie at the Facing Race Conference, she began conversations with Dance Exchange to commission a performance that would premiere in connection with the 2014 National Facing Race Conference taking place in Dallas. This began three years of work with Dallas artists and communities, in a project that would examine questions of racial justice relative to the city's past and present. Cassie contacted Paloma to co-lead the project because of her strengths as a dancemaker, her leadership in antiracist organizing practices through dance, and her experience as a Black woman creating collaborative performance projects that center Black voices. As a White-led organization, Dance Exchange could not have entered into this project without the leadership and contributions Paloma brought from this background. In collaboration with Paloma, the creative team began deeply engaging Dallas-based partners in determining the focus and content of the project. Sites for the work included historically African American neighborhoods in Dallas, the Dance Exchange 2014 Summer Institute in Maryland, and the 2014 Facing Race Conference in Dallas, where we engaged with attendees through performance plenaries and breakout sessions.

As co-artistic directors of the project, Paloma and Cassie held a shared commitment to cultivating local relationships and centering the work on the contributions of Dallas partners. Our ability to uphold this value throughout the project was possible because shared antiracist frameworks existed among Paloma, key members of the Dance Exchange team, and leaders in the Dallas community. In learning about the parts of Dallas's Black history that had been buried and dismissed for so long, we were sensitive to what it meant to be outsiders in relationship to these stories. The categories of "insider" and "outsider" are complex and, we would argue, insufficient. We all move back and forth between these categories and often even fail to experience a true sense of belonging in the spaces we call our homes. Still, during our time in Dallas there was no doubt that those of us who had traveled to be a part of *Bricks and Bones* needed to be intentional about the positions we were taking as well as the stories we were telling and how they were being told. This included being in conversation with existing Facing Race partners and developing avenues for connecting with the people whose stories, experiences, and contributions were not represented through previously established partnerships.

At the outset, it was essential to draw on our capacity to listen and recognize the significant ways in which Dallas-based artists and organizations were already gathering communities to advance racial equity. By participating in events led by artists in the neighborhoods of Vickery Meadow and the historic Tenth Street district, we heard stories of change experienced over lifetimes lived in these neighborhoods, as well as concern for further changes to come. We encountered artist/activists like vickie washington, Vicki Meek, Linda Jones, and Iv Amenti who had extensive experience in organizing across Dallas communities to resist erasure of Black neighborhoods and history. They in turn alerted us to other individuals and institutions who had been organizers in this resistance, including oral historian Donald Patton and the African American Museum of Fair Park.

The visioning and work of this project was made possible by our team and, significantly, the Black women, both on our team and in the community. Seeing and valuing the ways communities in Dallas were leading efforts to fight gentrification and engage people across generations in oral history, storytelling, and performance, our team was able to begin collaboratively visioning an arc for the project that began from the strength of what was working among artists in these communities.

The values cultivated by the use of the Critical Response Process brought support to the creative team's interactions as visiting artists in a vital and active local community. The practice of naming what is already of value in response to a given context is a frequent product of step one of CRP, often called "statements of meaning." Within the formal Process this emerges in expressions of what is interesting, meaningful, provocative, memorable, or compelling when responding to a work in process. This practice asks us to notice what is working, and to work from it. It also asks us to recognize the information and wisdom that can be utilized from a group when we take the time to name the value already present and what holds positive meaning for us. Attuning to this practice supported us in shaping and reshaping our project in Dallas in significant ways. First, it guided us to recognize what practices were already effectively being applied on the ground. This recognition, along with the cultural organizing practices Paloma brought to the project, led us to form a cohort of local artists deeply invested in the work of engaging their communities. Second, it guided Paloma and Cassie to prioritize the importance this cohort identified in having time to build and deepen relationships across neighborhoods and experiences, influencing the creative team to extend its research and development phase to over a three-year period to create ample time for relationship-building across geographic boundaries. This desire was first shared in response to some of the questions, phrased in the spirit of a step one prompt, that we asked during one of our early reflection and visioning times with the cohort: What have you found meaningful or significant about our work together so far? How might we advance what you are already finding valuable? This query called on the creative team to listen for the places and spaces where the cohort members and partners felt our work together would be most meaningful, leading to multiple sites across the city where engagements and performances took place, including community centers, a museum, schools, a church, and a cemetery. Our job is always, first and foremost, to listen, to witness, and to support that which is already flourishing in the communities where we're working. This is the beauty of the first step of CRP, which insists that we acknowledge what is meaningful, viable, and enduring before jumping to conclusions and offering opinions. Beyond the formal Process, this becomes a life practice that can help us to build from the full spectrum of value in our lives.

The Role of Inquiry

At Dance Exchange we value a responsive relationship with place—the people, environments, and histories that shape us, leading us to discover and contribute to expanded ways of seeing, collaborating, and questioning. Inquiry is at the heart of our work and process, driving our creative research and our dancemaking and action in the world. The practice of inquiry was central to *Bricks and Bones* as we entered a community that was not our own, while negotiating our particular racialized experiences and history as a White-led organization.

Step two of the Critical Response Process, "Artist as Questioner," and step three, "Neutral Questions from Responders," were particularly key in helping the creative team navigate the early stages of developing the project, which necessitated that we surface the many questions that our diverse experiences were bringing into the work and also turn our own internal and interpersonal discomforts into sites of productive tension and growth.

Essential research and visioning for the project took place in the context of two gatherings that drew together artists and other stakeholders in the project: the 2014 Dance Exchange Summer Institute in Takoma Park, Maryland, and Facing Race, hosted in Dallas during the same year. These events pursued creative research into methods for dismantling racism, with movement-and-dialogue approaches to discerning the issues and content that the project would address. During this visioning phase of the project, step two of CRP, "Artist as Questioner," became a central practice in expanding who shaped the direction of the work by creating space for multiple perspectives and opportunities to work from the full wisdom of the room. One of the ways we brought the "Artist as Questioner" into the research and rehearsal process was through an experience we call the "Walking Question Structure." Allowing participants to encounter several dialogue partners in succession, this structure offered the creative team an opportunity to articulate our driving questions connected to the research and work in Dallas. Among the questions we entered with were:

- What do the personal stories and experiences of those gathered through this project tell us about the racial history of Dallas?
- Where do we need to go to connect or surface the stories that aren't visible?

At the rehearsals and public engagements that followed the Dance Exchange Institute and Facing Race events, community members gathered to reflect and respond to these questions through dialogue and dance-making. In each of these encounters, we led a process for individuals to develop and share their own emerging/burning questions arising from their experience and discoveries. Each person had the opportunity to step into the role of "Artist as Questioner," their inquiry guiding the course of the work. This surfacing of experiences and history gave us information about where to dig deeper, and in some cases it led us to change course and reorient the project.

At an important juncture, the inquiry proved to be important for what it had not surfaced. As the creative team engaged these questions, cohort member vickie washington, a veteran theater artist and foundational presence in the North Texas arts scene, expressed her keen discomfort with the absence of any mention of the history of the Dallas Arts District, which is the largest continuous arts district in the United States. From vickie the team learned that prior to mid-twentieth-century urban "development," the site had been a thriving center for creative, intellectual, and political African American life, growing up from Freedman's Town, a settlement established in 1869 by formerly enslaved people. Our comprehension was subsequently deepened by Donald Patton, whose guided tour of the area told a story of displacement and resistance that could be read in the expressway that had replaced a burial ground and the few remaining buildings that attested to hardship and resilience. The creative team had been on several tours of the Arts District during our prior visits to Dallas without hearing any mention of this history. The absence of this narrative in the city's official history of the Arts District, which only starts in the 1970s, amounts to an erasure of the area's deeper history as a cohesive and flourishing African American cultural hub. For many of the White Dallas cohort members, this discovery was also unsettling as they faced how their racial conditioning can lead to an inability to see historic truths.

It was in light of this seemingly intentional omission that the creative team realized that *Bricks and Bones* needed to be about erasure and the process of recovering the lost stories of Black Dallas and also the acts of resilience and resistance against this erasure. Our work took place at the African American Museum of Dallas, where the creative team conducted embodied research and led moments of public intersection and reflection to contend with this history, and at Saint Paul Methodist Church, Billy Dade Middle School, the South Dallas Cultural Center, and Southern Methodist University. Some of the questions that became central as the project evolved included:

> Why do we learn lost/missing histories? How do we learn these histories? How do we teach or pass down these histories? How do we carry history in our bodies? What do we do with the excavated materials? Where does the history of Dallas begin? Who holds the deeper history?

The project did not result in a singular performative outcome but rather in several performances, which occurred at multiple sites, creating reflective space for emerging stories and a way to carry them forward through shared audience movement. Each performance site included fragments of the other sites through imagery and voices of a variety of Dallas community members, both live and in audio recordings that lived in conversation with the choreography. Performers included Dance Exchange creative team members, the cohort of Dallas-based artists and advisors, and people of all ages whom we met during the community engagements. Anchored in material that called on the audience to continue looking back as we face the journey ahead, themes explored in the performances included notable Freedman's Town figures, the demolition and restoration of Freedman's cemetery, Dallas's urban renewal and intentional erasure that destroyed much of Freedman's Town, and police brutality.

In the end, *Bricks and Bones* was about stimulating critical thinking and inspiring action. It was about the ways movement and making can help us access buried forms of knowledge we didn't even know we had and connect with our ancestors. It was about remembering and grieving. It was about honoring our individual and shared perspectives and experiences. It was about stepping back and acknowledging what we cannot know. It was about resisting silence and cultivating resilience among generations.

CONCLUSION: CRITICAL RESPONSE BEYOND *BRICKS AND BONES*

The usefulness of the Critical Response Process extends beyond the sequence of the steps practiced in their entirety in formal feedback settings. Even though the creative team did not practice the formal four-step Process during *Bricks and Bones*, we recognize that the values and practices embedded within the Process influenced the ways the team came to work throughout the project. In addition, the roles of artist, responder, and facilitator became fluid, as the members of the creative team stepped into these roles at different times, disrupting and expanding who shapes, influences, and leads the development of the work. This supports the possibility for an emergent process among the group, one in which the product is not determined at the beginning, one in which we are discovering the value and outcomes of the work together. It is not only the outcomes that change; we also change. We believe that we are here to be in process with our world, to work with what is working, to lead and be led, to bring our experience and histories to this work. This also allows us to deeply examine the source of our own opinions and perspectives.

Considering the project in retrospect and from the perspective of Dance Exchange's ongoing process of becoming an antiracist organization, we can also pose the following questions about how the principles of CRP might have been more fully applied or how they might be considered for the future:

- How could Dance Exchange have utilized the Process in more effective ways to sustain listening within the project's multiracial creative team and accountability toward our community partners in Dallas?
- How did our use of CRP principles under compressed residency timelines prioritize step one statements of meaning over opinions that might have been engaged and addressed together? Specifically, in what ways did our focus on what was working among the collaborators obscure our ability to address what was not working, or at work in more complex and challenging ways?
- In what ways can the Critical Response Process support the cultivation of antiracist practice? What are the limits of the Process in this work? How can the consideration of this project, with its benefits and challenges, inform the ongoing conversation about CRP as an antiracist practice?

Creating and supporting the making of art about the trauma, resistance, and resilience of a city you're not from, with or without permission from local partners, is a complex and difficult endeavor, one that requires creating the conditions for different ways of knowing and, at times, not knowing at all. When doing this kind of work, it is necessary to remind partners and ourselves that we cannot be experts on the experiences of others, and that it is not our job. We can bring curiosity to our own experiences and opinions, to their source and influences, creating ways of seeing and being in the world that have the power to change the environments we live and work in, and the encounters along the way. This requires us to sit with our discomforts and encounter and address our own relationships to privilege and power with honesty, especially as they apply to race, class, and access. Engaging our opinions and discomforts with inquiry is the foundational practice of CRP. When you hold privileges that allow your viewpoints to be more readily heard and validated by our society, you risk losing the awareness and ability to question your opinions fully and engage with their sources. This is a dangerous and unnecessary loss of creativity, which impairs our abilities to seek deeper levels of understanding and possibility, ultimately cutting off the creative potential of being influenced and inspired by others. Interrogating the source of the opinions we hold draws us privately into reflection and publicly into transformative dialogue.

To learn a new city through its erasures and silences is to have a very specific understanding of that city, one that forces you to reckon with the history you have been told and the history that may be hidden. We recognized that aspects of the Critical Response Process unified as one practice of resistance against erasure by bringing us together across communities to move beyond the dominant narrative and bring to light the history and experiences of people in Dallas. The values of CRP support us in acknowledging and engaging with place as something that is always in process because CRP embraces the work as subject to continued change and offers skills for relating and understanding content based on that emergent nature. When you view place, and your relationship to it, as something in constant development, you immediately have a different way of relating to your choices and actions in that place. It forces you to examine the implications of your relationship to the changes in that place and take an active role in the changes to come. These ways of navigating our relationship to place came into greater perspective for the creative team during our work in Dallas, and the Critical Response Process was one tool that helped us navigate this by giving us space to have and notice our experiences through the lens of curiosity and self-interrogation.

The authors would like to express thanks to MK Abadoo, Paloma McGregor, and Silvia Roberts for their thoughtful review and input on this essay.

ADVANCING EQUITY: CRP AT CULTURAL PLURALISM IN THE ARTS MOVEMENT ONTARIO

Charles C. Smith, Kevin A. Ormsby, and Shula Strassfeld

Cultural Pluralism in the Arts Movement Ontario (CPAMO) is a movement of indigenous and racialized artists engaged in empowering Canada's arts communities. CPAMO seeks to open opportunities for indigenous and racialized artists and arts organizations to build capacity through access and working relationships with cultural institutions in Canada resulting in constructive, implementative change. Employed in CPAMO's Pluralism in Organizational Change initiative, Liz Lerman's Critical Response Process has been an integral tool in meeting this mission.

CPAMO works to establish approaches that uphold the particular versus the universal and the abstract, that challenge homogeneity with heterogeneity and invites those interested and committed to enter into an exploratory process to both discover and create new ways of seeing and assessing art, and new ways of seeing, assessing, and engaging historically marginalized artists and their communities.

The story of how CPAMO began to use the Critical Response Process highlights the continuous growth of CPAMO's interventions in the arts ecology. It exemplifies CPAMO's use of diverse methodologies to promote the values, practices, and importance of pluralism and equity in contemporary arts in order to transform the Canadian arts ecology into one that meaningfully engages indigenous, racialized, the deaf, disabled, mad, and other historically marginalized artists, arts practices, and communities.

CPAMO formally began its journey in 2010, emerging in partnership with Ontario Presents (formerly Community Cultural Impresarios). It began as an initiative in research, documentation, and education involving multidisciplinary venue presenters and artists in the performing arts. From 2010 to 2012, CPAMO held workshops and town halls to focus on these functions and produced *Pluralism in the Arts in Canada: A Change Is Gonna Come* (Smith 2011), a book of essays, toolkits, and organizational strategies addressing the challenges of promoting pluralism in the arts.

While this book was making the rounds, CPAMO was busy organizing workshops, artist showcases, and research to continue promoting pluralism in the arts. These projects helped to build CPAMO's understanding and resources and led to the creation of Pluralism in Organizational Change (CPAMOPOC), a comprehensive pluralism/equity organizational change initiative involving forty-eight arts organizations in Canada committed to fostering pluralism and organizational change. At its monthly gatherings, each organization was represented by its executive director, in some cases accompanied by a second staff member. The passionate leaders of these artistically diverse organizations committed to addressing past practices of exclusion and developing viable strategies to include historically marginalized artists and their communities in the organization's lifeblood. General approaches included:

- Developing organizational commitment and personal leadership;
- Engaging pluralist aesthetic practices/artists and diverse communities;
- Involving indigenous, racialized, and other historically marginalized artists and communities in organizational program decision-making and promotion;
- Building staffing, membership, and/or audiences from indigenous, racialized, and historically marginalized artists and communities to support a continuum of engagement.

The participating organizations varied greatly: some were Ontario regional organizations, some Canada-wide; most were small, some with a staff of one or two; some with individual artist members and/or arts organization members; some had been around for years while others were fairly new. All the administrators in the group answered to a board. Those who committed to participation in CPAMOPOC were the visionaries, leaders who recognized the need for change and were seeking guidance, tools, and strategies to create this change.

The group met one day a month to share ideas about action plans that they hoped to see implemented within their organizations. Given the program's structure and intentions, a key concern for CPAMO was how to engage these organizations in a needs assessment that would familiarize participants with one another's self-perceived strengths, desires, and needs related to pluralism and equity. For CPAMO, this meant considering an appropriate and vital pedagogical approach that would emphasize collaborative sharing to support the creation of a community of practice while providing tools to discuss sensitive issues among themselves and in public forums. Based on these experiences and the learning from its recent reports and workshops and how they were received, CPAMO saw the need to create an environment to unlearn past practices, learn new ones, and focus on, address, and take responsibility for actions that promote pluralism and are thereby antiracist, anti-oppressive, anti-homophobic, anti-ableist, and so on. To facilitate this, CPAMO elected to use the Critical Response Process developed by Liz Lerman.

Considered as a pedagogical practice, CRP emphasizes inquiry, dialogue, and participant agency, bringing an inclusive spirit to feedback encounters. Like cultural pluralism, CRP has been applied to artistic work with a social justice agenda and dimensions of community engagement. In these contexts CRP reveals its capacity to mediate diverse viewpoints and promote civil conversation. As such, CPAMO has found it to be a valuable tool in our work.

CHARTING CPAMO'S WORK WITH CRP: HOW WE BEGAN

CRP was introduced into CPAMO's working process by program manager Kevin A. Ormsby, who had experienced and researched the artistic and administrative use of the Process in 2009 while a visiting artist at Dance Exchange, then CRP's home institution. In 2012, he applied CRP in an administrative capacity as part of the Ontario Arts Council's Ontario Dances Program and while functioning as a dance animator at the Living Arts Centre in Mississauga, Ontario. Inspired by the success of these uses, and recognizing for himself a distinctive experience with CRP, Ormsby sought to apply his knowledge and training in CRP to embed its values into CPAMO's work.

In 2012, most of his CPAMO colleagues were unfamiliar with CRP. As such, the idea of embedding CRP into CPAMO's working culture offered a way of enacting Liz Lerman's archetypal phrase "turn discomfort into inquiry." What ensued was an exploration of how CRP could be a valuable tool to support CPAMO's "commitment to a grassroots approach, always shaping its programs and activities from its members' needs and understanding across the lines of artistic and cultural difference." Joining Ormsby in the work was Shula Strassfeld, who had recently assumed the role of program facilitator at CPAMO, bringing past experience with CRP gained as an ensemble member and adjunct artist with Dance Exchange.

After cofacilitating CRP at the Dance Exchange summer institute, Ormsby and Strassfeld led a workshop and work-in-progress session focused on the Process with racialized artists in Toronto.

Since then, CPAMO has used CRP in its communications, planning, design phase, facilitation, and programming. Most concrete perhaps have been its applications within CPAMOPOC, where it has supported the "big ideas" of pluralism and equity of the participating arts organizations.

APPLYING CRP TO PLURALISM IN ORGANIZATIONAL CHANGE (CPAMOPOC)

In convening CPAMOPOC, CPAMO used the first few sessions for participants to get to know one another and learn more about the various organizations. CPAMO set the tone by doing a cake demo, a standard method for introducing CRP using a role-play in which the group practices the steps and roles of the Process with a cake as the artwork receiving feedback. Through this low-stakes practice, CPAMO worked to make the framing of neutral questions almost second nature.

After this initial practice, CRP was applied to the core work of CPAMOPOC. During the central months of the project, participating organizations presented their action plans and Kevin A. Ormsby and Shula Strassfeld alternated facilitating CRP in response to the presentations.

Through these sessions, CRP helped to reveal contextual sources of meaning and support mutually beneficial dialogue in many ways as CPAMOPOC participants:

- Talked about what stood out as memorable or surprising or meaningful without placing a value judgment on it.
- Responded to questions from the presenter about issues that they found challenging.
- Heard what they were asking and respectfully answered that question, not another.
- Asked neutral questions because we wanted to gain information in order to shape thoughtful and reasoned opinions.
- Talked to each other with an awareness of how we might be heard. We listened well, and we thought before we spoke.
- Recognized that a person's work matters to them and that even if we totally disagreed with what they were doing, we needed to be caring in how we responded.
- Asked before sharing an opinion, and even when invited to share it gave care to what we said and how we said it.

Once the session was complete, the group would move on to what we now call "CPAMO Step Five," a general, facilitated discussion with the whole group. The origin of this extra step arrived out of a unique opportunity created through the gatherings, and the fact that many of the executive directors of the participating organizations had not convened in this manner before. Conversation was important for galvanizing the "networking" that the CPAMOPOC programming supported. For the most part, participants sustained the values of CRP throughout these discussions, leading from the principles of neutral questions, deep listening, and inquiry rather by starting with opinion. They kept in mind the overall goals of each organization to effect important organizational change that would increase pluralism and equity within their organization. The group recognized that each organization's situation was different and that each plan would work only for that organization, although there were many things the groups learned from each other.

In spite of this prevailing spirit, some challenges emerged. In hindsight, CPAMO might have been more explicit about the goal of shifting the lens and the culture of discourse through which all the encounters within the group occurred and were seen. While all the participants did a great job with the cake demo, the principles sometimes got lost in the CRP sessions geared at looking at individual action plans. In a few instances during the step five discussions, old histories, hierarchical relationships, and routine patterns of interaction sneaked in, making the conversation increasingly difficult to facilitate. Through their organization action plans, CPAMOPOC participants were challenged to arrive with ideas that the organizations were curious to implement. Due to their established familiarity and history of interaction, however, participants did not always apply the same attentiveness to following the steps of the Process, often desiring to arrive at the opinion step earlier. CPAMO facilitators came to the conclusion that this highlighted some of the habitual ways the participants were working in the field. There were two instances when CPAMO staff had to insist on reframing the conversation in a nonaggressive way, and once that required a separate outside meeting with the participants involved.

It is interesting to assess CRP itself while using it as a framework for developing pluralism and equity projects. Further questions arise in assessing the efficacy of the initiative. Did it matter that CPAMO's program manager, a racialized man, and program facilitator, an older Jewish woman, were the facilitators of the Process? Does CRP imply an "expert" in the facilitator?

CRP: BENEFITS FOR CPAMO, IMPLICATIONS FOR PLURALISM

The use of CRP to flesh out each organization's plans had two goals. The first was to look at the plans as "work in progress" and to apply a method of feedback that assisted in continuing working on an idea, plan, or artistic work. The second was to create within the working group ways of interacting based on the principles of CRP that would allow for open, honest communication in a thoughtful framework.

For CPAMO, the original intention was that the Process would become second nature in the operations of the participating organizations. Some of CPAMO's main principles are rooted in listening to the voices of marginalized artists and discovering who has been historically missing from the conversation in the arts. A critical element in practicing these principles is the creation and support of a platform where feedback, opinions, and ideas can be actualized.

CRP offered a means of honoring change in radical, fundamental ways that fostered support, nurturing, and commitment in building community through allyship. It inspired inquiry and reflection among participants at an unprecedented level: a significant factor in this project was the fact that most of the participants were White and were attempting to lead the charge for pluralism. At a session someone asked, "How much do you want to see this change happen? Are you willing to give up your present job to make it happen?" Among organizations that already had internal challenges and inter-organizational histories with each other, these CRP-based dialogues supported the creation of new organizational alliances and collaborative ventures. An example was the convening of a group to foster emerging women administrators in the field, an idea that took shape through the CPAMOPOC CRP sessions. Other dialogues afforded opportunities for participants to share what they learned and experienced as well as the knowledge they gained from previous exercises focused on pluralism and equity, and from literature, case studies, and data sources. Effectively, each project participant became both a learner and a teacher as the unique expertise of each was shared with the others.

Perhaps naive or not at all, the principles on which CRP is based are not culture-specific, although we can assume that they are talked about in different ways in different cultures. The Process firmly demonstrated that the artist ultimately decides what their "best work" will look like, that the artist controls the conversation and teaches us all to respect the work and opinions of everyone. The experience of the work may vary greatly based on the frame of reference, but the agreement in CRP is to respond to the work the artist made, as well as the culture and worldview from which that work has emerged. This understanding is fostered when responders use questions to learn more about form, context, and perspective, as well as to offer comments to the artist. Throughout, it is a learning experience for all. Of extreme importance is that in facilitation or participation, no one is singled out as having more or better knowledge. In one instance, CPAMO's facilitations supported the comfort required in bringing up a nonjudgmental, non-defensive conversation around problematic language that was no longer used in equity, diversity and inclusion (EDI) work. The preparation received through CRP allowed for a presenter and a participant to arrive, with seamless comfort, at a place of shared understanding of how bureaucratic language shapes relationship in equity and pluralism. In this instance, by assuming no knowledge, everyone is a creator and supporter of information that shapes plural ideas.

From the perspective of equity and pluralism, some in the field have expressed concern that CRP's requirement for neutral questions in step three could suppress voices and silence important truths. CPAMO facilitators discovered, however, that framing of neutral questions in CRP is not necessarily limiting or exclusionist. The whole intent is to find a mutually acceptable format for asking questions that will keep the feelings of both the questioner and "questionee" in mind. As CPAMO pursued this ideal, we found ourselves asking, "Can we collectively reframe a question to make it neutral?" The practice soon emerged that when questions were not posed neutrally, CPAMOPOC participants together explored what support would be needed to help the questioner retool the inquiry in a neutral form. Behind the concept of the neutral question is an intention of inclusion and, by extension, a gentle challenge of all participants' knowledge.

In fact, perhaps thinking of CRP as "feedback" or "criticism" does not reflect what the Process accomplishes. Both those terms imply that the responders have information that the artist needs to hear and take into consideration. CRP says instead that the artist is at work on something; responders, by entering into dialogue, help inform, shape, and frame the development of the work, but ultimately it is the artist who chooses. Our CPAMOPOC experience suggests that when this principle can be embedded in the processes of arts organizations, artists, facilitators, and presenters, CRP becomes an integral tool in engaging with equity, inclusion, and pluralism.

REFERENCE

Smith, Charles C., ed. *Pluralism in the Arts in Canada: A Change Is Gonna Come* (Toronto: Canadian Centre for Policy Alternatives, 2011).

HUMAN WORKS IN PROGRESS: CRP AND PERSONAL CHANGE

Phil Stoesz

Sitting in a circle, teaching CRP, I start by asking a simple question: What's a work in progress in your life?

"I'm trying to learn how to trust people after I got a divorce." "I'm wondering how to connect better with my grandchildren." "How do I support my roommate? Because their friend was killed two weeks ago." "How do I make friends as an adult?"

As an educator and facilitator, I'm constantly faced with the question of how to have better conversations. I long to connect with people in ways that elicit openness, curious inquiry, and personal development. But humans are creatures of pattern—once we find ourselves in a loop of thinking, it's hard to break out. It's difficult enough to think about how to change our relationship with a problematic coworker, a troublesome relative, or a sexist friend. If we don't have the tools to reimagine our relationship with people close to us, how could we ever do the deep work of changing our relationship to racism, global warming, or sexual injustice?

When I was first introduced to the Critical Response Process in an undergraduate playwriting class, I wasn't particularly moved. I was just starting to write plays, and I didn't want feedback of any kind, much less structured feedback. Do I have questions about my own work? Sure . . . um, is it good?

It wasn't until I spent more time with Liz and John, learning the heart of the Process and watching the practice unfold in daily life, that I truly started to embrace it. I watched firsthand as audience members discovered curiosity by asking questions, as artists felt embraced by statements of meaning, as groups of people realized there were new ways to enter difficult conversations.

As I deepened my work as a facilitator, I started considering that perhaps CRP may not just be a tool for facilitating better feedback in art contexts, but is perhaps also a tool for personal growth, perhaps even for furthering justice in the world. If practicing step ones made me more grateful and asking neutral questions made me more empathetic, perhaps these tools could be used to usher groups of people closer to their own discomfort.

The best CRP sessions I've facilitated have an abundance of vulnerability and curiosity. Most often the vulnerability is someone speaking honestly about their pain related to a piece of work, and in turn the curiosity is everyone ready to engage, learn, and grow. At its root, CRP is a method for approaching a difficult thing. During CRP we are asked to speak honestly (sometimes with strangers) about how we think, what we feel and see, what we're curious about, what we don't understand, and sometimes what we love or hate. If CRP could be used in artistic contexts to teach a new relationship with difficult matters and the discomfort they engender, what would happen if we took the art out of it and just thought about deepening personal inquiry? Could I guide people through using the method in relationship to challenges in their own lives?

My first foray into answering this question came in the form of a three-day class at a local Unitarian Universalist Church (UUC). I hosted a CRP class explicitly to approach vulnerability and curiosity in our own lives. The structure was simple: teach the basics of CRP with the classic cake demo, then slowly apply the practice to situations of anger, fear, or discomfort in the participants' lives.

The class met at 10:00 a.m. on three consecutive Saturdays. We gathered in the cafeteria, seated in a circle of foldout chairs, and talked about our lives. Instead of describing the class beat by beat (I write exhaustive reflections after each facilitation session), I'll share two observations and two questions I came away with.

OBSERVATION 1: CRP CULTIVATES VULNERABILITY

My favorite introduction to CRP sessions is this question, which originated with CRP practitioner Margot Greenlee: "What's a work in progress in your own life and what's a question you have about it?" This acts both as an introduction to the concept of personal works in progress and as a primer for step two.

In the UUC class, I set the tone by describing my own mildly vulnerable work in progress, trying to figure out my business taxes, which is a point of fear for me. As we went around during the session, people shared deeply and emotionally: divorce, disconnection, fear, and loneliness.

The question "What's a work in progress you have and what are you asking yourself about it?" exemplifies two key aspects of CRP: awareness and intentionality. Consider "How do I make friends?" First, by simply naming that as a work in progress, you're naming it as a path you're on. Second, by asking a question, we open up an imagination space where we might intentionally move toward finding an answer. A pit becomes a path, and a question forces us to unlock the possibility of intentional movement and development.

OBSERVATION 2: CRP IS A WAY TO REHEARSE NEW CONVERSATIONS

Starting by identifying such works in progress, many in the class moved forward by imagining a conversation they needed to have (with their roommate, their friend, their ex-husband). As a performance-maker, I knew that imagination and conceptualization can only get us so far; we needed to get down to practicing!

I placed members of the group in one-on-one conversations, which I anticipated would more closely resemble actual, difficult conversations we might have in real life. While they weren't in full-on role-play, the pairings set up a new frame for entering what might be a conversation within a significant relationship. Participants started by sharing their personal works in progress, and then I guided them through a conversation that followed the steps.

The structured nature of the conversation required some adjustment, but slowly people started practicing the difficult conversations they'd been struggling to have. They practiced suspending judgment to give a series of step ones. I asked them to do five each, then later ten. They practiced forming a good question about their work. They practiced asking permission to give opinions, suggestions, or advice.

In this way, the structure of CRP can act as a rehearsal for how we might start communicating differently. Instead of imagining being honest or theorizing about how two people might listen to one another, CRP says: Get in there! Try something out! Rehearsals are places we can screw up, forget our lines, attempt something bold, and get supported by others. Perhaps if we first rehearsed having conversations about sex, or dying, or our own fears, we might start finding new ways of talking.

QUESTION 1: CAN CRP CHANGE DEEPLY ROOTED PATTERNS?

Whenever people spend time together, they build assumed norms of feedback over hundreds of small interactions. Sometimes the norms are beautiful and healthy (thanking each other regularly or asking questions before giving feedback), but often they can be painful and insidious, keeping the power structures imbalanced and critique far away from those who need it most. Does change look like a cataclysm or a small step?

This question has shown up a lot in my marriage. When I first started trying to introduce CRP into daily conversation, it was really rocky. "Can you talk about your definition of 'clean'?" does not sound like a neutral question after living with someone for seven years. But we have found that "statements of meaning" work wonders to help us stop taking each other's work for granted ("It's so meaningful that you take time to pay the bills each month"), and "permissioned conversations" are wonderful for clarity ("Can I complain about my day for ten minutes?")

Any group, whether a business organization of two hundred or three people living together, builds its own culture of feedback. How does that culture have a relationship with CRP in a way that's healthy?

QUESTION 2: WHAT IS THE RELATIONSHIP BETWEEN CRP, PERSONAL INQUIRY, AND JUSTICE?

One of the first inspirations for this question was a consideration of justice, asking myself big questions (How do we reimagine masculinity?) and small questions (How do I talk to my friend about his use of the word "rape"?). As we try to understand what justice in the world may look like, is the journey inward helpful? Is it necessary?

Practicing CRP is a master class in inquiry: What am I curious about? What stood out to me? What opinions do I have? How can I turn that opinion into a question? Participants are constantly faced with questions, and every answer produces more questions.

In my work in male-oriented spaces focused on dismantling violent masculinity, the talk can so easily turn to how bad other men can get or how we need to protect women. I try to turn the conversation toward personal inquiry. When have I been violent? When have I made someone feel scared? What steps can I take to heal?

Perhaps if we build the capacity to understand and question our own assumptions, practices, and biases, we can move toward better answers to those questions.

The space I ventured into at the Unitarian Church was the first step of many toward understanding the relationship between personal discomfort, CRP, and building justice in the world. There are times when I feel like CRP is too structured a tool, that the path toward justice is too messy to use it. But in teaching CRP, people can step into spaces of vulnerability that may otherwise be difficult to get into. Or perhaps easy to get into, but hard to find a path out of. Perhaps having better conversations doesn't require knowing the whole journey, but we may be able to find our way forward after step one.

CIVIC DRAMATURGY: UNDOING RACISM THROUGH THE CRITICAL RESPONSE PROCESS

Isaac Gómez

THE EVENT

House lights rise to a slow dim.

The stark and jolting ending of Marcus Gardley's searing historical parable *An Issue of Blood*, directed by Victory Gardens Theater's artistic director Chay Yew, is still visibly present in the watery eyes of a second-preview audience at the historic Biograph Theater on Lincoln Avenue in Chicago.

My heart races as I wait to begin a post-show discussion, as I have done for countless other post-show discussions in my time as Victory Gardens Theater's director of new play development.

Why am I so nervous?

When working on a world premiere of a new play it's hard to assess how an audience will respond, especially in a city like Chicago; previews are a time of exploration, of risk-taking, of trying things on their feet and seeing how they land with thoughtful and critical audiences hungry to be included in the play's development. And this particular audience was still collecting itself, sitting in the wake of an unrelenting story unearthing our country's deep-rooted history of oppression, violence, and police brutality.

My palms are sweaty but I keep them clasped tight, compressing my anxieties as I take the temperature of the room. As facilitator, it is impossible to shake away my nerves, but it's less important to shake them away as much as it is crucial to ensure the audience feels cared for amid my anxiety and theirs. I sit at the lip of the stage, which brings me closer to the audience physically and emotionally; it's important to begin these conversations by breaking any barrier of "us" versus "them." This instills an audience's ability to be honest in their feedback without fear of needing to "perform intelligence" in front of the ominous dramaturge who isn't so ominous at all.

In my periphery, I can see playwright Marcus Gardley sitting in the corner seat of the last row, notebook out, scratching his head, anxious to hear how audiences are responding to his work so he can assess what changes, if any, are inspired by this exchange.

The majority of the audience sticks around, not an unusual site at Victory Gardens. I clear my throat and begin.

I introduce myself and break the ice with a resonance exercise I have shamelessly borrowed from acclaimed playwright and teacher Steven Dietz, who was one of my professors at the University of Texas in Austin. I start by asking, "So, you're leaving the theater and you get a phone call. And it's from your mom, dad, brother, cousin, best friend—whomever. And they say, 'Hey, I've been trying to get ahold of you, but your phone was off.' And then you say, 'Oh, sorry. I was at Victory Gardens watching this play called *An Issue of Blood*.' And then they say, '*An Issue of Blood*? That's an interesting title. What's it about?'"

I take a breath.

Then I continue, "What do you say? What was this play about? You can shout words and phrases at me."

It doesn't take long before words are shouted in my direction like bricks against glass windows.

"Race."

"Police brutality."

"Pain."

"American legacy."

"History repeating itself."

"Blackness."

"Truth."

And on and on they go. I let this go on for a moment, repeating each word as it's shouted at me so the audience in the back of the house can hear. After a few minutes of this, I push them a little further: "What images, sounds, lines of dialogue, perhaps, are still resonating with you from what you just saw?"

After a brief moment of contemplation, an audience member shouts, "When the police officer pinned the young man to the ground."

"Why or in what ways did that moment resonate for you?" I respond.

"Because it's something that's still happening today," the patron says. A variety of responses from other audience members share similar sentiments, their nodding heads and vocal agreements painfully familiar.

"Good, good," I continue. "Anyone else?"

A subscriber's hand shoots up. "Why are we seeing this play?" they ask. "I see enough of this in the news. I don't come to the theater for this."

I take quick stock of the body language in the room. Many audience members have shifted in their seat by now, paying close attention to how I respond to this. Especially the patrons of color. I cannot continue the discussion until this statement is addressed.

I take a deep breath.

"Now, what we're hearing over here is a sense of oversaturation of police brutality against Black bodies in news outlets and media and entertainment," I said. "What resonances do folks find in that sentiment?"

Instantly, another hand shoots up. As I'd hoped, my reframing of our subscriber's sentiment is a crucial bridge to a new idea. "This is my life every day. It will never be oversaturated for me."

What then transpired was an exchange I had never experienced in a post-show discussion before. As these two patrons engaged in an intense intergenerational conversation centered on race in America, I found myself organically implementing Liz Lerman's Critical Response Process as a navigation tool to guide us in and out of that exchange. CRP requires a neutralized environment in which both artist and audience are equal. With works that center on race, we are entering a dialogue in which artist and audience may hold differing levels of power, socially. We had to establish an antiracist framework first because we did not have a shared language around the themes and topics the art was addressing. It was only then that we could move toward a more equitable conversation around the art. How could we engage in statements of meaning, questions, and then ultimately permissioned opinion if the guided facilitation does not provide equitable access for all participants?

I glance over at playwright Marcus Gardley. There he is, taking notes at furious speed, documenting resonant moments of his own from this discussion that would ultimately inform minor changes he would make prior to opening night the following week. But the thing I remember most was him smiling, inspired by a conversation around race that was asking an audience to push its growing edge to meet the playwright within his creative process.

UNPACKING THE PROCESS

A typical discussion for a work in development using CRP is conducted with the framework that the work presented is still in progress, and the participants may be selected to match the critical response needs of the artist; they are rarely members of the general public, at least in my experience of CRP. At Victory Gardens Theater, preview performances of a new play are very much still a work in progress, but the participants in the conversations that follow are members of the general public (patrons of the theater), with their experience of this post-show facilitation curated to meet the needs of the artist as they continue to work on this new play in process. That curation entails a purposeful adaptation of CRP.

In the course of step one, in which I ask for moments of resonance, I am often on the receiving end of declarations of discomfort or trauma, especially when the work centers on themes of race and racism. An audience's own cultural contexts shaped by their lived experiences greatly inform their interpretation and analysis of live performance, so it is important that with each moment of resonance, the facilitator follow up with a "How or in what ways did that moment resonate with you?" This helps the audience member identify (and articulate) in greater detail the perspective from which their moment of resonance derives. This is a unique divergence from standard CRP, but is important to implement as it is one of the earliest opportunities to neutralize power by assessing where the audience is in order to shape where an audience can go and how that can inform an artist's process.

Additionally, as a typical framework using CRP, the artist is often on stage with the facilitator, as steps two through four ask for a direct conversation to take place between artist and audience. For plays such as this one, to help neutralize power dynamics that might be present between artist and audience when race is involved and to protect the artist from experiencing direct harm by racist statements of meaning or questions fueled by unconscious bias, I have the artist's questions at hand instead, acting as a liaison between the audience and the playwright (who may be absent or unidentified), guiding the conversation to incite the feedback necessary for the artist to move forward in their process. Prior to the discussion, I check in with the artist, asking them if there's anything in particular they want to hear thoughts on or any questions they would like me to ask the audience about their experience. They are still present in the room for the discussion, of course, often sitting in the back of the house while I take this journey on their behalf.

In the context of Marcus Gardley's *An Issue of Blood* and the case study above, an audience member shared a question/moment of meaning by asking, "Why are we seeing this play? I see enough of this in the news. I don't come to the theater for this." Here is a moment of rich complexity involving race and race relations where I, the facilitator, must help the audience unpack this sentiment couched in aversive racism before we can move on in CRP. Through an antiracist framework, the facilitator must be well versed in receiving heated sentiments like this, and then rephrasing them so as to not perpetuate the harm that the statement or question embodies. Then, the facilitator directs that statement of meaning back to the audience so as not to declare their own racial bias or shut down any opportunity for growth.

And that is when I respond with, "Now what we're hearing over here . . ." (this is where I'm saying, "I did not say the following, someone else did") ". . . is a sense of oversaturation . . ." (the word "oversaturation" being a more fluid and positive alternative to what was initially stated) ". . . of police brutality against Black bodies . . ." (stating the thematic resonance explicitly helps an audience understand that the theme itself is not debatable) ". . . in news outlets and media and entertainment" (again, more positive alternatives to allow room for growth). "What resonance do folks find in that sentiment?" (throwing it back to the audience so that the opportunity for learning and growth is not the responsibility of the facilitator, but rather the collective responsibility of all of us, so that we can continue the work we are there to do, which is to help Marcus identify, without bias, what his play is doing, how it's resonating, and how it can still grow).

Lastly, for steps three and four in CRP, much adaptation must occur. Typically, step three carves out space for the audience to ask neutral questions of the artist (not couched in opinion), who then responds. Step four is an opportunity for audiences to offer an opinion of the work if direct permission from the artist is granted. Now, in my experiences working with writers at Victory Gardens, steps three and four remain crucial but are reframed to match the needs of the antiracist framework.

For step three, the audience is still welcome to ask neutral questions of the artist with the artist present in the room (in the case of *An Issue of Blood,* Marcus Gardley remained present for these moments, sitting in the back of the house and listening intensely). But to help protect Marcus from experiencing direct harm from seemingly neutral questions couched in unconscious bias, we allow time to dissect these neutral questions before moving on in the discussion, asking audience members to respond to the intentionality of what is said in the room. For instance: "Where is this question coming from? How does that resonate with you and why? What do others think?" and so on. This allows Marcus to hear feedback from the audience in a protected way while allowing the audience to engage with one another, and myself, about the questions that may arise from the work.

It is important for the facilitator to be watching for questions that, even if intended neutrally, are based on culturally privileged assumptions and internalized misconceptions of who the people onstage are and how they function. The experience of one narrative does not apply to all and, unfortunately, when responding to work centering on the experiences of people of color, questions from audiences may reflect a lack of cultural context. Seemingly neutral questions, though well-intended, may come from a place of assumption and stereotype and not from a place of deep understanding of who these characters are in the context of their social circumstances.

But then, of course, there are actual neutral questions introduced in the discussion, in which case the playwright, the director, and the dramaturge will assess afterward to identify whether or not those questions inform any necessary rewrites, clarity in direction, or are questions the artist wants the audience to walk away with.

Step four of CRP is complex in circumstances like these. It is challenging to divorce the social location of the participants in the room with the opinions they may offer in the final part of CRP; what does it mean for a White audience member to offer an opinion on the experiences of Black characters? How might an artist of color be receptive to opinions from White audience members, when the artist is not sure of the intentionality of the opinion offered? It's not until power in the space is neutralized through direct interrogation in steps one through three that permissioned opinion can occur. Given most time frames of post-show discussions, it is not often that we even reach permissioned opinion, and there are many instances in which the artist has expressed explicitly that they are not interested in that, which is absolutely okay. The adaptation of CRP in this context includes, at times, not including steps when they are not of use.

CONCLUSION

Here's the thing: Racist statements are made in post-show discussions all the time. When an artist of color is trying something new that might feel unfamiliar to an audience that is largely upper-middle class, over the age of fifty, and White, offensive comments or questions will undoubtedly make their way into the discussion. And more often than not, most facilitators shy away from this discomfort.

Through this case study, I am calling my fellow gatekeepers in the development of new work to claim the responsibility needed in order to sit in this discomfort long enough to ensure that power is neutralized and an artist's intent is more closely identifiable to an audience before moving forward in the Critical Response Process. The intention of CRP is not to absolve discomfort, but to help artist and audience navigate it and partner it. And as facilitator, we are encountering our own discomfort rather than skirting around it, our anxiety in post-show facilitation used as a bridge between ideas and ideologies. This is Civic Dramaturgy: a conducting of dramaturgical practices through a sociopolitical framework. And in this particular case, an antiracist one.

It goes without saying that the Critical Response Process, in all its incredible significance, will still be flawed in practice when uncritically applied with a false expectation of equal social power between a given artist and audience. Without thoughtful adaptation and firm, sensitive facilitation, it potentially puts the artist at risk of experiencing harm that might ultimately stifle a creative process.

But what might happen if we used that same process as a tool to dismantle racism? What might happen if we adapt those steps to address potentially problematic statements in the room, as they're spoken? What might happen if the Critical Response Process functioned as a tool for antiracism for both artist and audience?

I guess you'll have to try it out and see for yourself.

THE CRITICAL RESPONSE PROCESS: AESTHETICS OF TIME

Cristóbal Martínez

Contextualized within the increasing velocity of capitalism, this essay considers the potential implications of time in the Critical Response Process, and recommends considerations of time and place that are informed by an indigenous knowledge systems approach to knowing and being. As a critical pedagogy CRP emphasizes certain sociopolitical protocols and rhetoric[1] designed to catalyze peer relationships and discourses required for generative critiques of creative productions. Typically scaled to meet the cultural expectations of its participants within today's fast-paced world, CRP is subject to the metaphor "time is money." To problematize ideas of time embodied by this metaphor, I will argue that CRP is most productive when it is understood as a sacred conversation that transcends the aesthetic of time-space as commodity. To do this CRP must constitute the experience of a ceremony where there is a high consciousness and well-considered set of ethics associated to the power of context, listening, and speaking. In the future, I envision the development of CRP as a knowledge exchange facilitated by a patient aesthetic of time, and adapted to the various lands on which it is situated.

This essay extends the potential of CRP in part by offering considerations for the role of the time-space process as embodied in Resolana, an indigenous mestizo ceremony of northern New Mexico. Applying a definition by indigenous knowledge scholar Bryan McKinley Jones Brayboy, the term "aesthetics" refers to what a people believe to be good, beautiful, and true. A people's aesthetics are largely grounded by Discourse with a capital "D." In addition to language and grammar, Big "D" Discourses are combinations of saying, doing, being, and believing in a given context (Gee 2015).

An aesthetic of time defined by patience matters if a pedagogical process is going to benefit from an indigenous research methods approach emphasizing the importance of relationships, respect, reciprocity, and responsibility (Brayboy et al. 2012). In the aesthetic perception of some indigenous peoples, it takes patience and longer durations of practice to embody, enact, and achieve these four Rs. In the spirit of connected-knowledge, I am offering this chapter as a mestizo artist-scholar with the intention to proliferate CRP with an indigenous worldview, specifically that with which I grew up. I believe that such an offering strengthens CRP as a tool for thinking transparently, complexly, and responsibly about the things we, as individuals and groups, create and maintain in our world. To achieve accountability and complexity in the Western Hemisphere, such a process must aspire in good faith to connect with indigenous worldviews, since CRP is often facilitated on the lands of our hemisphere's indigenous peoples. (I often wonder how my vision of CRP might be useful to indigenous youth who are commonly expected to connect the dots between worlds.[2])

Connected-knowledge as part of the CRP ethos is vital, since it addresses varying levels of literacy, including arts literacies within the greater public. Where artistic education is lacking, it responds with the opportunity to participate in a critique that is also a pedagogy for the public decoding, comprehension, and oratory of art. This is an important framing as social and political attitudes toward education and intellectualism advance in ways that undermine literacy, and include the US government's defunding of the arts.

CRP AND CEREMONY

While complex, the Critical Response Process can be understood as a social gathering for providing critical feedback about some sort of creative production by an individual or collective. In such a gathering, an artist, such as a painter, might *go public* with a work of art through CRP. This may be a work in progress or something that is already on exhibition. In CRP, a "public" is assembled and organized via several protocols or rules of play for providing generative critical feedback for the creative process and/or production under consideration.

An act of "going public" requires one to face the intended and unintended consequences of one's actions by eliciting responses from an organized group of people. Operationalizing the public requires rhetorical ceremony—a persuasive oratory or demonstration of an idea to a body politic, further ritualized with protocols that potentially offer up the idea for public discussion. We can observe these kinds of ceremonies throughout the world in diverse forms of expression that range across many peoples and cultures.

Important outcomes that help define this type of ceremony include exchanging knowledge, recovering knowledge, generating knowledge, or deliberation/consensus-building across complexity. During CRP, these outcomes of rhetorical and political[3] ceremony may play out as an individual or group receives a public's critical feedback. CRP, at the same time and upon the permission of the creator, is the organized public's forum to issue a critique. CRP understands that knowledge is political, and, to elicit generative feedback, it is structured for deliberative knowledge production. For CRP to be generative as a social gathering, it requires participants, regardless of perspective, to respect a mediated set of prescriptive protocols for how to participate in ways that concern uses of language.

"Rules of play" describes the conventions of CRP because its protocols are refereed, just as in a game of soccer. Game theorist Katie Salen argues that games are an invitation and social contract (Salen and Zimmerman 2004), meaning that those invited to participate must abide by the rules so the game may function in a way that is productive and just. This type of facilitative and deliberative framework also appears to characterize CRP.

In CRP the contract is laid out and stewarded by a referee called the facilitator in a keeping of the ceremony, similar to how a judge interprets what is permissible in a court of law. The difference here is that a game of soccer and courtroom justice reflect a zero-sum game of winners and losers, whereas with creative output in the arts, sciences, and humanities, life is much more complicated.

Often acts of creativity arrive not at winning or losing, but at aesthetic-discursive consequences that are more intricate than binaries. In cases of abstraction and complexity, understanding and seeing require an art of listening and speaking, such as that which CRP potentially holds within the context of an indigenous aesthetic of time.

While the words "ritual" and "ceremony" may offer interesting ways to think about CRP, it is important to note that these words have been overspent with connotations of religion, primitivism, the supernatural, magic, or New Age spirituality. Less often do people think of pragmatism, but it is precisely this notion that inspires me to frame CRP as ceremony. CRP's pragmatism achieves clarity through language and discourse, within a context of "going public," and public critique.

To return to games as a reference point, an example of a ceremony can be baseball, with certain rituals that a baseball player might conduct before, during, and after a game in order to bring about clarity, focus, and success. An example of an in-game ritual is the high five for a teammate as he walks into the dugout after having scored a home run. Baseball fans ritualize the sport with body paint, team apparel, unison chants from the stands, prayers, and, as with the players, certain protocols for acceptable behavior. Disrespecting protocols means disrespecting the game, and this can lead to a consequence such as getting ejected from the park.

When I think about baseball as ceremony, I think about neoliberal capitalism and the exchange of money for commodities as an epic globalizing ceremony. I also think about neoliberal capitalism as ceremony for the disciplining of bodies and the structuring of society, which is what ritual practices do. I participate when I go to the game and visit the team shop to buy a jersey with the team logo, making me feel a part of a group when I wear it alongside other fans at the home field of my team. More than a utility for covering the body, the jersey becomes a fast and furious fetish for belonging and acquiring certain privileges both within a city and at the ballpark.

We participate in ceremonies because they transform the world and us. For transformation of thoughts, feelings, and expectations to occur, we share and receive knowledge. Through an indigenous worldview, transformation occurs not through knowledge for knowledge's sake, but for the purposes of life, living, and stewardship. All acts of recovering, generating, sharing, and connecting knowledge are sacred. Since knowledge is power, it is imperative to human survival that we steward our knowledge with great reverence and respect. It remains to be seen whether or not various peoples respect the sanctity of knowledge, especially when considering context and the stewarding of land. In the neoliberal context, where people attempt to engineer society through capitalism, the sanctity of knowledge is almost never respected, but is mostly usurped to serve the logics of frenetic and irrational market systems.

I would like to propose that the Critical Response Process is a ceremony, but one that differs from sports and justice systems in that the purpose of CRP is not winning or losing. Instead it is a ceremony designed to facilitate nuanced and complex meanings about creative phenomena, while resisting simplicity.

If CRP resists oversimplified models of aesthetic truth, notions of time must be considered as integral to its protocols. In today's fast capitalism,[4] which infuses itself into all aspects of contemporary life, the key value or aesthetic of time is frenetic at best. I imagine CRP short-circuiting this ontology by reimagining new stretched aesthetics of time. I am proposing that for a practice of CRP, we make a good faith effort toward patience and low speed. Patience, as opposed to instant resolution, is a pragmatic choice toward care in learning, teaching, and understanding, which, according to human experience, are processes that require time so that we may be thoughtful and artful in our communicative approach with one another. I am suggesting that CRP strive toward relationship with knowledge during ceremony that transcends the aesthetics of fast capitalism. This proposition is so that all who gather may bless, dignify, and humanize each other (Martínez 2018).

RESOLANAS AND THE CRITICAL RESPONSE PROCESS

My thinking about time and ceremony in relationship to the Critical Response Process derives more from my place of origin than from my work as an artist or scholar. I am from Alcalde, New Mexico, located in the Upper Rio Grande Valley. Not too far north of Alcalde, my mother was born in a place called Embudo, New Mexico, and grew up in the nearby village named Dixon. As a child I often visited and stayed with my grandparents in Dixon. When I was a child, mestizos of Genizaro, Pueblo, Manito, and Chicano heritages comprised most of the population of this small village.

All geographies contain ways of knowing that define place. One such way of knowing is a cultural practice called Resolana. Both a place and a process, Resolana is a dialogical ceremony rooted in my mother's pueblo, and throughout northern New Mexico. Resolanas have numerous roles in the traditional societies of New Mexico, such as diplomacy and cooperative consensus-building for the equitable distribution of water in a high desert region. It is through the lens of Resolana that I have grown interested in thinking about the Critical Response Process. For clarity, I am not inviting CRP into Resolana or any indigenous ceremony, but I am challenging CRP to consider a philosophical underpinning of time that often circulates in the presence of indigenous knowledge systems. My concerns and interests specifically lie in terms of CRP's rhetorical power and potential to rest within the continuum of being harmful and productive.

From my perspective, much of CRP's potential is centered in the aesthetics of time, and how we choose to locate and perform these aesthetics when we approach each other with feedback, as well as how we choose to view ourselves and our relationships to each other within moments of human communication. From the perspective of *Speed and Politics* theorist Paul Virilio, the accelerating aesthetic of time may very well be one of the greatest crises of the emerging present. His theory of speed, in the context of "Emergency," can be applied to suggest that in today's status quo the synergies between money, politics, and technology have increased the velocity of processes well beyond our human cognitive capacities to keep up (2006). In other words, the systems we have developed outpace our ability to make thoughtful decisions. Indigenous elders in the United States have also been talking about this for several hundred years of colonization.

An implication of these observations by some indigenous elders is that we don't take enough time to enter into patient and meaningful relationships with each other. Instead of being accountable to each other, we monetize our relationships in order to accelerate today's neoliberal market logics. This might be the reason why, during CRP, someone is almost always thinking about the clock—or at least feeling uneasy with how long the Process is taking. Even if there were a CRP gathering where all participants were able to remove themselves from the "time is money" metaphor, it would remain inherent to the experience, since CRP contains no protocol that mitigates it. Nor has training, in my experience, addressed how time is implicated in whether CRP can be successful in contexts of diplomacy where the outcomes are extremely consequential for many people.

Our world today moves so fast, in fact, that we rely on technologies to make accelerated decisions on our behalf. We have even created abbreviated language through applications like instant messaging simply because face-to-face and phone conversations have become inconvenient and require too much accountability for speed. Perhaps CRP might mitigate the crisis of speed by repositioning the metaphor "time is money" to one that sounds more like "time is knowledge," where knowledge is framed by patience, love, and care.

Traveling further into the aesthetics of time, place, and land, a consideration of Resolana will prompt some new knowledge, including implications for the Critical Response Process. Surviving from colonial dialects of archaic Spanish due to the historic isolation of northern New Mexico, the word "Resolana" means "under the glare of the sun," or "place where sunlight hits." According to the late Chicano scholar Tomás Atencio, Resolanas are outdoor places along adobe structures that receive direct sunlight. In pueblos and villages, community members gather at these spaces during the winter months for warmth and protection from the cold (Atencio et al. 2009). These spaces vary with differing architectural settings, but what remains consistent is the quality of the light in these spaces, and the heat that emanates from the sun in combination with the heat from the adobes warmed by the sun. When gathered together within these spaces of warmth that are locally perceived as beautiful, northern New Mexicans often reflect upon community issues through impromptu ceremonial dialogues. Although these gatherings are referred to by a Spanish name, they are the legacy of mestizaje in the region.

Social scientist Miguel Montiel, Atencio's colleague, often speaks about Resolanas as a metaphor for awareness or coming into consciousness, for illuminating knowledge or "shedding light upon a subject" (Martínez and Montiel). This metaphor articulates ideas about a place and process for learning communities where serious discussions about significant matters are encouraged. More traditionally, Resolana refers to the physical cultural space, community gathering, and processes of discourse. The ceremony of Resolana is emerging from a long-view history of time and cumulative knowledge to foster meaningful experiences that are co-determined by participants, and generate community knowledge and awareness through reflection and sharing.

Beyond the scholarly perspective, a Resolana is a place where people care for one another. It is a place where co-intentional free associative oratory is expressed across the members of a community. This oratory is patient and thoughtful, never conscious of "time as money," and always aware of physical context. Resolanas never acknowledge an agenda, but instead honor language as a randomly determined phenomenon during which knowledge and ideas emerge via the mediation of time and place.

Traditional Resolanas never begin with an agreed upon topic for discussion. Instead people gather as a collective to listen and finish each other's statements through speech, gesture, silence, and stillness—and in the presence of humor and intense listening/contemplation. It is through a prolonged, chance-based, co-intentional, and repetitive assemblage of sociocognitive oratory that shared knowledge circulates within the Resolana. This shared knowledge represents group consensus and resolution in the ceremony.

In a Resolana, hours can pass and no one will look at the time. Having transferred knowledge, people will reenter the world from a Resolana simply when it collectively feels right. This feeling is unspoken, but wholly known. For a Resolana the land mediates the group's relationships to each other and is the place from which protocols were received. Through land, in the context of northern New Mexican indigenous agrarian societies, time is a slow, patient, caring, and transformative aesthetic that facilitates balanced relationships that depend on stability, endurance, and interdependence. This aesthetic was once necessary for survival, and many indigenous peoples continue to believe it is the only sustainable lifeway for our future.

Resolanas are similar to CRP, but not the same. Both are gatherings of the public and are structured by protocols for knowledge recovery, creation, and exchange—though in a Resolana, protocols are not stewarded by a referee. As a participant, a Resolanero/a comes into a relationship with unspoken protocols through lifelong experiential acquisition that occurs by learning-while-watching and learning-while-doing pedagogies, allowing the ceremony to drift and flow somewhere in time. In contrast to Resolanas, which are collective dialogues with no premeditation or specific goal, CRP has an agenda to provide feedback to a group or individual. Despite these contrasts, as social ceremony governed by protocols, Resolanas and CRP are both quests to understand the world. This overlap points to certain indigenous ideas that might benefit CRP.

Within the world, the creative processes of art and science require a high degree of ethics, which today often appear absent. The outcomes of human creativity have led to earth-changing ecological effects and caused unprecedented stress and suffering of all species of life on our planet. In the midst of the negative consequences of human creativity, the artist and scientist are vulnerable by nature of their reciprocal status with the public. The public is made vulnerable by the creative output of artists and scientists, while the public's critique also renders creative actors vulnerable.

The relationship between creative knowledge-producers and the public exists in a political state of emergence, and needs time if it is to be constructive, diplomatic, reflexive, and reflective.

Resolanas, along with many indigenous dialogical ceremonies, inform us that without a patient aesthetic of time, CRP can become subject to malpractices. Fast capitalism has led to miscalculations and misunderstandings not emblematic of respect, reciprocity, relationships, and responsibility. In our high-speed world, we are experiencing severe unintended consequences, where, as the earth warms and rivers dry,[5] our communications knowledge systems are deteriorating. In terms of communication, many languages are going extinct, and contemporary politics, media, and online anonymity are betraying the stability of language itself.

With a certain fast-capitalistic aesthetic of time, CRP can become commoditized and, as commodities often do, produce disassociations, bad health, and landfill. CRP must be careful, and may be particularly vulnerable because of its nonplace status—irreverent to land and the sovereignty of context[6]—as it becomes further entrenched as a global phenomenon.[7] My assessment of CRP as a potential nonplace in this essay is specifically an indigenous critique, stemming from my perception that the current state of CRP does not legibly connect to the given biomes in which it finds itself situated. In other words, in CRP relationships do not appear to be mediated by the land.

An indigenous worldview might argue that people cannot be accountable to one another in a social ceremonial gathering without knowledge and acknowledgment of the land underneath their feet. Without this level of accountability within all aspects of creativity, an indigenous person might ask: without stewardship of land, memory, and context, how can we be truly respectful of one another?

RELATIONSHIPS, TRUST, DIPLOMACY, AND TIME

The Critical Response Process is a gathering that relies on the power of trust. Because of the political nature of language and knowledge, much of the Process is about building trust within an organized public, where all participants, guided by a facilitator, must respect a prescribed level of diplomacy. If the Process is artfully conducted, a person receiving feedback will likely be more willing than not to listen to the voices of a public, and members of a public more comfortable with sharing their perspectives. This reciprocity in giving and receiving is likely to take place with the greatest level of generosity in the presence of trust.[8]

CRP was originally created as a way to structure critiques so that feedback is vetted with care, meaning that both artists and members of the critical public have agency by carefully considering, reflectively and reflexively, the nature of their rhetorical expressions when asking questions, providing feedback, presenting ideas, and listening. To me this means that all verbal interactions require justification, according to certain philosophical criteria, for CRP to be productive in accordance with certain values and politics of what is believed to be "useful feedback."

Permitting an external, speedy aesthetic of time to imbue a system of care, which requires a high level of trust and thoughtfulness, is antithetical within many indigenous aesthetics of time. Watching the clock or keeping track of time only breaks the ceremony, or prevents it from transcending fast capitalism. Meaningful relationships based on love and care are unlikely to thrive within the conditions of high speed.[9] I personally struggle with this issue every day when I communicate with my family, friends, and students.

In CRP an aesthetic of time must be defined, valued, and protected. It is difficult for a ceremony's values of time to transcend fast capitalism, if the ceremony has no connections to place (or more specifically, no connection to land). Perhaps CRP can turn to place-contextualized Resolanas for inspiration on how to reimagine itself outside the neoliberal paradigm. Resolanas show us that rhetorical spaces have the potential to be place-based. In Resolana, it is the context of land that yields a patient aesthetic of time.[10]

CRP entrenches itself as an instrument of fast capitalism in cases when it is solely positioned to discipline rhetoric and bodies to monetize knowledge. In these instances CRP is positioned to create instrumental relationships for a type of resource extraction. For CRP to aspire to the goal of becoming more socially and culturally responsible, I recommend that the critique no longer become the means to an end, but instead that critique itself serve the purpose for building strong relationships. If CRP were to meet this vision, like Resolanas, its applications have to resemble a people responding to the various lands, contexts, histories, and politics they gather in. To support this shift, critiques must become the catalyzing mechanism for the creation of publics founded upon the four Rs. I also envision CRP as using critiques as a catalyst for building publics that are based on caring, compassion, empathy, and love. If learning communities exist for the purpose of loving and caring for each other, connected-knowledge will flow in abundance.

HONORING TIME IN CRP: A CONCLUSION AND POTENTIAL DIRECTIVE

In our contemporary society, time is never on our side. Communication systems demand our attentions from so many different directions. Speed is frenetic. Tools, language, and ideas are misused every day against the earth's ecosystems as an outcome of human desire and fear. Powerful ideas can lead to intentional and unforeseeable disastrous outcomes, which I have often personally witnessed in art critiques that are not well structured. Critiques devolve into anger, resentment, frustration, insecurities, subjugation, inequitable power, weaponized rhetoric, and miscalculated inaccuracies falsely presented as knowledge. These are many of the same outcomes that we see replicated today through capitalism and politics.

I believe that CRP is justified in its original intention to fill the pedagogical gap for facilitating diplomatic, productive, and useful critiques. CRP is a strong idea, but, like everything, it is vulnerable to the whims of capitalism. Despite these susceptibilities, I also believe CRP can, like some art, resist simplicity and achieve much more than originally intended. But for this to happen, I would like to encourage all who practice CRP to turn toward a higher-level moral and ethical accountability to make the ceremonial gathering more than just about generating feedback loops that are governed by people's limited availability (fast capitalism's aesthetic of time). Let's use CRP as an excuse to generate, recover, and connect knowledge—not merely for knowing or applying knowledge, but for the extended purpose of catalyzing the creation of publics based upon the importance of relationships, respect, reciprocity, and responsibility in relationship to land and the sovereignty of its historical and emergent contexts. These things take time, commitment, and diligence.

NOTES

1. Forms of persuasive language are often used within a sociopolitical scenario. CRP represents such a scenario, as it is an organized social gathering meant to accomplish a certain kind of work that in the arts is called a critique.

2. It is not uncommon for indigenous youth in the United States to be encouraged by their communities to seek educations. This is often with the expectation that youth will use the Western and indigenous knowledge that they acquire along the way in order to help strengthen indigenous self-determination and sovereignty.

3. In this essay I use the term "political" to refer to ideas, which are always contested, and I use the term "rhetorical" to signify the use of careful listening and generative language for diplomatic communication.

4. Fast capitalism is mediated by high-speed communications systems that are globally networked. This capitalism responds to a society whose expectations of real-time capitalism are disciplined by speedy communications networks that outpace the human ability for decision-making—thus computer automation provides the assistance we require.

5. As of 2020, the southwestern United States has been suffering a mega-drought, during which the water in aquifers located in northern New Mexico have not been significantly replenished in relationship to the water being drawn. Additionally, the Rio Grande is drying up.

6. In 2015, poet Roberto Bedoya delivered a keynote address at a symposium at the Mexican Consulate in Douglas, Arizona, to mark Postcommodity's installation of *Repellent Fence / Valla Repellent*, asserting that in order for us to respect the land, we must know its history, and that we must not subjugate or simplify history.

7. Depending on how CRP is framed, it may lack the guidance of a land-based cumulative memory that defines a sense of place and requires a responsibility to place.

8. The following statements represent an interesting and humorous paradox I would like to offer, considering the context of my advocacy for CRP to adopt a slower and more patient aesthetic of time. The maxim "trust must be earned" takes time and patience. Trust has value because it takes time to achieve because "time is money."

9. CRP may produce anxieties for a participant about how they are perceived by others. Although CRP works to mitigate competitive or zero-sum game rhetorics during its structured critiques, actors within CRP will focus a great deal of energy on what they want to say; the anxieties of feeling socially pressured to say something; weighing the social consequences of their statements; or the desire to be heard when time is limited, that there may not be an equitable amount of energy given to reflective, reflexive, and focused listening within the Process. These arguments beg the following questions: What are the values and protocols for listening in CRP? What is the role of silence in CRP? Here's a rhetorical question: Should we time listening and silence?

10. From my perspective, it is unfortunate that the classic pedagogical model of a nonplace is the school classroom. My belief is that CRP's

intention is to emerge beyond the pedagogical models of schooling to create something more effectively transformative. One set of education theories suggests that schools are mostly pathways for organizing society into labor pipelines (Gee 2015).

REFERENCES

Bedoya, Roberto. "Sovereignty of Context." Repellent Fence / Valla Repelente Symposium. October 2015, Mexican Consulate, Douglas, AZ.

Brayboy, Bryan McKinley Jones, Heather R. Gough, Beth Leonard, Roy F. Roehl II, and Jessica A. Solyom. "Reclaiming Scholarship: Critical Indigenous Research Methodologies," in *Qualitative Research: An Introduction to Methods and Designs*, edited by Stephen D. Lapan, MaryLynn T. Quartaroli, and Frances J. Riemer, 423–50 (San Francisco: Jossey-Bass, 2012).

Gee, James Paul. *Social Linguistics and Literacies: Ideology in Discourses*, Fifth Edition (London: Routledge, 2015).

Martínez, Cristóbal. "Art is Tecpatl, A Flint Knife Tongue." Visiting Artist Lecture Series 13, February 2018, Kresge Theatre, Carnegie Mellon University, Pittsburgh, PA.

Martínez, Cristóbal, and Miguel Montiel. Transborder Practicum: Resolana, Arizona State University undergraduate class. Spring 2010.

Montiel, Miguel, Tomás Atencio, and E. A. "Tony" Mares. *Resolana: Emerging Chicano Dialogues on Community and Globalization* (Tucson: University of Arizona Press, 2009).

Salen, Katie, and Eric Zimmerman. *Rules of Play: Game Design Fundamentals* (Cambridge, MA: The MIT Press, 2004).

Virilio, Paul. *Speed and Politics*. Translated by Mark Polizzotti (Los Angeles: Semiotext(e), 2006).

Closing Ritual

Liz Lerman

My move to the Southwest in 2016 brought me into contact with people and land that I have come to love. The enduring contrasts of this amazing world with its deep blue sky, large stretches of dirt and sand, the compelling display of chaotic beauty in the shapes of the plants, and the always present sense of spirit. I feel lucky to have been invited and fortunate to make it home for a while.

I say "for a while" because I am a nomad. I come from a people who are nomads. My awareness of this has been a part of a long, slow conversation that I have been having with Cristóbal Martínez, whose preceding essay is the final guest entry in our book. Cristóbal and I met when I first moved to Arizona, and his ideas and worldview have been a consequential influence in my life. In naming the Critical Response Process as ceremony and reflecting on it as a form of ritual, he has enlivened some previously latent perceptions about the Process. Cristóbal's contribution to the book and his conversations with me have made me "suddenly" aware of why ritual matters in contemporary life, and how thinking of CRP as a form of ritual might also help us understand the ongoing resourcefulness of the Process itself.

Perhaps because I was raised in a Reform Jewish home, the aspect of ritual within religion was downplayed. It's not that we didn't have it. Rather, I think, my father in his growing-up years had experienced most forms of ritual as a kind of false piety or as a reason to withdraw from the world and the urgent issues of the day. Activism was his declared form of Jewish life, and thus the rituals borne out in our family were of a social justice nature. We also practiced certain traditions that reflected my parents' values. For example, we were expected to be at Friday night family dinners before going out and socializing. Staying home from school on the High Holidays was another. And he loved performing full-on Seders at Passover with plenty of non-Jewish guests so that he could tell the story of freedom in his own manner. For my mother, who had given up on most things Jewish, spring cleaning was her form of preparation for Passover, a way, she said, of following the rules on her own terms. It would be years before I could understand that she had taken the idea of ritual and completely remade it to fit her needs and her will. I loved her for this quiet rebellion and her way of reclaiming meaning by mashing unlikely things together.

For the longest time, I thought of the word "ritual" only in relation to religion. Slowly, though, I began to think of it as a way to characterize certain repetitive habits that served me by helping me achieve something of personal meaning. For example, in one period of my performing life I had forms of preparation that I see now were quite ritualistic. On the day of a performance I would sit with a piece of paper and pencil, close my eyes, imagine my part, and draw a line on the paper, picturing every second in an exercise that was both calming and decisive. Or just before every single performance, I brought my mother to mind and placed her in the audience, long after she had departed this earth.

So I had ritual in my life, even as I was developing and building CRP as a practice. But despite these ongoing acts of ceremony, it would be a long time before I understood or saw the value in perceiving the Process in this manner.

Ritual functions in many ways. And as I began to more carefully examine its presence in my own life I began to also understand that by naming it we might be able to more fully harvest its gifts. I noticed that it served different valuable functions. When I placed a small china doll on my shelf with care, the act was giving me a chance to remember my mother and her women friends who gave this token to me just before my younger brother's birth. In one tiny gesture I was able to bring to mind so much history, pain, and love. When I carve out a full day to prepare for a holiday meal, I am claiming time, our most rare commodity, and putting it to use for something that stands apart from the rest of everyday life. I am making space for people, stories, and the repetition of memory as I attempt to separate my mind, imagination, and body from the urgency of normal living. I can see in these two small acts that I am transformed by doing the ritual. In fact, it is the transformation I seek.

I can recognize from this vantage point that the Critical Response Process does the same. We sit in a circle. Each step prepares us for the next. The accumulation of knowledge, ideas, and shared recognition of our journey contributes to a sense of purpose, which is essential to the ritual and one of its outcomes. In the midst of this, we can observe that CRP enacts an idea of critique as generative and a nourishing way to experience daily life. We judge, and we are judged. No one is exempt. Seen in this light, CRP is a ritual that both allows for critique in different phases of our lives, and gives us a way to preserve the time and place and company to make it happen.

Each of the steps of CRP calls for some mental preparation. If participants think of the whole session as a kind of ritual of openness, one can see again how each step aides them in sustaining the space of curiosity, generosity, and discovery. The act of filtering out the negative in step one, the active form of listening in step two, the transformation of opinion to inquiry in step three, and the formality of the permissioned opinion in step four each provide a protocol that mirrors ritual. Paying attention to doing it well generates a better outcome and reenergizes the artist and responder alike in comprehending the amazing capacity of people's creativity.

In my teaching during the Covid-19 pandemic, I found so many of my students bringing their personal lives into the work they were doing. Given the opportunity, for example, to apply the creative tools I was sharing to a current project, many started out with ideas for their degree capstone work or their master's thesis, but the further we got into the semester the more they moved to personal subject matter. In response, I consistently asked them to consider the relationship between artmaking, symbol making, performance, and ritual. This was surprising to some who had been raised in secular homes, and it was surprising for those coming from religious settings to hear the word "ritual" in a public university. But then I mentioned CRP, which is a through line in my courses, and they softened and began to see possibility. Yes to repetition. Yes to saying, "While I do this . . . I mean to be addressing that." But mostly I think the invocation of CRP as ritual gave them permission to be publicly human, by which I mean to be imperfect.

CRP actually asks us to be that. To let the flaws, the early thinking, the messy potential show, and not only to show, but also to receive others' commentary. Somehow this openness and vulnerability leads to relief, discovery, and even joy. That seems like good ritual to me.

I think ritual is ultimately an attempt to codify some kind of transformative act. Or if not the act itself, then a hoped-for outcome if one repeats the practice. This is why CRP as a whole and in its parts can be seen as ritual. As my coauthor John has often said, it's not just the work of art that is in process; our opinions are in process as well. And that can be as wondrous as any spiritual act. Staying open to influence, regarding our ideas as moving and shifting rather than locked in, and finding a regular reciprocal way of moving through what might be a challenging situation is where we hope the ritual asserts its power to hold us to our work at hand.

People are always asking me about how to do CRP faster. I've learned from Cristóbal to say: "No . . . do it slower, it's not transactional. It is ceremony. It is human. It is relational." When I pass this idea on to people, the same thing happens every time. They settle into their seats as if they are preparing for a really good story (they are, actually, because CRP sessions are full of story). And they take a breath.

There is a story I have been telling myself. I once caught it on a science podcast I was listening to while I was driving: Our earth used to spin faster. But once we got a moon, we slowed down.

So I like to remind people: get a moon, and settle in for the ceremony.

ABOUT THE AUTHORS AND CONTRIBUTORS

Liz Lerman is a choreographer, performer, writer, educator, and speaker, and the recipient of honors including a 2002 MacArthur "Genius Grant" and a 2017 Jacob's Pillow Dance Award. Key to her artistry is opening her process to various publics, resulting in research and outcomes that are participatory, urgent, and usable. She founded Dance Exchange in 1976 and led the organization until 2011. Her recent work *Healing Wars* toured the United States. Liz teaches Critical Response Process, creative research, the intersection of art and science, and the building of narrative within dance at institutions such as Harvard, Yale School of Drama, and Guildhall School of Music and Drama. Her previous book was *Hiking the Horizontal: Field Notes from a Choreographer* (Wesleyan University Press, 2014). She has been an Institute Professor at Arizona State University since 2016.

John Borstel is a maker, writer, and facilitator of experiences in critique and learning whose award-winning artistic work combines imagery, performance, and text. On the administrative staff of Liz Lerman Dance Exchange from 1993 to 2015, he coordinated numerous projects in documentation, communication, and evaluation, reflecting the stage and community work of this innovative performance company. Coauthor and illustrator of *Liz Lerman's Critical Response Process* (2003), John has traveled widely to teach and facilitate this unique feedback system. As project advisor and director of CRP Certification for Liz Lerman LLC, he continues to collaborate with Lerman on online, education, and writing projects. John's writing on the arts has appeared in *Youth Drama Ireland, Generations, Parterre Box,* and multiple projects for Animating Democracy. John holds a BA in English from Georgetown University and an MFA in interdisciplinary arts from Goddard College.

Bimbola Akinbola is an assistant professor in the department of Performance Studies at Northwestern University. Dr. Akinbola has been collaborating with Dance Exchange since 2012 and has contributed to several movement-based projects exploring racism, memory, and historical erasure with communities across the country. She is currently at work on her first book manuscript, which examines the creative work of contemporary Nigerian diasporic women artists whose work, she argues, strategically utilizes disbelonging as a critical tool and strategy for queer worldmaking.

Mark Callahan is the artistic director of Ideas for Creative Exploration, an interdisciplinary initiative for advanced research in the arts at the University of Georgia, and serves on the faculty of the Lamar Dodd School of Art.

Founder of American Lyric Theater (ALT), and artistic and general director of Opera Saratoga, director and dramaturge **Lawrence Edelson** is a ceaseless advocate for emerging artists. Edelson studied voice and musicology at the University of Ottawa and holds degrees in Directing and Arts Administration from New York University. At ALT, he created the first full-time program in the country to mentor opera composers and librettists. He is nationally consulted on best practices in developing new operas.

Isaac Gómez is an award-winning playwright and television writer originally from El Paso, Texas/Ciudad Juárez, Mexico. His plays include *La Ruta* (Steppenwolf), *the way she spoke* (Audible Theater), and *I Am Not Your Perfect Mexican Daughter* (Steppenwolf), among others. He is under commission with Alley Theatre, South Coast Repertory, and Denver Center for the Performing Arts. His television writing credits include *Narcos: Mexico* on Netflix. He was also a proud member of the pilot certification cohort for Liz Lerman's Critical Response Process.

Lekelia "Kiki" Jenkins is associate professor at Arizona State University in the School for the Future of Innovation in Society. She is an award-winning scientist, dancer, and choreographer. She earned a PhD in marine conservation from Duke University. Her research includes the human dimensions of solutions for sustainable fisheries, the use of dance as a form of science engagement, and active learning—including music and movement—to reform collegiate STEM education.

Elizabeth Johnson Levine (EJ) is a socially engaged choreographer and facilitator. Johnson connects communities through choreography, creating dance that promotes civic dialogue and designing participatory experiences that apply artistic practices in multiple contexts. She has practiced the Critical Response Process since beginning with Dance Exchange in 1998, and is currently a certified CRP trainer with particular expertise in using the Process with teenagers and investigating applications of CRP as a trauma-informed practice.

Carlos Lopez-Real is a saxophonist, composer, coach, educator, and senior fellow of the Higher Education Academy. Since 2005 he has taught at the Guildhall School, founding the BA in Performance & Creative Enterprise program and leading the PGCert in Performance Teaching, playing a key role in developing collaborative and transformative teaching and learning approaches. He has recorded and toured extensively, composed music for silent film, curated several club venues, and in 2007 he founded the E17Jazz Collective.

Cristóbal Martínez is an artist and publishing scholar in interdisciplinary liberal arts and sciences. He is a member of the indigenous artist collective Postcommodity, and founded the artist-hacker performance ensemble Radio Healer. As an artist and scholar, Martínez positions metaphors to mediate complications within sites of dromological, spatial, social, cultural, political, ecological, and economic anxiety. Within these locations, Martínez often aestheticizes complexity to engage publics in co-intentional generative inquiry and deliberation for recovering and connecting knowledge.

Gesel Mason is artistic director for Gesel Mason Performance Projects and associate professor of dance at University of Texas at Austin. She was a member of Liz Lerman Dance Exchange and Ralph Lemon/Cross Performance Projects. Over fifteen years in the making, Mason's solo performance and digital archival project, *NO BOUNDARIES: Dancing the Visions of Contemporary Black Choreographers*, features work by Kyle Abraham, Rennie Harris, Donald McKayle, Bebe Miller, and Jawole Willa Jo Zollar, among others. More information can be found at Mason's website: www.geselmason.com.

Cassie Meador is a Maryland-based choreographer, educator, and the executive artistic director of Dance Exchange. Her work cultivates intergenerational engagement and supports environmental connection, stewardship, and advocacy through dance and performance. Cassie's *How to Lose a Mountain* was created along a five-hundred-mile walk from Washington, DC, to West Virginia to expose the impacts of mountaintop removal mining. Cassie continues to collaborate with the National Park Service, USDA Forest Service, and public schools to develop arts-integrated environmental programs.

Rachel Miller Jacobs, D. Min., is associate professor of Congregational Formation at Anabaptist Mennonite Biblical Seminary in Elkhart, Indiana, where she teaches in the areas of worship, Christian formation, and pedagogy. Trained as a high school English teacher, she formerly served as a pastor, spiritual director, and worship resources coordinator for Mennonite Church USA's *Leader* magazine.

Program manager at Cultural Pluralism in the Arts Movement Ontario (CPAMO) and artistic director of KasheDance, **Kevin A. Ormsby** has performed with companies in Canada, the United States, and the Caribbean. Recipient of a Canada Council for the Arts' Victor Martyn Lynch-Staunton Award and a TAC Cultural Leaders Fellow, Kevin has been a guest artist at the University of Wisconsin at Madison and Northwestern University. Kevin is on the boards of DCD, Toronto Alliance for the Performing Arts, and Nia Centre for the Arts.

Multidisciplinary artist **CJay Philip** is artistic director of Dance & Bmore, an ensemble of singers, dancers, and theater-makers fusing movement, original music, and spoken word to create interactive and socially conscious performances. Dance & Bmore also designs innovative programs for all ages that stimulate the imagination and foster human connections through the arts while building a sense of community and well-being. After being introduced to the Critical Response Process in 2014, CJay was convinced CRP would strengthen her artistic practice and collaboration. She utilizes CRP to give and receive feedback from creatives and community members. CJay introduces students to CRP at Baltimore School for the Arts and Peabody Conservatory, where she is a faculty member. CJay is also a member of the first cohort of CRP Certified Practitioners.

Kathryn Prince is director of theatre studies (BA and MA) at the University of Ottawa. She has published widely in the fields of Shakespeare in performance, emotions in the theater, and, more recently, the emotion of hope in the literature of climate change and apocalypse. She is the editor of *Shakespeare Bulletin* (the international journal of Shakespeare in performance), and several collections, including (with Peter Kirwan) *The Arden Research Handbook of Shakespeare and Contemporary Performance.*

Violinist **Sean Riley** maintains a career throughout the United States, Europe, and Asia as a performer, entrepreneur, and educator. As a performer he was most recently featured on a score for the Netflix original series *Eden*. As an entrepreneur Riley created an award-winning project, 3D printing a six-string electric violin. As an educator Riley gives lectures globally, specializes in creating performance training programs in higher music education, and teaches violin performance.

Charles C. Smith is a poet, playwright, and essayist who has written and edited fourteen books. He studied poetry and drama at the Frank Silvera Writers' Workshop in Harlem and with William Packard at New York University and Herbert Berghof Studios. He is the executive director of Cultural Pluralism in the Arts Movement Ontario (CPAMO) and artistic director of the wind in the leaves collective. He lectures at the Humber College post-graduate program in arts administration.

Shula Strassfeld was a dancer, teacher, choreographer, and writer. From 2006 to 2015 she was a member of the Maryland-based Dance Exchange, founded by Liz Lerman, where she was a regular CRP facilitator. Earlier in her career Shula directed her own company, Meirimdance, in Toronto; performed for five years with Mirali Sharon in Tel Aviv; and was a contributor to the *Jewish Catalog* series. At the time of her death in 2018, Shula was based in Toronto, where she taught and facilitated CRP with CPAMO and the In[heir]itance Project.

Phil Stoesz is a queer Mennonite facilitator, educator, and creator. His practice in CRP was developed through teaching with Liz Lerman at Arizona State University. He has applied CRP in community-based theater-making, sexual violence prevention activism, visual art critiques, graduate science labs, and his own multifaceted artmaking. He is particularly interested in how CRP may be used to teach the skill of following to people who have only ever been taught to lead.

After studying social work (CICSA, Amsterdam), **Gerda van Zelm** became a professional singer and pursued a career combining solo and ensemble performance. Since 1992 she has been a voice teacher at the Royal Conservatoire in The Hague, where she has developed and facilitated a teachers' development program since 2016. She is a member of the creative directors team of Innovative Conservatoire (ICON).

Jill Waterhouse is a Minnesota-based artist, writer/performer, community activist, and curator. Former executive director of WARM (Women's Art Resources of Minnesota), Jill was a member, mentor, CRP facilitator, exhibit coordinator, and MAX program director during the organization's decades of creating, redefining, and fighting for a place for women in the arts. Her own work spans sculpture/installations, performance/social practice art, and "dances on the frayed edges of the American social fabric." She has exhibited in local, national, and international museums and galleries, including the Walker Art Center and Minneapolis Institute of Art. She remains dedicated to CRP facilitation and mentoring, and to her work as a certified life coach. In recent work with Phipps Center for the Arts in Hudson, Wisconsin, she has explored approaches for facilitating CRP for a large number of artists simultaneously.

Engaging internationally with a variety of spaces, people, and perspectives, **Rebekah West** is an American artist, writer, filmmaker, designer, musician, and dance professional. West served as producing director for Boulder Dance Alliance/Space for Dance and the University of Colorado's ATLAS Center for Arts, Media and Performance. She holds an interdisciplinary MA combining writing and poetics with visual art, and BAs in dance therapy and dance movement studies. West follows currents and patterns of play across disciplines. More information can be found at West's website: www.rebekahwest.com.

INDEX